MAINE
HIKING

MAINE
HIKING

First Edition

Michael Lanza

AVALON
TRAVEL

FOGHORN OUTDOORS MAINE HIKING

First Edition

Michael Lanza

Printing History
1st edition—May 2005
5 4 3 2 1

Avalon Travel Publishing
An Imprint of
Avalon Publishing Group, Inc.

AVALON
publishing group incorporated

ISBN: 1-56691-934-7
ISSN: 1553-6114

Editor and Series Manager: Ellie Behrstock
Acquisitions Editor: Rebecca Browning
Copy Editor: Donna Leverenz
Graphics Coordinator: Deborah Dutcher
Production Coordinator: Darren Alessi
Cover and Interior Designer: Darren Alessi
Map Editors: Olivia Solís, Naomi Adler Dancis, Kat Smith, Kevin Anglin
Cartographers: Kat Kalamaras, Mike Morgenfeld
Indexer: Ellie Behrstock

Front cover photo: Baxter State Park, © Phil Schermeister/Network Aspen

Printed in the USA by Malloy, Inc.

About the Author

An avid four-season hiker, backpacker, climber, skier, and road and mountain biker, Michael Lanza first fell in love with hiking and the outdoors in New Hampshire's White Mountains 20 years ago. For years, he spent weekend after weekend hiking in the Whites, then branched out all over New England. During the year that he researched and wrote the first edition of *Foghorn Outdoors New England Hiking,* he figures he hiked 1,200 miles, covering all six New England states. He's now hiked and climbed extensively in the West and Northeast and as far afield as Nepal, but still returns regularly to New England to hike.

Michael is the Northwest Editor of *Backpacker* magazine and writes a monthly column and other articles for *AMC Outdoors* magazine. His work has also appeared in *National Geographic Adventure, Outside,* and other publications. He is also the author of *Foghorn Outdoors New England Hiking, Foghorn Outdoors Massachusetts Hiking, Foghorn Outdoors New Hampshire Hiking,* and *Foghorn Outdoors Vermont Hiking.*

During the mid-1990s Michael syndicated a weekly column about outdoor activities in about 20 daily newspapers throughout New England and co-hosted a call-in show about the outdoors on New Hampshire Public Radio. A native of Leominster, Massachusetts, Michael has a B.S. in photojournalism from Syracuse University and spent 10 years as a reporter and editor at various Massachusetts and New Hampshire newspapers. When he's not hiking the trails of New England, he can be found in Boise, Idaho, with his wife, Penny Beach, and their son, Nate, and daughter, Alex.

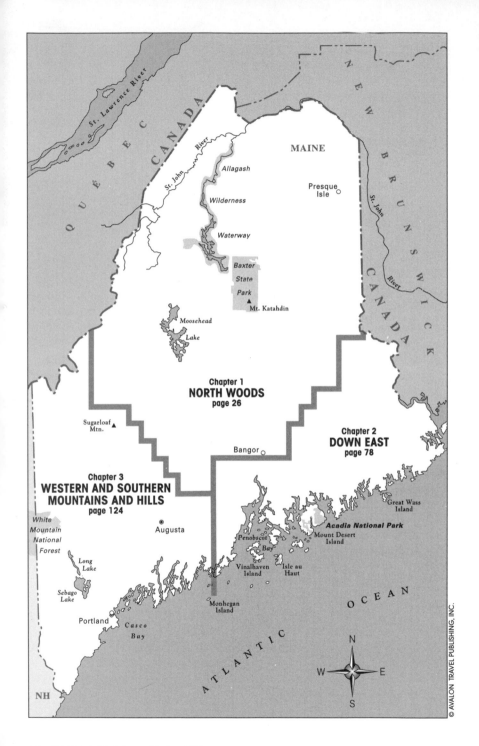

St. Lawrence River

QUEBEC

CANADA

MAINE

St. John River

Allagash

Wilderness

Waterway

Presque Isle ○

NEW BRUNSWICK

St. John River

CANADA

Baxter State Park

▲ Mt. Katahdin

Moosehead Lake

Chapter 1
NORTH WOODS
page 26

Sugarloaf Mtn. ▲

Bangor ○

Chapter 2
DOWN EAST
page 78

Chapter 3
WESTERN AND SOUTHERN
MOUNTAINS AND HILLS
page 124

White Mountain National Forest

Augusta ◉

Great Wass Island

Acadia National Park

Penobscot Bay

Mount Desert Island

Long Lake

Vinalhaven Island

Isle au Haut

Sebago Lake

Portland

Casco Bay

Monhegan Island

OCEAN

ATLANTIC

N
W   E
S

NH

© AVALON TRAVEL PUBLISHING, INC.

COURTESY OF THE MAINE OFFICE OF TOURISM

Contents

Our Commitment

We are committed to making *Foghorn Outdoors Maine Hiking* the most accurate and enjoyable hiking guide to the state. With this first edition you can rest assured that every hiking trail in this book has been carefully reviewed and is accompanied by the most up-to-date information. Be aware that with the passing of time some of the fees listed herein may have changed, and trails may have closed unexpectedly. If you have a specific need or concern, it's best to call the location ahead of time.

If you would like to comment on the book, whether it's to suggest a trail we overlooked, or to let us know about any noteworthy experience—good or bad—that occurred while using *Foghorn Outdoors Maine Hiking* as your guide, we would appreciate hearing from you. Please address correspondence to:

Foghorn Outdoors Maine Hiking, first edition
Avalon Travel Publishing
1400 65th Street, Suite 250
Emeryville, CA 94608

email: atpfeedback@avalonpub.com
If you send us an email, please put "Maine Hiking" in the subject line.

How to Use This Book

Foghorn Outdoors Maine Hiking is divided into three chapters, based on major regions of the state. Regional maps show the location of all the hikes in that chapter.

For North Woods trails: see pages 23–74
For Down East trails: see pages 75–119
For Western and Southern Mountains and Hills trails: see pages 121–179

There are two ways to search for the perfect hike:
1. If you know the name of the specific trail you want to hike, or the name of the surrounding geographical area or nearby feature (town, national or state park, or forest, mountain, lake, river, etc.), look it up in the index and turn to the corresponding page.
2. If you want to find out about hiking possibilities in a particular part of the state, turn to the map at the beginning of that chapter. You can then determine the area where you would like to hike and identify which hikes are available; then turn to the corresponding numbers for those hikes in the chapter.

Trail Names, Distances, and Times
Each trail in this book has a number, name, mileage information, and estimated completion time. The trail's number allows you to find it easily on the corresponding chapter map. The name is either the actual trail name (as listed on signposts and maps) or a name I've given to a series of trails or a loop trail. In the latter cases, the name is taken from the major destination or focal point of the hike.

Most mileage listings are precise, though a few are very good estimates. All mileages and approximate times refer to round-trip travel unless specifically noted as one-way. In the case of one-way hikes, a car or bike shuttle is advised.

The estimated time is based on how long I feel an average adult in moderate physical condition would take to complete the hike. Actual times can vary widely, especially on longer hikes.

What the Ratings Mean
Every hike in this book has been rated on a scale of 1 to 10 for its overall quality and on a scale of 1 to 10 for difficulty.

The quality rating is based largely on scenic qualities, although it also takes into account how crowded a trail is and whether or not you see or hear civilization.

The difficulty rating is calculated based on the following scale:

10 —The hike entails all of the following qualities: climbs 3,000+ feet in elevation, covers at least seven miles, and has rugged and steep terrain with some exposure.

9 —The hike entails at least two of the following qualities: climbs 2,500+ feet in elevation, covers at least seven miles, and/or has rugged and steep terrain with some exposure.

8 —The hike entails one or more of the following qualities: climbs 2,000+ feet in elevation, covers at least seven miles, or has rugged and steep terrain with possible exposure.

7 —The hike entails at least two of the following qualities: climbs 1,500+ feet in elevation, covers at least five miles, and/or has steep and rugged sections.

6 —The hike entails one of the following qualities: climbs 1,500+ feet in elevation, covers at least five miles, or has steep and rugged sections.

5 —The hike covers at least four miles and either climbs 1,000+ feet in elevation or has steep, rugged sections.

4 —The hike entails one of the following qualities: climbs 1,000+ feet in elevation, covers at least four miles, or has steep, rugged sections.

3 —The hike has some hills—though not more than 1,000 feet of elevation gain—and covers at least three miles.

2 —The hike either has some hills—though not more than 1,000 feet of elevation gain—or covers at least three miles.

1 —The trail is relatively flat and less than three miles.

Hike Descriptions

The description for each listing is intended to give you some idea of what kind of terrain to expect, what you might see, and how to follow the hike from beginning to end. I've sometimes added a special note about the hike or a suggestion on how to combine it with a nearby hike or expand upon your outing in some other way.

There are a couple of terms used throughout the book that reflect the land usage history in the region. Forest roads are generally dirt or gravel roads maintained by the land manager and are typically not open to motor vehicles except those of the manager. Woods roads, or "old woods roads," are abandoned thoroughfares—many were formerly public routes between colonial communities—now heavily overgrown, but recognizable as a wide path. Their condition can vary greatly.

User Groups

I have designated a list of user groups permitted on each trail, including hikers, bicyclists, dogs, horses, hunters, cross-country skiers, snowshoers, and wheelchair users.

While this book is intended primarily as a hiking guide, it includes some trails that are mediocre hikes yet excellent mountain biking or cross-country skiing routes. The snowshoe reference is intended as a guide for beginners; experienced snowshoers know that many of Maine's bigger mountains can be climbed on snowshoes in winter, but this book indicates when snowshoeing a trail may require advanced winter hiking skills. As always, the individual must make the final judgment regarding safety issues in winter.

Wheelchair accessibility is indicated when stated by the land or facility manager, but concerned persons should call to find out if their specific needs will be met.

The hunting reference is included to remind hikers to be aware of the hunting season when hiking, and that they may be sharing a trail with hunters, in which case they should take the necessary precautions (wearing a bright color, preferably fluorescent orange) to avoid an accident in the woods. Hunting is a popular sport in Maine and throughout New England. The hunting season generally extends from fall into early winter. The state department of fish and game and state parks and forests offices can provide you with actual dates (see Resources in the back of the book for contact information).

Access and Fees

This section provides information on trail access, entrance fees, parking, and hours of operation.

Maps

Information on how to obtain maps for a trail and environs is provided for each hike listing. When several maps are mentioned, you might want to ask the seller about a map's detail, weatherproofness, range, and scale when deciding which one to obtain. Consider also which maps will cover other hikes that interest you. Prices are usually indicative of quality and detail. I've also listed the appropriate United States Geologic Survey (USGS) map or maps covering that area. Be advised that many USGS maps do not show trails or forest roads, and that trail locations may not be accurate if the map has not been updated recently. Maine is covered by the standard 7.5-minute series maps (scale 1:24,000). An index map also covers Maine, showing the 7.5-minute and 15-minute maps.

See Resources in the back of the book for map sources. To order individual USGS maps or the New England index maps, write to USGS Map Sales, Federal Center, Box 25286, Denver, CO 80225.

Directions
This section provides mile-by-mile driving directions to the trailhead from the nearest major town.

Contact
Most of the hikes in this book list at least one contact agency, trail club, or organization for additional information. Many hikes will give you a sample of something bigger—a long-distance trail or public land. Use the contact information to explore beyond what is found in these pages. And remember to support the organizations listed here that maintain the trails you hike.

Introduction

COURTESY OF THE MAINE OFFICE OF TOURISM

Author's Note

Dear fellow hiker,

I have a single black-and-white photograph from what was probably my first hike up a mountain. It shows two friends and me—young, dressed in flannel shirts and jeans—standing on a rocky New England summit. In the distance, clouds blot out much of the sky. The wind lifts our hair and fills our shirts; it appears to be a cool day in early autumn.

I no longer recall what peak we hiked, only that the hike had been the idea of one of my friends; I was tagging along on an outing that seemed like something I might enjoy. In fact, my recollection of the entire day amounts to little more than a lingering sense of the emotions it generated for me—kind of an artifact of memory, like an arrowhead dug up somewhere.

I was perhaps 18 or 20 years old, and standing on top of that little mountain struck me as quite possibly the most intense and wonderful thing I'd ever done.

Of course, at that age most people have limited experience with things intense and wonderful. But I found that as my fascination with high places grew, so did the inspiration that began on that first summit.

I have since done much hiking all over Maine and the rest of New England and taken my thirst for that feeling to bigger mountains out West—hiking, backpacking, and climbing in the Sierra Nevada, the Cascades and Olympics, the Tetons and Wind River Range, the Rockies from Colorado to Alberta, and Alaska. My work allows me to spend many days and nights every year in wild country.

When asked to write *Foghorn Outdoors New England Hiking,* I realized I would spend a summer hiking trails I had not yet visited but which belong in a guide this comprehensive. While I expected to sorely miss the West, where I'd been spending summers hiking and climbing, instead I found myself enjoying a reunion of sorts with my hiking roots. I finally got to many places that had been on my checklist for some time. And, to my surprise, the hikes I relished most were those I had known the least about, those scattered trails that for various reasons attract relatively few hikers.

Foghorn Outdoors Maine Hiking is the product of many days on the trail and a reflection of many personal memories. As you use it to explore Maine's trails, I urge you to walk lightly, to do your part to help preserve these fragile places, and to venture beyond the popular, well-beaten paths to lesser-known destinations.

I also invite you to let me know about any inaccuracies by writing to my publisher, Avalon Travel Publishing, at the following address: Foghorn Outdoors Maine Hiking, Avalon Travel Publishing, 1400 65th Street, Suite 250, Emeryville, CA 94608.

I hope this book helps you find the same kind of experiences I have enjoyed in these mountains and forests—to discover your own arrowhead.

—Michael Lanza

Maine Overview

Sprawling over more than 33,000 square miles—roughly the area of the other five New England states combined—Maine offers a variety of hiking experiences unmatched in New England.

Maine's most prominent mountains comprise the northernmost reaches of the Appalachian chain, stretching from the White Mountain National Forest in western Maine to Baxter State Park in the far north. The Appalachian Trail (AT), extending 281 miles through Maine alone, forms the backbone of the trail network through this region of vast wilderness lakes and rugged peaks.

Maine's North Woods offers the most remote, and in many ways the wildest, hiking experience one can find in this part of the country. Baxter State Park and the 100-Mile Wilderness stretch of the Appalachian Trail are highlights of the North Woods region. Both are well-known destinations for hikers from out of state as well as Mainers. Maine's highest peak, Katahdin, in Baxter State Park, especially is a draw. Much North Woods hiking is rugged, harder than the distance or elevation change would imply, and often highlighted by encounters with wildlife. Loons (often seen on and around the lakes) and moose are two of the region's defining species.

Down East Maine is another major destination for hikers from both inside and outside Maine. Adventurers are primarily drawn to the unique, eminently accessible, and incredibly scenic hiking at popular Acadia National Park. Acadia harbors some of the best seaside hiking in the country, not to mention a rich and complex history. Acadia's neighbor, Camden Hills State Park, remains more of a local destination and doesn't quite compare to Acadia—but most places don't. Nonetheless, the Camden Hills are stellar local trails.

The Western and Southern Mountains and Hills is a varied area ranging from the higher, more rugged eastern edge of the White Mountains to smaller hills with good views of southern Maine. This area includes three of Maine's most popular destinations for hikers from throughout New England and New York: The Mahoosuc, Bigelow, and Saddleback Ranges, which have the kind of big-mountain terrain only matched by the White Mountains and parts of Baxter State Park. Consequently, these places are all popular, especially on nice weekends from early summer through early October.

The Appalachian Trail

Perhaps the most famous hiking trail in the world, the Appalachian Trail (AT) runs 2,174 miles from Springer Mountain in Georgia to Mount Katahdin in Maine, along the spine of the Appalachian Mountains in 14 states.

About 281 miles of the Appalachian Trail passes through Maine, which boasts some of the trail's finest and most famous stretches, including the Saddleback and Bigelow Ranges, the 100-Mile Wilderness, and Katahdin.

A few hundred people hike the entire Appalachian Trail end to end every year, but countless thousands take shorter backpacking trips and day hikes somewhere along the Appalachian Trail. Well maintained by various hiking clubs that assume responsibility for different sections, the trail is well marked with signs and white blazes on trees and rocks, or cairns above treeline. Shelters and campsites are spaced out along the Appalachian Trail so that backpackers have choices of where to spend each night, but those shelters can fill up during the busy season of summer and early fall, especially on weekends.

The prime hiking season for the Appalachian Trail in Maine generally runs from June into October.

Hiking Tips

Climate

With micro-climates ranging from some of New England's highest peaks in the state's interior, smaller hills in the southern part of the state, and an ocean moderating the Seacoast climate, Maine hardly has a statewide "hiking season." But the good news is that fair-weather hikers can find a trail to explore virtually year-round. Still, the wildly varied character of hiking opportunities here also demands some basic knowledge of and preparation for hitting the trails.

In the Maine mountains, the prime hiking season stretches from late spring or early summer through mid- to late autumn. In Baxter State Park, the season isn't really underway at least until late June and snowflakes may start appearing by early October, while southern Maine's smaller hills often remain snow-free into November or even December, and are passable again when the mud dries up sometime between May and June. The ocean generally keeps coastal areas a little warmer in winter and cooler in summer than inland areas; snow is uncommon at Acadia and Camden Hills. Otherwise, any time of year, average temperatures typically grow cooler as you gain elevation or move northward. In general, summer high temperatures range from 60–90°F with lows from 50°F to around freezing at higher elevations. Days are often humid in the forests and lower elevations and windy on the mountaintops. July and August see occasional thunderstorms, but July through September are the driest months.

Black flies, or mayflies, emerge by late April or early May and pester hikers until late June or early July, while mosquitoes come out in late spring and dissipate (but do not disappear) by midsummer. No-see-ums (tiny biting flies that live up to their name) plague some wooded areas in summer (the 100-Mile Wilderness is notorious for them). September is often the best month for hiking, with dry, comfortable days, cool nights, and few bugs. Fall foliage colors peak anywhere from mid-September or early October. The period from mid-October into November offers cool days, cold nights, no bugs, few people, and often little snow.

In the higher peaks of the eastern White Mountains and along the Appalachian Trail, high-elevation snow disappears and alpine wildflowers bloom in late spring; by late October, wintry winds start blowing and snow starts flying (though it can snow above 4,000 feet in any month of the year). Spring trails are muddy at low elevations—and best avoided so as not to accelerate erosion during this "mud season"—and buried under deep,

Cross-Country Skiing and Snowshoeing

Many hikes in this book are great for cross-country skiing or snowshoeing in winter. But added precaution is needed. Days are short and the temperature may start to plummet by mid-afternoon, so carry the right clothing and don't overestimate how far you can travel in winter.

Depending on snow conditions and your own fitness level and experience with either snowshoes or skis, a winter outing can take much longer than anticipated—and certainly much longer than a trip of similar distance on groomed trails at a cross-country ski resort. Breaking your own trail through fresh snow can also be very exhausting—take turns leading, and conserve energy by following the leader's tracks, which also serve as a good trail to return on.

The proper clothing becomes essential in winter, especially the farther you wander from roads. Wear a base layer that wicks moisture from your skin and dries quickly (synthetics or wool, not cotton), middle layers that insulate and do not retain moisture, and a windproof shell that breathes well and is waterproof or water-resistant (the latter type of garment usually breathes much better than something that's completely waterproof). Size boots to fit over a thin, synthetic liner sock and a thicker, heavyweight synthetic-blend sock. For your hands, often the most versatile system consists of gloves and/or mittens that also can be layered, with an outer layer that's water- and windproof and preferably also breathable.

Most importantly, don't overdress: Remove layers if you're sweating heavily. Avoid becoming wet with perspiration, which can lead to you cooling too much. Drink plenty of fluids and eat snacks frequently to maintain your energy level; feeling tired or cold on a winter outing may be an indication of dehydration or hunger.

As long as you're safe, cautious, and aware, winter is a great time to explore Maine's trails. Have fun out there.

slushy snow up high, requiring snowshoes. Winter conditions set in by mid-November and can become very severe, even life-threatening. Going above tree line in winter is considered a mountaineering experience by many (though these mountains lack glacier travel and high altitude), so be prepared for harsh cold and strong winds—and, in the higher mountains, few if any people around.

In the smaller hills, the snow-free hiking season often begins by early spring and lasts into late autumn. Some of these trails, particularly on the Seacoast, are occasionally free of snow during the winter, or offer opportunities for snowshoeing or cross-country skiing in woods protected from strong winds, with warmer temperatures than you'll find on the bigger interior peaks. Still, they can get occasional heavy snowfall and be icy.

For more information about weather-related trail conditions, refer to the individual hike listings.

Basic Hiking Safety

Few of us would consider hiking a high-risk activity. But like any physical activity, it does pose certain risks, and it's up to us to minimize them. For starters, make sure your physical condition is adequate to your objective—the quickest route to injury is overextending either your skills or your physical abilities. You wouldn't presume that you could rock climb a 1,000-foot cliff if you've never climbed before; don't assume you're ready for one of Maine's hardest hikes if you've never—or not very recently—done anything nearly as difficult.

Build up your fitness level by gradually increasing your workouts and the length of your hikes. Beyond strengthening muscles, you must strengthen the soft connective tissue in joints like knees and ankles that are too easily strained and take weeks or months to heal from injury. Staying active in a variety of activities—hiking, running, bicycling, Nordic skiing, etc.—helps develop good overall fitness and decreases the likelihood of an overuse in-

---

 ## First-Aid Checklist

Although you're probably at greater risk of injury while driving to the trailhead than you are on the trail, it's wise to carry a compact and lightweight first-aid kit for emergencies in the backcountry, where an ambulance and hospital are often hours, rather than minutes, away. Many are available at outdoor gear retailers. Or prepare your own first-aid kit with attention to the type of trip, the destination, and the needs of people hiking (for example, children or persons with medical conditions). Pack everything into a thick, clear plastic resealable bag. And remember, merely carrying a first-aid kit does not make you safe; knowing how to use what's in it does.

A basic first-aid kit consists of:

❑ 2 large cravats
❑ 2 large gauze pads
❑ 4 four-inch-square gauze pads
❑ 1 six-inch Ace bandage
❑ roll of one-inch athletic tape
❑ several one-inch adhesive bandages
❑ several alcohol wipes
❑ safety pins
❑ tube of povidone iodine ointment (for wound care)
❑ Moleskin or Spenco Second Skin (for blisters)
❑ knife or scissors
❑ paper and pencil
❑ aspirin or an anti-inflammatory medication
❑ SAM splint (a versatile and lightweight splinting device available at many drug stores)
❑ blank SOAP note form

---

jury. Most importantly, stretch muscles before and after a workout to re-
duce the chance of injury.

Maine's most rugged trails—and even parts of its more moderate paths—
can be very rocky and steep. Uneven terrain is often a major contributor
to falls resulting in serious, acute injury. Most of us have a fairly reliable
self-preservation instinct—and you should trust it. If something strikes you
as dangerous or beyond your abilities, don't try it, or simply wait until you
think you're ready for it.

An injury far from a road also means it may be hours before the victim
reaches a hospital. Basic training in wilderness first aid is beneficial to
anyone who frequents the mountains, even recreational hikers. New England happens to have two highly respected sources for such training, and
the basic course requires just one weekend. Contact SOLO (Conway, NH;
603/447-6711, website: www.soloschools.com) or Wilderness Medical As-
sociates (Bryant Pond, ME; 888/945-3633, website: www.wildmed.com)
for information.

Clothing and Gear

Much could be written about how to outfit oneself for hiking in Maine,
with its significant range of elevations and weather, alpine zones, huge sea-
sonal temperature swings, and fairly wet climate. But in the simplest of
terms, you should select your clothing and equipment based on:

- the season and the immediate weather forecast
- the amount of time you plan to be out (a couple of hours, a full day,
  more than one day)
- the distance you'll be wandering from major roads
- the elevation you will hike to
- the abilities of your hiking companions

At lower elevations amid the protection of trees or on a warm day, you
may elect to bring no extra clothing for an hour-long outing, or no more
than a light jacket for a few hours or more. The exception to this is in the
Seacoast region, where hikes are more exposed to cool wind. But higher elevations, especially above tree line, get much colder than the valleys—about
three degrees Fahrenheit per thousand feet—and winds can grow much
stronger. Many a hiker has departed from a valley basking in summer-like
weather and reached a summit wracked by wintry winds and lying under a
carpet of fresh snow, even during the summer months. Insulating layers, a
jacket that protects against wind and precipitation, a warm hat, and gloves
are always a good idea when climbing Maine's highest peaks.

Acadia National Park

Occupying 47,633 acres of granite-domed mountains, woodlands, lakes, ponds, and ocean shoreline, Acadia is one of the country's smallest, yet most popular, national parks.

Glaciers carved a unique landscape here of mountains rising as high as 1,500 feet virtually out of the ocean—most of them thrusting bare summits into the sky. Innumerable islands, bays, and coves collaborate to create a hiking environment unlike any other in New England.

Human history dates back at least 6,000 years. The Wabanaki Indians knew Mount Desert Island as Pemetic, "the sloping land." In the late 19th century, Mount Desert Island became a retreat for wealthy families like the Rockefellers, Morgans, Fords, Vanderbilts, Carnegies, and Astors, who built mansions they called their summer "cottages." After the turn of the century, conservationist George B. Dorr began a lifelong effort to preserve land on the island for the public, acquiring and donating to the government the first 6,000 acres in 1913.

In 1916, President Woodrow Wilson declared the Sieur de Monts National Monument. Three years later, Wilson established Lafayette National Park—the first national park established east of the Mississippi. The name was changed to Acadia in 1929.

The most important piece of gear may be well-fitting, comfortable, supportive shoes or boots. Finding the right footwear requires trying on various models and walking around in them in the store before deciding. Everyone's feet are different, and shoes or boots that feel great on your friend won't necessarily fit you well. Deciding how heavy your footwear should be depends on variables like how often you hike, whether you easily injure your feet or ankles, and how much weight you'll carry. Generally, I recommend hiking in the most lightweight footwear that you find comfortable and adequately supportive.

Above all, use good judgment and proceed with caution. When you're not sure, take the extra layer of clothing, just in case.

Foot Care

At an Appalachian Mountain Club seminar on winter backpacking that I attended years ago, one instructor told us that, besides the brain, "Your feet are the most important part of your body." Hurt any other body part and you might conceivably still make it home under your own power. Hurt your feet, and you're in trouble.

Take care of your feet. Wear clean socks that wick moisture from your skin while staying dry. If you anticipate your socks getting wet from perspiration or water, bring extra socks; on a multiday trip, have dry socks for each day, or at least change socks every other day. Make sure your shoes or boots fit properly, are laced properly, and are broken in if they require it. Wear the appropriate footwear for the type of hiking you plan to do.

Whenever I stop for a short rest on the trail—even if only for a few minutes—I sit down, pull off my boots and socks, and let them and my feet dry out. When backpacking, wash your feet at the end of the day. If you feel any hot spots developing, intervene before they progress into blisters. A slightly red or tender hot spot can be protected from developing into a blister with an adhesive bandage, tape, or a square of moleskin.

If a blister has formed, clean the area around it thoroughly to avoid infection. Sterilize a needle or knife in a flame, then pop and drain the blister to promote faster healing. Put an antiseptic ointment on the blister. Cut a piece of moleskin or Second Skin (both of which have a soft side and a sticky side with a peel-off backing) large enough to overlap the blistered area. Cut a hole as large as the blister out of the center of the moleskin, then place the moleskin over the blister so that the blister is visible through the hole. If done properly, you should be able to walk without aggravating the blister.

Water and Food

Streams and brooks run everywhere in Maine. If you're out for more than a day in the backcountry, finding water is rarely a problem (except on ridgetops and summits). But protozoans and bacteria occur in backcountry water sources, and campers do not always maintain an appropriate distance between their messes and the stream. Assume you should always treat water from backcountry sources, whether by using a filter or iodine tablets, boiling, or another proven method. Day hikers will usually find it more convenient to simply carry enough water from home for the hike.

Most of us require about two liters of water per day when we're not active. Like any physical activity, hiking increases your body's fluid needs by a factor of two or more. On a hot, sticky summer day, or even on a cold, dry winter day (when the air draws moisture from your body even though you may not be perspiring), you'll need even more water than you would on a cool autumn afternoon. A good rule of thumb for an all-day hike is two liters of water per person, but that could even leave you mildly dehydrated, so carry a third liter if you think you may need it. Dehydration can lead to other, more serious problems, like heat exhaustion, hypothermia, frostbite, and injury. If you're well hydrated, you will urinate frequently and your urine will be clear. The darker your urine, the greater your level of dehydration. If you feel thirsty, dehydration has already commenced. In short: Drink a lot.

Similarly, your body burns a phenomenal amount of calories walking up and down a mountain. Feed it frequently. Carbohydrates like bread, chocolate, dried fruit, fig bars, snack bars, fresh vegetables, and energy bars provide a source of quick energy. Fats contain about twice the calories per pound than carbs or protein, and provide the slow-burning fuel that keeps you going all day and warm through the night if you're sleeping outside; sate your need for fats by eating cheese, chocolate, canned meats or fish, pepperoni, sausage, or nuts.

Animals

While the mountains and forests of Maine have an abundance of wildlife, including black bears and thousands of moose (not to mention more rare species like wildcat and bald eagle), for the most part, you don't have to worry for your safety in the backcountry. In years of hiking, I've seen two bears in Maine—and both were running across the gravel Perimeter Road in Baxter State Park as I drove it. I've never encountered a bear on the trail, though I've seen scat and other signs of their presence.

Still, a few sensible precautions are in order. If you're camping in the backcountry, know how to hang or store your food properly to keep it from bears and smaller animals like mice, which are more likely to be a problem. If you're fortunate enough to see a moose or bear, you certainly should never approach either. These creatures are wild and unpredictable, and a moose can weigh several hundred pounds and put the hurt on a much smaller human.

The greatest danger posed by moose and other wildlife is that of hitting one while driving on dark back roads at night; hundreds of collisions occur in Maine and New Hampshire every year, often wrecking vehicles and injuring people. At night, drive more slowly than you would during daylight.

Low-Impact Practices

Many of Maine's trails receive heavy use, making it imperative that we all understand how to minimize our physical impact on the land. The nonprofit organization Leave No Trace (LNT) advocates a set of principles for low-impact backcountry use that are summarized in these basic guidelines:

- Plan ahead and prepare
- Travel and camp on durable surfaces
- Dispose of waste properly
- Leave what you find
- Minimize campfire impact
- Respect wildlife
- Be considerate of other visitors

Below are more-specific recommendations that apply to many backcountry areas:

- Choose a campsite at least 200 feet from trails and water sources, unless you're using a designated site. Make sure your site bears no evidence of your stay when you leave.
- Avoid building campfires; cook with a backpacking stove.
- Carry out everything you carry in.
- Do not leave any food behind, even buried, as animals will dig it up. Learn how to hang food appropriately to keep it from bears. Black bears have spread their range over much of New England in recent years, and problems have arisen in isolated backcountry areas where human use is heavy.
- Bury human waste beneath six inches of soil at least 200 feet from any water source. Burn and bury, or carry out, used toilet paper.
- Wash your cooking gear with water away from any streams or ponds. Even biodegradable soap is harmful to the environment.
- Avoid trails that are very muddy in spring; that's when they are most susceptible to erosion.
- And last but not least, know and follow any regulations for the area you will be visiting.

LNT offers more in-depth guidelines for low-impact camping and hiking on its website, www.lnt.org. You can also contact them by mail or phone: Leave No Trace Inc., P.O. Box 997, Boulder, CO 80306; 303/442-8222 or 800/332-4100, website: www.lnt.org.

Trail Etiquette

One of the great things about hiking—at least for as long as I've been hiking—has always been the quality of the people you meet on the trail. Hikers generally do not need an explanation of the value of courtesy, and I hope that will always ring true.

Personally, I yield the trail to others whether I'm going uphill or down. All trail users should yield to horses by stepping aside for the safety of everyone present. Likewise, horseback riders should, whenever possible, avoid situations where their animals are forced to push past hikers on very narrow trails. Mountain bikers should yield to hikers, announce their approach, and pass non-bikers slowly. During hunting season, non-hunters should wear blaze orange, or an equally bright, conspicuous color. Most of the hunters I meet are responsible and friendly and deserve like treatment.

Many of us enjoy the woods and mountains for the quiet, and we should

Hiking Blazes

New England's forests abound with blazes—slashes of paint on trees used to mark trails. Sometimes the color of blazes seems random and unrelated to other trails in the same area, but most major trails and trail systems are blazed consistently.

The Appalachian Trail bears white blazes for its entire length, including its 281 miles within Maine. Most side trails connecting to the Appalachian Trail are blue-blazed. Although not all trails are well blazed, popular and well-maintained trails usually are—you'll see a colored slash of paint at frequent intervals at about eye level on tree trunks. Double slashes are sometimes used to indicate a sharp turn in the trail.

Trails are blazed in both directions, so whenever you suspect you may have lost the trail, turn around to see whether you can find a blaze facing in the opposite direction; if so, you'll know you're still on the trail.

Above tree line, trails may be marked either with blazes painted on rock or with cairns, which are piles of stone constructed at regular intervals.

keep that in mind on the trail, at summits, or backcountry campsites. Many of us share the belief that things like cell phones, radios, CD players, and hand-held personal computers do not belong in the mountains; if you must use them, use discretion.

This region has seen some conflict between hikers and mountain bikers, but it's important to remember that solutions to those issues are never reached through hostility and rudeness. Much more is accomplished when we begin from a foundation of mutual respect and courtesy. After all, we're all interested in preserving and enjoying our trails.

Large groups have a disproportionate impact on backcountry campsites and on the experience of other people. Be aware of and respect any restrictions on group size. Even where no regulation exists, keep your group size to no more than 10 people.

Dogs can create unnecessary friction in the backcountry. Dog owners should respect any regulations and not presume that strangers are eager to meet their pet. Keep your pet under physical control whenever other people are approaching.

Best Hikes in Maine

Can't decide where to hike this weekend? Here are my picks for the best hikes in several categories:

Top Trails for Fall Foliage Viewing

Penobscot and Sargent Mountains, Down East, page 98. Surrounding hills will show a kaleidoscope of colors, but the flaming red blueberry bushes in the alpine zone may be the highlight.

Bigelow Mountain, Western and Southern Mountains and Hills, page 129. One of Maine's greatest peaks, the view from its summit ridge extends across vast stretches of forest from western Maine to the White Mountains.

Tumbledown Mountain via any trail, Western and Southern Mountains and Hills, page 149. From the top of this peak, you'll have a blanket of colors spread out before you as far as New Hampshire's Mount Washington.

Table Rock, Grafton Notch, Western and Southern Mountains and Hills, page 152. The abrupt drop from this high ledge amplifies the drama of the notch awash in fall colors.

Sabattus Mountain, Western and Southern Mountains and Hills, page 172. This short hike leads to a sheer drop of hundreds of feet, overlooking a tremendous view of nearly unbroken forest and mountains.

Top Coastline or Island Hikes

Ocean Lookout, Down East, page 83. Short and sweet, this hike offers easy access to expansive views of the islands of Penobscot Bay.

Isle au Haut: Duck Harbor Mountain/Merchant Point Loop, Down East, page 88. Lucky hikers will spot seals and other marine life in the scenic coves visible from this loop trial.

Acadia Traverse, Down East, page 111. By traversing Mount Desert Island's east side, ambitious hikers can hit the six major peaks of Acadia National Park.

Great Head, Down East, page 116. This short cliff-top walk provides superb views from Frenchman Bay to Otter Cliffs.

Ocean Path, Down East, page 118. When you hear the thunderous surf pound the craggy shoreline, you'll know why this is a favorite among Acadia National Park visitors.

Top Hikes to Waterfalls

Katahdin Stream Falls, North Woods, page 47. You'll cross Katahdin Stream on a wooden bridge as you make the easy walk to this 50-foot cascade.

Gulf Hagas, North Woods, page 71. Maine's "Little Grand Canyon" is a deep, narrow gorge along the West Branch of the Pleasant River with sheer walls and numerous waterfalls and cascades.

Screw Auger Falls, Western and Southern Mountains and Hills, page 155. The Bear River tumbles through an impressive waterfall and a tight gorge of water-sculpted rock reminiscent of Southwestern slot canyons.

Step Falls, Western and Southern Mountains and Hills, page 158. Take a leisurely stroll to this spectacular set of falls, just half a mile from the parking lot.

Mount Caribou, Western and Southern Mountains and Hills, page 167. The Caribou Trail–Mud Brook Trial, a 7.3-mile loop, is dotted with several lovely waterfalls.

Top Hikes to Lakes and Swimming Holes

Sandy Stream Pond/Whidden Ponds Loop, North Woods, page 36. Dogs aren't permitted on this loop trail, but hikers will pass by two ponds that are frequented by moose.

100-Mile Wilderness, North Woods, page 60. An expedition along this remote and lengthy route passes by scores of alpine ponds and cold mountain streams.

Gulf Hagas, North Woods, page 71. You'll find plenty of cool, calm pools on a hike through this spot, known as Maine's "Little Grand Canyon."

Jordan Pond Loop, Down East, page 102. This easy walk around Jordan Pond affords great views of wooded slopes.

Screw Auger Falls, Western and Southern Mountains and Hills, page 155. The Bear River pours over smooth stone slabs and through an impressive, narrow gorge—a favorite spot for families.

Top Hikes for Children

Isle au Haut: Duck Harbor Mountain/Merchant Point Loop, Down East, page 88. Kids will love the adventurous terrain, rugged coastline, and scenic coves, plus possible sightings of seals, ducks, and cormorants.

The Bubbles/Eagle Lake Loop, Down East, page 101. The short climb to the top of The Bubbles can be done by almost anyone, and the view is among the best in Acadia.

The Beehive, Down East, page 113. Older children will be thrilled by the vertical scramble up this rocky trail.

Piazza Rock and the Caves, Western and Southern Mountains and Hills, page 146. Just a couple miles from the road, Piazza Rock is an enormous horizontal slab protruding improbably from a cliff, and the Caves are passageways through giant boulders that scream, "Explore here!"

Sabattus Mountain, Western and Southern Mountains and Hills, page 172. Keep energetic kids in sight along the wide path of this short ascent.

Top Short, Scenic Walks

Sandy Stream Pond/Whidden Ponds Loop, North Woods, page 36. This flat walk explores two ponds where moose are frequently seen in early morning and evening.

Kidney Pond Loop, North Woods, page 56. A relaxed ramble on this lovely loop trail will lead you to Kidney Pond and several other small bodies of water.

Great Head, Down East, page 116. From tall cliffs rising virtually out of the ocean, the views stretch from the islands of Frenchman Bay to Otter Cliffs.

Screw Auger Falls, Western and Southern Mountains and Hills, page 155. Minutes from the parking lot, this is a favorite swimming spot for families with small children.

Step Falls, Western and Southern Mountains and Hills, page 158. A 0.5-mile stroll leads to a spectacular series of waterfalls.

Top Hikes Under Five Miles

South Turner Mountain, North Woods, page 34. The very steep haul up this little neighbor of Katahdin's offers rare views of the big mountain.

the view of Jordan Pond from The Bubbles, Acadia National Park

Acadia Mountain, Down East, page 95. At 681 feet, the biggest hill on the west side of Somes Sound offers excellent views of the sound, and the islands south of Mount Desert.

The Bubbles/Eagle Lake Loop, Down East, page 101. This loop trail provides unforgettable views of Jordan Pond from a collection of exposed ledges.

Dorr and Cadillac Mountains, Down East, page 109. You'll hit two great Mount Desert Island peaks in this three-mile hike.

Table Rock, Grafton Notch, Western and Southern Mountains and Hills, page 152. A steep climb is rewarded by a view from a flat ledge a thousand feet above the floor of dramatic Grafton Notch.

Top Easy Backpacking Trips

Russell Pond/Davis Pond Loop, North Woods, page 32. A relatively flat trail looping through a remote portion of Baxter State Park, with several ponds along the way.

Nesuntabunt Mountain, North Woods, page 59. Continue past Nesuntabunt to the Wadleigh Stream lean-to and the isolated shore of Nahmakanta Lake for a relatively short overnight trip.

Half a 100-Mile Wilderness (northern half), North Woods, page 67. A multiday hike through remote and rugged territory.

Piazza Rock and the Caves, Western and Southern Mountains and Hills, page 146. A nearby lean-to and camping area invites an easy overnight trip—ideal for new backpackers and children.

Top Difficult Backpacking Trips

100-Mile Wilderness, North Woods, page 60. The longest stretch of roadless trail in New England.

Half a 100-Mile Wilderness (southern half), North Woods, page 67. Only have four or five days? Hike the more-rugged half of the Wilderness.

Bigelow Range, Western and Southern Mountains and Hills, page 126. Don't underestimate this steep climb, but the payoff is big views of the Maine mountains and as far off as New Hampshire's Mount Washington.

Saddleback Range, Western and Southern Mountains and Hills, page 140. Up and down, up and down, up and down... bring the trekking poles for this hike.

The Mahoosuc Range, Western and Southern Mountains and Hills, page 162. Mahoosuc Notch is called "the hardest mile on the Appalachian Trail," but the rest of this range is no walk in the park.

Top Summit Hikes

North Traveler Mountain, North Woods, page 29. Don't get discouraged by several false summits on the way to the peak of Traveler Mountain—the views only improve as you ascend up the ridge.

The Owl, North Woods, page 48. A little-visited part of Baxter State Park, with imposing views of Katahdin to the east.

Bigelow Mountain, Western and Southern Mountains and Hills, page 129. A great trek for fit hikers, with the option of adding a second summit on day two.

Mount Abraham, Western and Southern Mountains and Hills, page 138. Like Vermont's Mount Abraham, Maine's peak by the same name also rises above the tree line and provides expansive views.

Saddleback Mountain and The Horn, Western and Southern Mountains and Hills, page 144. On a clear day, hikers who undertake this challenging ascent are rewarded with views of Katahdin to the north and Mount Washington to the southwest.

Top Hikes for Solitude and Remoteness

North Traveler Mountain, North Woods, page 29. You're likely to have this trail to yourself as you take in sweeping ridge-top views.

Peak of the Ridges, North Woods, page 31. A challenging and isolated ridgeline hike with a 2,500-foot elevation gain.

100-Mile Wilderness, North Woods, page 60. For nearly 100 miles, this multiday trek weaves along a remote, northern section of the Appalachian Trail.

White Cap Mountain, North Woods, page 69. This 3,654-foot summit can be reached via a two- or three-day tromp through a remote, roadless area.

Old Blue Mountain, Western and Southern Mountains and Hills, page 147. A challenging day hike to a 3,600-foot summit on a remote stretch of the Appalachian Trail.

Top Hikes on Mountain Ridges

Katahdin: Knife Edge Loop, North Woods, page 39. A tough trail on rugged terrain, but one of the best ways for ambitious hikers to take in the mother of all Maine mountains.

Doubletop Mountain, North Woods, page 55. A challenging hike with expansive views on the alpine portion of the trail.

Cadillac Mountain: South Ridge Trail, Down East, page 108. Explore the highest peak on Mount Desert Island by way of this spectacular seven-mile hike.

Acadia Traverse, Down East, page 111. It's not one continuous ridge, but this traverse of Mount Desert Island's six major peaks is one of the best "ridge-top" hikes in New England.

Saddleback Mountain and The Horn, Western and Southern Mountains and Hills, page 144. The three-mile ridge linking these two summits offers continuous long views.

Top Hikes for Rugged Mountain Terrain

Katahdin Traverse, North Woods, page 41. Best as an overnighter with a scramble up Cathedral Trail to Katahdin's summit on the second day.

Katahdin: Abol Trail, North Woods, page 43. Perhaps the oldest existing trail up Katahdin, this route climbs a whopping 4,000 feet in 7.6 miles.

Mount O-J-I, North Woods, page 53. Aside from Katahdin, this is one of the most grueling treks in Baxter State Park, but you'll be rewarded with several fine viewpoints just below the summit.

Bigelow Range, Western and Southern Mountains and Hills, page 126. This traverse of nearly 17 miles could be the hardest two days of hiking you'll ever do.

Tumbledown Mountain Loop Trail, Western and Southern Mountains and Hills, page 150. Although this trail tops out just over four miles, a steeply graded trail strewn with boulders makes the terrain tough to navigate.

Top Hikes to Watch the Sunrise

Katahdin: Abol Trail, North Woods, page 43. You'll want to start your day early when tackling this 4,000-foot elevation gain.

Cadillac Mountain via any trail, Down East, page 107. Begin your day with a view of the sun rising up out of the Atlantic and casting its light down on a collection of nearby islands.

The Beehive to Gorham Mountain/Cadillac Cliffs, Down East, pages 113 and 115. Catch the dawn from atop the Beehive, then combine that hike with Gorham Mountain/Cadillac Cliffs for wonderful views during the best light of the day.

The Mahoosuc Range, Western and Southern Mountains and Hills, page 162. Break up this multiday hike by catching a glorious sunrise from the summit of Fulling Mill Mountain.

Pleasant Mountain, Western and Southern Mountains and Hills, page 174. Start this hike by heading up Bald Peak to catch a big view of dawn over the western Maine hills.

Top Hikes to Watch the Sunset

North Traveler Mountain, North Woods, page 29. The 360-degree views from this remote summit take in a sprawling wilderness of mountains, lakes, and forests.

a hiker atop Tumbledown Mountain

Maiden Cliff, Down East, page 80. From atop the high cliff, a view due
west of wooded hills assures a great sunset.

Isle au Haut: Eben's Head, Down East, page 84. Usher in the evening
from this rocky, surf-pounded bluff.

Tumbledown Mountain via any trail, Western and Southern Mountains and
Hills, page 149. The view from the East Peak extends in every compass direction but north, reaching as far as New Hampshire's Mount Washington.

Burnt Meadow Mountain, Western and Southern Mountains and Hills,
page 175. Watch the sunset over the distant White Mountains from this
little hill.

Chapter 1

© MICHAEL LANZA

North Woods

North Woods

The 26 hikes described in this chapter all lie on public land and fall within two of Maine's greatest hiking areas: Baxter State Park and the 100-Mile Wilderness stretch of the Appalachian Trail. This chapter covers the part of Maine east of U.S. 201 and north of Routes 2 and 9.

With 204,733 acres remaining as close to true wilderness as managed lands come, Baxter is Maine's flagship state park. It provides a hiking experience that's rare in New England: remote and untamed. Maine's highest peak, 5,267-foot Katahdin, dominates the park's south end and attracts the bulk of hiker traffic. But Baxter Park boasts more than 47 other peaks, many of them with trails to overlooked summits as nice as anything east of the Rockies. I've hiked peaks like the Brothers, Coe, Doubletop, and Traveler on a sunny Labor Day weekend and seen few other people. You'll never grow tired of hiking Katahdin, but don't miss out on Baxter's other gems.

At busy times in summer, some parking lots at popular trailheads—usually Katahdin trails—fill up, and the park will not allow any more vehicles in those lots on that day, effectively forcing visitors who come later to choose other trailheads and hikes. There are no overflow parking areas, but trailhead parking north of Katahdin rarely fills, so you can always find someplace to hike. The park's Tote Road is not open to vehicles in winter, when access is by ski or snowshoe and reaching anyplace within the park requires a multiday trip. Millinocket Road is maintained in winter as far as Abol Bridge Campground. The road to the park's Matagamon Gate entrance is maintained only as far as a private campground about four miles east of the gate.

There are no public water sources in Baxter Park; treat your water or bring an adequate supply with you.

Advance reservations for campground sites and backcountry campsites are recommended, and in winter a permit is required for staying overnight; in addition, park authorities require that visitors show that they have winter backcountry experience.

The 100-Mile Wilderness stretch of the Appalachian Trail is neither officially designated federal wilderness nor true wilderness as found in the American West or Alaska—you may hear the distant thrum of logging machinery while hiking here. But the Wilderness does offer some of the most remote hiking in New England, and the big lakes here are home to loons and many other birds and a favorite haunt of moose. The peaks along the Appalachian Trail are not as tall as elsewhere in New England, but they are rugged. The 100-Mile Wilderness stretch is also the longest hike you can do on trail in the region without crossing a paved or public road (it crosses several logging roads). It has seen a tremendous growth in popularity since the 1990s.

The busiest month is August, when you're likely to encounter lots of other backpackers, though still not as many as on Bigelow Mountain or on popular White Mountains trails. The hiking season begins with the disappearance of snow in late spring—though the black flies, no-see-ums, and mosquitoes also emerge—and extends into October, when the first snow may start flying.

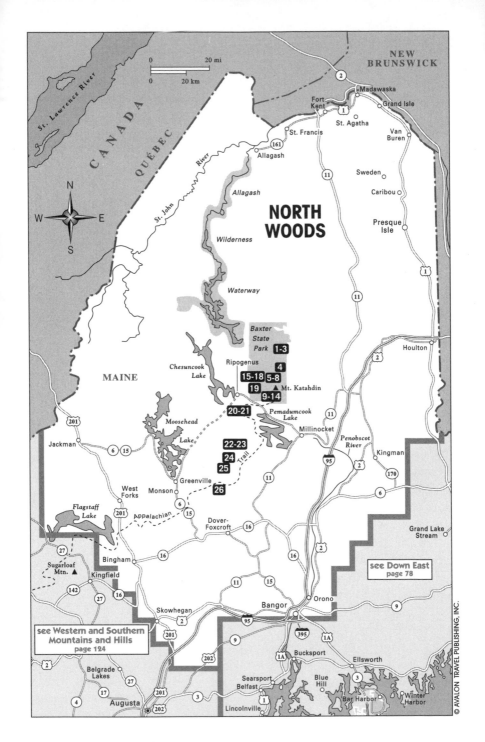

Contents

1 SOUTH BRANCH FALLS
in northern Baxter State Park

Total distance: 1 mile round-trip   **Hiking time:** 1 hour

Difficulty: 2   **Rating:** 8

This stretch of South Branch Ponds Brook might more aptly be called South Branch Gorge, since the biggest vertical drop the stream makes is only about four feet. But the stream cuts a narrow channel through rock in a scenic gorge about a quarter mile long. From the parking area, follow the trail for 0.5 mile, descending gently at first, then somewhat steeply for the last 0.1 mile to the stream. Take one of the short side paths that lead to views of the gorge before heading back the way you came.

User Groups
Hikers only. No wheelchair facilities. Bikes, dogs, and hunting are prohibited.

Access and Fees
Baxter Park is open from May 15 to November 1 (no camping in the park after October 15) and from December 1 to March 31. An entrance fee of $12 per vehicle is charged at the gatehouse, but vehicles bearing Maine registration can enter at no charge. During the summer season, the park's Togue Pond Gate opens at 6 A.M. and closes at 10 P.M.—though it may open at 5 A.M. some summer days—and the Matagamon Gate opens at 6 A.M. and closes at 10 P.M. The road is not maintained to the trailhead in winter, but it can be skied.

Maps
For a park trails map, get the *Baxter State Park and Katahdin* map for $7.95 from the DeLorme Publishing Company, 800/642-0970; or the *Rangeley-Stratton/Baxter State Park-Katahdin* map, $7.95 in waterproof Tyvek, from the Appalachian Mountain Club, 800/262-4455, website: www.outdoors.org. For topographic area maps, request Wassataquoik Lake and the Traveler from USGS Map Sales, Federal Center, Box 25286, Denver, CO 80225, 888/ASK-USGS (888/275-8747), website: http://mapping.usgs.gov.

Directions
Take I-95 in Maine to Exit 56 for Medway/Millinocket. Drive west on Route 157 through East Millinocket to Millinocket. Follow signs for Baxter State Park; the park's Togue Pond gatehouse is 18 miles from Millinocket. Just beyond the gatehouse, take the gravel Tote Road's left fork and drive 34.8

miles. Turn right at a sign for South Branch Pond Campground. Drive 1.3 miles to a turnout on the right. Or from the junction of Routes 11 and 159 in Patten, drive west on Route 159 to Shin Pond and follow the access road to Baxter State Park's Matagamon gatehouse, which is 24 miles from Patten. From the gatehouse, drive about 7.3 miles and turn left at the sign for South Branch Pond Campground. Drive 1.3 miles to a turnout on the right.

Contact
Baxter State Park, 64 Balsam Drive, Millinocket, ME 04462-2190, 207/723-5140, website: www.baxterstateparkauthority.com.

2 NORTH TRAVELER MOUNTAIN
in northern Baxter State Park

Total distance: 5 miles round-trip **Hiking time:** 3.5 hours

Difficulty: 8 **Rating:** 10

Traveler Mountain feels less like New England than any other mountain in the region. With much of its sprawling upper ridges denuded by fires decades ago and kept bare by a harsh climate, I half expect to see mountain goats grazing and hear the whistling of marmots up here. What you hear, however, is next to nothing. You can enjoy blissful solitude for several hours on Traveler. The North Traveler Trail climbs more than 2,000 feet in elevation up a ridge to the 3,144-foot north peak, with almost continuous sweeping views.

From the parking area, walk the road into the campground, toward the northernmost South Branch Pond. (Traveler Mountain defines the skyline to the left, or east, above the pond.) Bear left through the campground, passing several sites, and turn right (south) onto the Pogy Notch Trail, which parallels the pond. In 0.1 mile, turn left onto the blue-blazed North Traveler Trail, immediately ascending the fairly steep, rocky ridge. Just 0.3 mile from the pond, you emerge onto open ledges with your first views of the two South Branch Ponds, across to the South Branch Mountains, and south toward Katahdin. The views only improve as you continue up the ridge, where loose stones can make footing difficult and false summits can make the hike seem longer than its five miles. The trail passes through a little birch grove with fresh blueberries in late summer (I ate my share on an early September hike). Follow the blazes and cairns to the open summit, where there are views in every direction, including north to the wilderness. Due south is the 3,541-foot summit of the Traveler, connected to North Traveler by a trailless, three-mile ridge. Descend the way you came.

User Groups

Hikers only. No wheelchair facilities. This trail should not be attempted in winter except by hikers experienced in mountaineering and prepared for severe winter weather, and is not suitable for skis. Bikes, dogs, horses, and hunting are prohibited.

Access and Fees

Baxter Park is open from May 15 to November 1 (no camping in the park after October 15) and from December 1 to March 31. An entrance fee of $12 per vehicle is charged at the gatehouse, but vehicles bearing Maine registration can enter at no charge. During the summer season, the park's Togue Pond Gate opens at 6 A.M. and closes at 10 P.M.—though it may open at 5 A.M. some summer days—and the Matagamon Gate opens at 6 A.M. and closes at 10 P.M. The road is not maintained to the trailhead in winter, but it can be skied.

Maps

For a park trail map, get the *Baxter State Park and Katahdin* map for $7.95 from the DeLorme Publishing Company, 800/642-0970; or the *Rangeley-Stratton/Baxter State Park-Katahdin* map, $7.95 in waterproof Tyvek, from the Appalachian Mountain Club, 800/262-4455, website: www.outdoors.org. For topographic area maps, request Wassataquoik Lake and the Traveler from USGS Map Sales, Federal Center, Box 25286, Denver, CO 80225, 888/ASK-USGS (888/275-8747), website: http://mapping.usgs.gov.

Directions

Take I-95 in Maine to Exit 56 for Medway/Millinocket. Drive on Route 157 west through East Millinocket to Millinocket. Follow signs for Baxter State Park; the park's Togue Pond gatehouse is 18 miles from Millinocket. Just beyond the gatehouse, take the gravel Tote Road's left fork and drive 34.8 miles. Turn right at a sign for South Branch Pond Campground. Drive 2.1 miles to a parking area on the left, before the campground. Or from the junction of Routes 11 and 159 in Patten, drive west on Route 159 to Shin Pond and follow the access road to Baxter State Park's Matagamon gatehouse, which is 24 miles from Patten. From the gatehouse, continue about 7.3 miles and turn left at the sign for South Branch Pond Campground.

Contact

Baxter State Park, 64 Balsam Drive, Millinocket, ME 04462-2190, 207/723-5140, website: www.baxterstateparkauthority.com.

3 PEAK OF THE RIDGES
in northern Baxter State Park

Total distance: 7.2 miles round-trip   **Hiking time:** 6 hours

Difficulty: 9   **Rating:** 10

Like the North Traveler hike, this 7.2-mile round-trip trek to Traveler Mountain's Peak of the Ridges follows a long, open ridge, but is longer and more arduous, making it even more remote and challenging than the North Traveler hike. It ascends about 2,500 feet in elevation.

From the parking area, walk the road into the campground, toward the northernmost South Branch Pond. Bear left through the campground, passing several sites, and turn right (south) onto the Pogy Notch Trail, which parallels the pond. In a mile, the trail passes a junction with the Howe Brook Trail and then crosses an often-dry streambed; follow the blue blazes to the left, eventually turning away from the streambed. Within another 0.4 mile, the trail turns left and ascends steeply 0.1 mile to another junction. Turn left onto the Center Ridge Trail, which climbs relentlessly and at times steeply. But you don't have to go far to enjoy your first views of the two South Branch Ponds, across to the South Branch Mountains and south toward Katahdin. After crossing an extensive talus field—where following the trail can be difficult, so watch carefully for blazes and cairns—the trail terminates at the Peak of the Ridges, a high point about a mile west of the 3,541-foot summit of the Traveler, and connected to it by a trailless ridge. Follow the same route back to your car.

User Groups
Hikers only. No wheelchair facilities. This trail should not be attempted in winter except by hikers experienced in mountaineering and prepared for severe winter weather. It is not suitable for skis. Bikes, dogs, horses, and hunting are prohibited.

Access and Fees
Baxter Park is open from May 15 to November 1 (no camping in the park after October 15) and from December 1 to March 31. An entrance fee of $12 per vehicle is charged at the gatehouse, but vehicles bearing Maine registration can enter at no charge. During the summer season, the park's Togue Pond Gate opens at 6 A.M. and closes at 10 P.M.—though it may open at 5 A.M. some summer days—and the Matagamon Gate opens at 6 A.M. and closes at 10 P.M. The road is not maintained to the trailhead in winter, but it can be skied.

Maps

For a park trails map, get the *Baxter State Park and Katahdin* map for $7.95 from the DeLorme Publishing Company, 800/642-0970; or the *Rangeley-Stratton/Baxter State Park-Katahdin* map, $7.95 in waterproof Tyvek, from the Appalachian Mountain Club, 800/262-4455, website: www.outdoors.org. For topographic area maps, request Wassataquoik Lake and the Traveler from USGS Map Sales, Federal Center, Box 25286, Denver, CO 80225, 888/ASK-USGS (888/275-8747), website: http://mapping.usgs.gov.

Directions

Take I-95 in Maine to Exit 56 for Medway/Millinocket. Drive on Route 157 west through East Millinocket to Millinocket. Follow signs for Baxter State Park; the park's Togue Pond gatehouse is 18 miles from Millinocket. Just beyond the gatehouse, take the gravel Tote Road's left fork and drive 34.8 miles. Turn right at a sign for South Branch Pond Campground. Drive 2.1 miles to a parking area on the left, before the campground. Or from the junction of Routes 11 and 159 in Patten, drive west on Route 159 to Shin Pond and follow the access road to Baxter State Park's Matagamon gatehouse, which is 24 miles from Patten. From the gatehouse, drive about 7.3 miles and turn left at the sign for South Branch Pond Campground.

Contact

Baxter State Park, 64 Balsam Drive, Millinocket, ME 04462-2190, 207/723-5140, website: www.baxterstateparkauthority.com.

◢ RUSSELL POND/DAVIS POND LOOP
in central Baxter State Park

Total distance: 19 miles round-trip   **Hiking time:** 3 days

Difficulty: 7   **Rating:** 9

Ever since I backpacked this Baxter Park loop with two friends several years ago, I've longed to get back and repeat it. Visitors to this magnificent park who hike only Katahdin—especially on a busy weekend like Labor Day—may not get a sense of remoteness. But Baxter is far enough removed from the rest of the world that if you wander away from the big mountain, you're in some real wilderness. And that's what this loop is all about. On a recent trip, my friends and I saw only a handful of other backpackers at Russell Pond and hikers on the popular Chimney Pond Trail, and one day we saw more moose (two) than people (none). The only steep stretches of this hike are the climbs to Davis Pond in the Northwest Basin and above Davis Pond to the Northwest Plateau, and the descent off Hamlin Peak. Much of this loop is easy hiking that fit backpackers can accomplish in a few hours of hiking per day. The loop hike is spread out over three days to take advantage of two excellent backcountry camping areas at Russell and Davis Ponds. At the latter, you have the lean-to and pristine hanging valley to yourself.

From Roaring Brook Campground, follow the Russell Pond Trail north a relatively flat seven miles to Russell Pond Campground, where a ranger is posted and canoes can be rented for a small fee. The hiking has small ups and downs, but is easy. Listen for early morning or evening splashes in the pond—it's probably a moose grazing. On day two, head southwest on the Northwest Basin Trail, which climbs gradually alongside a rock-strewn stream, passing small pools that invite a very chilly swim. It's a bit more than five miles and about 1,700 feet uphill to the Davis Pond lean-to.

The final day takes you up the Northwest Basin Trail onto the rocky, alpine Northwest Plateau area. At 2.2 miles past, and about 1,600 feet above Davis Pond, turn left onto the Hamlin Ridge Trail, soon passing over Hamlin Peak (4,751 feet), one of Maine's 14 4,000-footers. The trail descends the open, rocky Hamlin Ridge, with constant views down into the cliff-ringed North Basin to your left (north) and toward Katahdin on the right (south). About two miles from Hamlin Peak, you reach the North Basin Trail. To the right, it's less than a mile downhill to Chimney Pond (via the Chimney Pond Trail for the final 0.3 mile); this hike, however, turns left, following the North Basin Trail a short distance to the North Basin Cutoff, where you turn right. (For a view into the North Basin, continue straight ahead on the North Basin Trail for 0.3 mile to Blueberry Knoll; once you enjoy the vista, double back to the cutoff.) Follow the cutoff for a bit more than a half mile to the Chimney Pond Trail, turn left, and it's another 2.3 miles to Roaring Brook Campground.

User Groups

Hikers only. No wheelchair facilities. This trail should not be attempted in winter except by experienced skiers or snowshoers prepared for severe winter weather. The trail can be skied as far as Russell Pond, but it grows very steep on the climb to Davis Pond. Bikes, dogs, horses, and hunting are prohibited.

Access and Fees

Baxter Park is open from May 15 to November 1 (no camping in the park after October 15) and from December 1 to March 31. An entrance fee of $12 per vehicle is charged at the gatehouse, but vehicles bearing Maine registration can enter at no charge. During the summer season, the park's Togue Pond Gate opens at 6 A.M. and closes at 10 P.M.—though it may open at 5 A.M. some summer days. The road is not maintained to the trailhead in winter, but it can be skied. A fee of $9 per person per night is charged for lean-to shelters ($12 in winter) and tent sites (minimum $18 per night per shelter), and $10 per person per night for a bunkhouse ($18 in winter). Advance reservations for backcountry campsites are recommended. On this hike, Russell Pond has a bunkhouse (capacity 13), four tent sites, and four lean-tos (capacity four to eight); Davis Pond has one lean-to (capacity six).

Maps
For a park trails map, get the *Baxter State Park and Katahdin* map for $7.95 from the DeLorme Publishing Company, 800/642-0970; or the *Rangeley-Stratton/Baxter State Park–Katahdin* map, $7.95 in waterproof Tyvek, from the Appalachian Mountain Club, 800/262-4455, website: www.outdoors.org. For topographic area maps, request Mount Katahdin and Katahdin Lake from USGS Map Sales, Federal Center, Box 25286, Denver, CO 80225, 888/ASK-USGS (888/275-8747), website: http://mapping.usgs.gov.

Directions
Take I-95 in Maine to Exit 56 for Medway/Millinocket. Drive on Route 157 west through East Millinocket to Millinocket. Follow signs for Baxter State Park; the park's Togue Pond gatehouse is 18 miles from Millinocket. Just beyond the gatehouse, take the gravel Tote Road's right fork and drive 8.1 miles to Roaring Brook Campground. The Russell Pond Trail begins beside the ranger station (where there is a hiker register).

Contact
Baxter State Park, 64 Balsam Drive, Millinocket, ME 04462-2190, 207/723-5140, website: www.baxterstateparkauthority.com.

5 SOUTH TURNER MOUNTAIN
in southern Baxter State Park

Total distance: 4 miles round-trip   **Hiking time:** 3 hours

Difficulty: 7   **Rating:** 9

Though just 3,122 feet in elevation, South Turner's craggy summit gives a rare view of the entire Katahdin massif from the east side. It's so overshadowed by the big mountain that many hikers don't even know about it—enhancing your chances of summiting in solitude. Sandy Stream Pond is a good place for moose viewing in the early morning or at dusk. You could combine this four-mile hike with the Sandy Stream Pond/Whidden Ponds Loop.

From the ranger station, follow the Russell Pond Trail 0.25 mile and then turn right onto the South Turner Mountain Trail/Sandy Stream Pond Trail. You soon reach Sandy Stream Pond's southeast shore, which the trail follows. As you come around the pond's far end, the South Turner Mountain Trail turns right (the Whidden Pond Trail leads left) and soon begins the steep, 1,600-foot ascent of South Turner; much of the trail cuts through dense forest. The final stretch breaks out of the trees to wide views. Descend the same way you came.

User Groups

Hikers only. No wheelchair facilities. This trail may be difficult to snow-shoe because of its steepness and severe winter weather, and is not suitable for skis. Bikes, dogs, horses, and hunting are prohibited.

Access and Fees

Baxter Park is open from May 15 to November 1 (no camping in the park after October 15) and from December 1 to March 31. An entrance fee of $12 per vehicle is charged at the gatehouse, but vehicles bearing Maine registration can enter at no charge. During the summer season, the park's Togue Pond Gate opens at 6 A.M. and closes at 10 P.M.—though it may open at 5 A.M. some summer days. The road is not maintained to the trail-head in winter, but it can be skied.

Maps

For a park trails map, get the *Baxter State Park and Katahdin* map for $7.95 from the DeLorme Publishing Company, 800/642-0970; or the *Rangeley-Stratton/Baxter State Park-Katahdin* map, $7.95 in waterproof Tyvek, from the Appalachian Mountain Club, 800/262-4455, website: www.outdoors.org. For topographic area maps, request Mount Katahdin and Katahdin Lake from USGS Map Sales, Federal Center, Box 25286, Denver, CO 80225, 888/ASK-USGS (888/275-8747), website: http://mapping.usgs.gov.

Directions

Take I-95 in Maine to Exit 56 for Medway/Millinocket. Drive on Route 157 west through East Millinocket to Millinocket. Follow signs for Baxter State Park; the park's Togue Pond gatehouse is 18 miles from Millinocket. Just beyond the gatehouse, take the gravel Tote Road's right fork and drive 8.1 miles to Roaring Brook Campground. The Russell Pond Trail begins beside the ranger station (where there is a hiker register).

Contact
Baxter State Park, 64 Balsam Drive, Millinocket, ME 04462-2190, 207/723-5140, website: www.baxterstateparkauthority.com.

6 SANDY STREAM POND/ WHIDDEN PONDS LOOP
in southern Baxter State Park

Total distance: 1.5 miles round-trip   **Hiking time:** 1 hour

Difficulty: 1   **Rating:** 8

This relatively flat, easy loop hits two ponds where moose are often seen, especially early in the morning or around dusk. I sat with friends on rocks on the Sandy Stream Pond shore one morning and watched a huge bull moose casually grazing on underwater plants. And the view across the southernmost of the Whidden Ponds toward the North Basin of Hamlin and Howe Peaks is terrific. Start this hike early enough, and you could catch the sunrise hitting the North Basin and moose at Sandy Stream Pond. You might also want to combine it with a jaunt up South Turner Mountain.

From the ranger station, follow the Russell Pond Trail 0.25 mile, then turn right onto the South Turner Mountain Trail/Sandy Stream Pond Trail. You soon reach the southeast shore of Sandy Stream Pond, which the trail follows. As you come around the far end of the pond, the South Turner Mountain Trail leads right; this hike turns left onto the Whidden Pond Trail, following it for a mile to the first of the Whidden Ponds (also the largest and the only one directly accessed by a trail). You might turn right onto the Russell Pond Trail and walk along the pond's shore for a bit. Eventually, turn back (south) on the Russell Pond Trail for the easy hike of a bit more than a mile back to Roaring Brook Campground.

User Groups
Hikers only. No wheelchair facilities. Bikes, dogs, horses, and hunting are prohibited. This trail should not be attempted in winter except by experienced skiers or snowshoers prepared for severe winter weather.

Access and Fees
Baxter Park is open from May 15 to November 1 (no camping in the park

after October 15) and from December 1 to March 31. An entrance fee of $12 per vehicle is charged at the gatehouse, but vehicles bearing Maine registration can enter at no charge. During the summer season, the park's Togue Pond Gate opens at 6 A.M. and closes at 10 P.M.—though it may open at 5 A.M. some summer days. The road is not maintained to the trailhead in winter, but it can be skied.

Maps

For a park trails map, get the *Baxter State Park and Katahdin* map for $7.95 from the DeLorme Publishing Company, 800/642-0970; or the *Rangeley-Stratton/Baxter State Park-Katahdin* map, $7.95 in waterproof Tyvek, from the Appalachian Mountain Club, 800/262-4455, website: www.outdoors.org. For topographic area maps, request Mount Katahdin and Katahdin Lake from USGS Map Sales, Federal Center, Box 25286, Denver, CO 80225, 888/ASK-USGS (888/275-8747), website: http://mapping.usgs.gov.

Directions

Take I-95 in Maine to Exit 56 for Medway/Millinocket. Drive on Route 157 west through East Millinocket to Millinocket. Follow signs for Baxter State Park; the park's Togue Pond gatehouse is 18 miles from Millinocket. Just beyond the gatehouse, take the gravel Tote Road's right fork and drive 8.1 miles to Roaring Brook Campground. The Russell Pond Trail begins beside the ranger station (where there is a hiker register).

Contact

Baxter State Park, 64 Balsam Drive, Millinocket, ME 04462-2190, 207/723-5140, website: www.baxterstateparkauthority.com.

7 HAMLIN PEAK
in southern Baxter State Park

Total distance: 9.5 miles round-trip   **Hiking time:** 6 hours

Difficulty: 9   **Rating:** 10

Hamlin Peak, at 4,751 feet, is Maine's second highest peak and one of 14 4,000-footers in the state, though it's also considered part of the Katahdin massif. Swarms of hikers climb Katahdin on summer weekends, but far fewer venture up onto Hamlin—and they are missing a lot. The constant views along the Hamlin Ridge, both into the North Basin and back toward the South Basin and Katahdin, are among the most magnificent in Maine.

This 9.5-mile round-trip hike climbs about 3,200 feet in elevation and is fairly strenuous.

From Roaring Brook Campground, follow the Chimney Pond Trail an easy 2.3 miles to just beyond the Basin Ponds. Don't bypass the short side path leading right to the southernmost of the Basin Ponds, where there's a great view of your destination, Hamlin Ridge, and the North Basin. Turn right onto the North Basin Cutoff, which soon meets up with the North Basin Trail. To the right a short distance is Blueberry Knoll and views into the North Basin and South Basin. Experienced hikers will see that it's possible to bushwhack down to the pair of tiny ponds on the North Basin floor and explore that rugged glacial cirque. This hike turns left (southwest) onto the North Basin Trail, and soon takes a right and begins ascending the Hamlin Ridge Trail. Two miles farther you reach Hamlin Peak, a mound of rocks slightly higher than the vast surrounding tableland, or plateau. Descend the way you came.

Special note: For visitors making this peak part of an extended stay at Baxter State Park, another enjoyable way of hiking Hamlin is from Chimney Pond Campground, which is 3.3 miles from Roaring Brook Campground via the Chimney Pond Trail. Backpack in to Chimney Pond (be sure to make your camping reservations months in advance), and hike Hamlin Peak via the Chimney Pond, North Basin, and Hamlin Ridge trails (four miles, 2.5 hours). Chimney Pond is a good staging point for hikes of Katahdin, or even for beginning the Russell Pond/Davis Pond backpacking loop in the reverse direction.

User Groups

Hikers only. No wheelchair facilities. This trail should not be attempted in winter except by hikers experienced in mountaineering and prepared for severe winter weather. Bikes, dogs, horses, and hunting are prohibited.

Access and Fees

Baxter Park is open from May 15 to November 1 (no camping in the park after October 15) and from December 1 to March 31. An entrance fee of $12 per vehicle is charged at the gatehouse, but vehicles bearing Maine registration can enter at no charge. During the summer season, the park's Togue Pond Gate opens at 6 A.M. and closes at 10 P.M.—though it may open at 5 A.M. some summer days. The road is not maintained to the trailhead in winter, but it can be skied.

Maps

For a park trails map, get the *Baxter State Park and Katahdin* map for $7.95 from the DeLorme Publishing Company, 800/642-0970; or the

Rangeley–Stratton/Baxter State Park–Katahdin map, $7.95 in waterproof Tyvek, from the Appalachian Mountain Club, 800/262-4455, website: www.outdoors.org. For topographic area maps, request Mount Katahdin and Katahdin Lake from USGS Map Sales, Federal Center, Box 25286, Denver, CO 80225, 888/ASK-USGS (888/275-8747), website: http://mapping.usgs.gov.

Directions

Take I-95 in Maine to Exit 56 for Medway/Millinocket. Drive on Route 157 west through East Millinocket to Millinocket. Follow signs for Baxter State Park; the park's Togue Pond gatehouse is 18 miles from Millinocket. Just beyond the gatehouse, take the gravel Tote Road's right fork and drive 8.1 miles to Roaring Brook Campground. The Chimney Pond Trail begins beside the ranger station (where there is a hiker register).

Contact

Baxter State Park, 64 Balsam Drive, Millinocket, ME 04462-2190, 207/723-5140, website: www.baxterstateparkauthority.com.

8 KATAHDIN: KNIFE EDGE LOOP

In southern Baxter State Park

Total distance: 9.3 miles round-trip   **Hiking time:** 9 hours

Difficulty: 10   **Rating:** 10

This hike offers a mountain experience like no other in New England and is the best way to take in as much of Maine's greatest mountain as possible in a day. The hike encompasses Chimney Pond (set deep in the vast glacial cirque known as the South Basin), a challenging scramble up the Cathedral Trail, Katahdin's four peaks, the infamous Knife Edge, and the open Keep Ridge. Don't underestimate its length, difficulty, or dangers: Two of my several visits to the 5,267-foot Katahdin have come on the heels of hiker deaths on the Knife Edge (one fell, two were struck by lightning). This 9.3-mile loop gains 3,800 feet in elevation and covers some of New England's most rugged terrain—fit, experienced hikers often take eight hours or more. Once you're on the Knife Edge, there's no alternate descent route.

Follow the fairly easy Chimney Pond Trail 3.3 miles to the pond camping area (many visitors make this hike and go no farther, because the views from Chimney Pond are so beautiful). Behind the Chimney Pond ranger station, pick up the Cathedral Trail, which climbs steeply up a rockslide and the right flank of Katahdin's sweeping head wall, passing the

the view of Katahdin from South Turner Mountain in Baxter State Park

three prominent stone buttresses known as the Cathedrals. You can scramble off trail onto each of the Cathedrals for great South Basin views.

At 1.4 miles from Chimney Pond, bear left where the trail forks, soon reaching the Saddle Trail and more level ground. Turn left (southeast) and walk 0.2 mile to the main summit, Baxter Peak, where a large sign marks the Appalachian Trail's northern terminus. Continue straight over the summit (southeast) on the Knife Edge Trail, following an increasingly narrow, rocky ridge that runs 1.1 miles to Katahdin's Pamola Peak. The trail hooks left at South Peak, and the stretch from here to Pamola becomes precipitous. At times, the footpath is barely two feet wide, with sharp drops to either side. At Chimney Peak, you scramble down the vertical wall of a ridge cleft, a spot known to intimidate more than a few hikers. Then you scramble up the other side (not as difficult) onto Pamola Peak. From here, turn right (east) on the Helon Taylor Trail, which descends the Keep Ridge, much of it open, for 3.1 miles to the Chimney Pond Trail. Turn right and walk 0.1 mile to Roaring Brook Campground.

User Groups

Hikers only. No wheelchair facilities. This trail should not be attempted in winter except by hikers experienced in mountaineering and prepared for severe winter weather, and is only suitable for skis as far as Chimney Pond. Bikes, dogs, horses, and hunting are prohibited.

Access and Fees

Baxter Park is open from May 15 to November 1 (no camping in the park after October 15) and from December 1 to March 31. An entrance fee of $12 per vehicle is charged at the gatehouse, but vehicles bearing Maine registration can enter at no charge. During the summer season, the park's Togue Pond Gate opens at 6 A.M. and closes at 10 P.M.—though it may open at 5 A.M. some summer days. The road is not maintained to the trailhead in winter, but it can be skied.

Maps

For a park trails map, get the *Baxter State Park and Katahdin* map for $7.95 from the DeLorme Publishing Company, 800/642-0970; or the *Rangeley-Stratton/Baxter State Park-Katahdin* map, $7.95 in waterproof Tyvek, from the Appalachian Mountain Club, 800/262-4455, website: www.outdoors.org. For topographic area maps, request Mount Katahdin and Katahdin Lake from USGS Map Sales, Federal Center, Box 25286, Denver, CO 80225, 888/ASK-USGS (888/275-8747), website: http://mapping.usgs.gov.

Directions

Take I-95 in Maine to Exit 56 for Medway/Millinocket. Drive on Route 157 west through East Millinocket to Millinocket. Follow signs for Baxter State Park; the park's Togue Pond gatehouse is 18 miles from Millinocket. Just beyond the gatehouse, take the gravel Tote Road's right fork and drive 8.1 miles to Roaring Brook Campground. The Chimney Pond Trail begins beside the ranger station (where there is a hiker register).

Contact

Baxter State Park, 64 Balsam Drive, Millinocket, ME 04462-2190, 207/723-5140, website: www.baxterstateparkauthority.com.

9 KATAHDIN TRAVERSE

in southern Baxter State Park

Total distance: 10.9 miles one-way   **Hiking time:** 10 hours or 1–2 days

Difficulty: 10   **Rating:** 10

If my one lament about hiking the Katahdin Knife Edge Loop is that you miss the Hunt Trail, this traverse of Katahdin remedies that dilemma. Although this 10.9-mile hike, which ascends more than 4,100 feet, could be accomplished in a very long day (its length is compounded by the necessity of shuttling vehicles between Katahdin Stream and Roaring

Brook Campgrounds), you can also spread it out over two days, with an overnight at Chimney Pond Campground. On the second day, you may have time to make an early morning scramble up the Cathedral Trail (see previous listing) to catch Katahdin's summit free of the afternoon crowds, or to hike up onto the spectacular Hamlin Ridge (see the Hamlin Peak hike).

From Katahdin Stream Campground, follow the white-blazed Hunt Trail for 5.2 miles to Katahdin's main summit, 5,267-foot Baxter Peak. (See the Katahdin: Hunt Trail hike for a more detailed description.) Turn right (east) on the Knife Edge Trail, which continues for a mile over South Peak and Knife Edge's narrow crest to Chimney Peak, drops very steeply into a notch, and climbs a few hundred feet up onto Pamola Peak (see previous listing). From here, the Dudley Trail drops steeply 1.3 miles to Chimney Pond. On day two, the 3.3-mile hike out to Roaring Brook Campground is an easy couple of hours.

User Groups
Hikers only. No wheelchair facilities. This trail should not be attempted in winter except by hikers experienced in mountaineering and prepared for severe winter weather, and is not suitable for skis. Bikes, dogs, horses, and hunting are prohibited.

Access and Fees
Baxter Park is open from May 15 to November 1 (no camping in the park after October 15) and from December 1 to March 31. An entrance fee of $12 per vehicle is charged at the gatehouse, but vehicles bearing Maine registration can enter at no charge. During the summer season, the park's Togue Pond Gate opens at 6 A.M. and closes at 10 P.M.—though it may open at 5 A.M. some summer days. The road is not maintained to the trailhead in winter, but it can be skied.

Maps
For a park trails map, get the *Baxter State Park and Katahdin* map for $7.95 from the DeLorme Publishing Company, 800/642-0970; or the *Rangeley-Stratton/Baxter State Park-Katahdin* map, $7.95 in waterproof Tyvek, from the Appalachian Mountain Club, 800/262-4455, website: www.outdoors.org. For topographic area maps, request Mount Katahdin and Katahdin Lake from USGS Map Sales, Federal Center, Box 25286, Denver, CO 80225, 888/ASK-USGS (888/275-8747), website: http://mapping.usgs.gov.

Directions
Take I-95 in Maine to Exit 56 for Medway/Millinocket. Drive on Route

157 west through East Millinocket to Millinocket. Follow signs for Baxter State Park; the park's Togue Pond gatehouse is 18 miles from Millinocket. Just beyond the gatehouse, take the gravel Tote Road's right fork and drive 8.1 miles to Roaring Brook Campground, and leave a vehicle in the parking lot. The Chimney Pond Trail—where you will end this hike—begins beside the ranger station. Drive a second vehicle back to the fork in the Tote Road, turn right, and drive eight miles to Katahdin Stream Campground. Turn right onto the campground road and continue 0.1 mile to the day-use parking area. The Hunt Trail begins here.

Contact

Baxter State Park, 64 Balsam Drive, Millinocket, ME 04462-2190, 207/723-5140, website: www.baxterstateparkauthority.com.

10 KATAHDIN: ABOL TRAIL

in southern Baxter State Park

Total distance: 7.6 miles round-trip **Hiking time:** 7 hours

Difficulty: 10 **Rating:** 10

This trail follows the path of the 1816 Abol landslide, and may be the oldest existing route up the 5,267-foot Katahdin. It's the shortest way to Katahdin's main summit, Baxter Peak, but by no means easy: It climbs 4,000 feet, and the slide's steepness and loose rock make for an arduous ascent, complicated by the possibility of falling rock. And descending this trail is harder than going up, though not impossible (but believe me, it's rough on the knees).

From the day-use parking area on the Tote Road, walk to the back of the campground loop and pick up the Abol Trail. The trail leads through woods for more than a mile to the broad slide base. Pick your way carefully up the slide; watch for rockfall caused by hikers above, and take care not to kick anything down onto hikers below. At 2.6 miles, the trail reaches the level ground of the Tableland, a beautiful, sprawling alpine area, and 0.2 mile farther it connects with the Hunt Trail near Thoreau Spring. Turn right on the Hunt Trail for the final mile to Katahdin's summit, Baxter Peak, which is also the Appalachian Trail's northern terminus. By shuttling vehicles between Abol and Katahdin Stream Campgrounds, you can ascend the Abol and descend the Hunt Trail, a nine-mile hike if you go to Baxter Peak.

User Groups

Hikers only. No wheelchair facilities. This trail should not be attempted in winter except by hikers experienced in mountaineering and prepared for severe winter weather, and is not suitable for skis. Bikes, dogs, horses, and hunting are prohibited.

Access and Fees
Baxter Park is open from May 15 to November 1 (no camping in the park after October 15) and from December 1 to March 31.. An entrance fee of $12 per vehicle is charged at the gatehouse, but vehicles bearing Maine registration can enter at no charge. During the summer season, the park's Togue Pond Gate opens at 6 A.M. and closes at 10 P.M.—though it may open at 5 A.M. some summer days. The road is not maintained to the trailhead in winter, but it can be skied.

Maps
For a park trails map, get the *Baxter State Park and Katahdin* map for $7.95 from the DeLorme Publishing Company, 800/642-0970; or the *Rangeley-Stratton/Baxter State Park-Katahdin* map, $7.95 in waterproof Tyvek, from the Appalachian Mountain Club, 800/262-4455, website: www.outdoors.org. For topographic area maps, request Mount Katahdin and Katahdin Lake from USGS Map Sales, Federal Center, Box 25286, Denver, CO 80225, 888/ASK-USGS (888/275-8747), website: http://mapping.usgs.gov.

Directions
Take I-95 in Maine to Exit 56 for Medway/Millinocket. Drive on Route 157 west through East Millinocket to Millinocket. Follow signs for Baxter State Park; the park's Togue Pond gatehouse is 18 miles from Millinocket. Just beyond the gatehouse, take the gravel Tote Road's left fork and drive 5.7 miles to Abol Campground and day-use parking on the left, opposite the campground entrance.

Contact
Baxter State Park, 64 Balsam Drive, Millinocket, ME 04462-2190, 207/723-5140, website: www.baxterstateparkauthority.com.

11 LITTLE ABOL FALLS
in southern Baxter State Park

Total distance: 1.6 miles round-trip   **Hiking time:** 1 hour

Difficulty: 2   **Rating:** 8

This easy walk along a path of packed dirt and gravel ascends gently for 0.8 mile to where one of the Abol Stream branches drops over 12-foot falls into a pleasant little pool. This can be a popular hike, so if you want some solitude, go in the early morning or late in the day. From the parking area, walk up the campground road. The Little Abol Falls Trail begins at the rear of the campground, just to the right of the Abol Trail.

User Groups
Hikers only. No wheelchair facilities. This trail should not be attempted in winter except by experienced skiers or snowshoers prepared for severe winter weather. Bikes, dogs, horses, and hunting are prohibited.

Access and Fees
Baxter Park is open from May 15 to November 1 (no camping in the park after October 15) and from December 1 to March 31. An entrance fee of $12 per vehicle is charged at the gatehouse, but vehicles bearing Maine registration can enter at no charge. During the summer season, the park's Togue Pond Gate opens at 6 A.M. and closes at 10 P.M.—though it may open at 5 A.M. some summer days. The road is not maintained to the trailhead in winter, but it can be skied.

Maps
For a park trails map, get the *Baxter State Park and Katahdin* map for $7.95 from the DeLorme Publishing Company, 800/642-0970; or the *Rangeley-Stratton/Baxter State Park-Katahdin* map, $7.95 in waterproof Tyvek, from the Appalachian Mountain Club, 800/262-4455, website: www.outdoors.org. For topographic area maps, request Doubletop Mountain and Mount Katahdin from USGS Map Sales, Federal Center, Box 25286, Denver, CO 80225, 888/ASK-USGS (888/275-8747), website: http://mapping.usgs.gov.

Directions
Take I-95 in Maine to Exit 56 for Medway/Millinocket. Drive on Route 157 west through East Millinocket to Millinocket. Follow signs for Baxter State Park; the park's Togue Pond gatehouse is 18 miles from Millinocket. Just beyond the gatehouse, take the gravel Tote Road's left fork and drive 5.7 miles to the day-use parking area on the left, opposite the entrance to Abol Campground.

Contact
Baxter State Park, 64 Balsam Drive, Millinocket, ME 04462-2190, 207/723-5140, website: www.baxterstateparkauthority.com.

12 KATAHDIN: HUNT TRAIL
in southern Baxter State Park

Total distance: 10 miles round-trip   **Hiking time:** 8 hours

Difficulty: 10   **Rating:** 10

This is the trail I followed on my first hike of the 5,267-foot Katahdin, when I fell in love with this magnificent mountain. Were it not for the Knife Edge, I'd describe the Hunt Trail as the most interesting route up the mountain. The trail is rugged, gains 4,100 feet in elevation, and traverses a substantial area above timberline; it's not uncommon for people to spend a very long day on this hike.

From the campground, follow the white-blazed Hunt Trail (it's the Appalachian Trail's final stretch, so in the fall you may see some through-hikers finishing their 2,174-mile journey). Just over a mile from the campground, a side trail leads left to roaring Katahdin Stream Falls. The trail continues upward through the woods, with occasional views. It abruptly breaks out above the trees, where you use iron rungs drilled into the stone to scale a short but vertical rock face.

The trail ascends the rocky, open ridge crest to the Tableland, a mile-wide plateau at about 4,500 feet, a tundra littered with rocks. The trail passes Thoreau Spring near the Abol Trail junction before ascending the summit cone to the main summit, Baxter Peak, where on a clear day you enjoy one of the finest mountain views in New England. A large sign marks the Appalachian Trail's northern terminus. Some 2,000 feet below is the blue dot of Chimney Pond. To the right (east) is the serrated crest of the Knife Edge, and to the north lie Hamlin Peak, the Howe Peaks, and the vast Baxter Park wilderness. Descend the same way you came up.

User Groups

Hikers only. No wheelchair facilities. This trail should not be attempted in winter except by hikers experienced in mountaineering and prepared for severe winter weather, and is not suitable for skis. Bikes, dogs, horses, and hunting are prohibited.

Access and Fees

Baxter Park is open from May 15 to November 1 (no camping in the park after October 15) and from December 1 to March 31. An entrance fee of $12 per vehicle is charged at the gatehouse, but vehicles bearing Maine registration can enter at no charge. During the summer season, the park's Togue Pond Gate opens at 6 A.M. and closes at 10 P.M.—though it may open at 5 A.M. some summer days. The road is not maintained to the trail-head in winter, but it can be skied.

Maps

For a park trails map, get the *Baxter State Park and Katahdin* map for $7.95 from the DeLorme Publishing Company, 800/642-0970; or the *Rangeley-Stratton/Baxter State Park–Katahdin* map, $7.95 in waterproof Tyvek, from the Appalachian Mountain Club, 800/262-4455, website: www.outdoors.org. For topographic area maps, request Mount Katahdin and Katahdin Lake from USGS Map Sales, Federal Center, Box 25286, Denver, CO 80225, 888/ASK-USGS (888/275-8747), website: http://mapping.usgs.gov.

Directions

Take I-95 in Maine to Exit 56 for Medway/Millinocket. Drive on Route 157 west through East Millinocket to Millinocket. Follow signs for Baxter State Park; the park's Togue Pond gatehouse is 18 miles from Millinocket. Just beyond the gatehouse, take the left fork of the gravel Tote Road and drive eight miles to Katahdin Stream Campground. Turn right onto the campground road and continue 0.1 mile to the day-use parking area, where the Hunt Trail begins.

Contact

Baxter State Park, 64 Balsam Drive, Millinocket, ME 04462-2190, 207/723-5140, website: www.baxterstateparkauthority.com.

13 KATAHDIN STREAM FALLS

in southern Baxter State Park

Total distance: 2.4 miles round-trip   **Hiking time:** 1.5 hours

Difficulty: 2   **Rating:** 8

Katahdin Stream Falls tumbles about 50 feet and is visible from the trail after an easy walk of just over a mile. From the parking area, follow the white blazes of the Hunt Trail, which is the Appalachian Trail's final stretch. It ascends easily through the woods. After passing the Owl Trail one mile out, continue 0.1 mile on the Hunt Trail and cross Katahdin Stream on a wooden bridge. Just 0.1 mile farther, side paths lead to the waterfall. After enjoying the falls, head back the way you came.

User Groups

Hikers only. No wheelchair facilities. This trail should not be attempted in winter except by experienced skiers or snowshoers prepared for severe winter weather. Bikes, dogs, horses, and hunting are prohibited.

Access and Fees
Baxter Park is open from May 15 to November 1 (no camping in the park after October 15) and from December 1 to March 31. An entrance fee of $12 per vehicle is charged at the gatehouse, but vehicles bearing Maine registration can enter at no charge. During the summer season, the park's Togue Pond Gate opens at 6 A.M. and closes at 10 P.M.—though it may open at 5 A.M. some summer days. The road is not maintained to the trailhead in winter, but it can be skied.

Maps
For a park trails map, get the *Baxter State Park and Katahdin* map for $7.95 from the DeLorme Publishing Company, 800/642-0970; or the *Rangeley-Stratton/Baxter State Park–Katahdin* map, $7.95 in waterproof Tyvek, from the Appalachian Mountain Club, 800/262-4455, website: www.outdoors.org. For topographic area maps, request Doubletop Mountain and Mount Katahdin from USGS Map Sales, Federal Center, Box 25286, Denver, CO 80225, 888/ASK-USGS (888/275-8747), website: http://mapping.usgs.gov.

Directions
Take I-95 in Maine to Exit 56 for Medway/Millinocket. Drive on Route 157 west through East Millinocket to Millinocket. Follow signs for Baxter State Park; the park's Togue Pond gatehouse is 18 miles from Millinocket. Just beyond the gatehouse, take the gravel Tote Road's left fork and drive eight miles. Turn right into the Katahdin Stream Campground and continue 0.1 mile to the day-use parking area.

Contact
Baxter State Park, 64 Balsam Drive, Millinocket, ME 04462-2190, 207/723-5140, website: www.baxterstateparkauthority.com.

14 THE OWL
in southern Baxter State Park

Total distance: 6 miles round-trip   **Hiking time:** 6 hours

Difficulty: 9   **Rating:** 10

One of the most arduous hikes in Baxter State Park and one of its best-kept secrets, this six-mile round-tripper climbs some 2,600 feet to the

3,736-foot summit of the Owl, which is visible from the Hunt Trail/Appalachian Trail ridge on neighboring Katahdin. On the Thursday of a busy Labor Day weekend that saw hundreds of hikers on Katahdin, I encountered just seven other people on the Owl and spent a half hour at the summit completely alone.

From the parking area, follow the white blazes of the Hunt Trail, which is the Appalachian Trail's final stretch, ascending easily through the woods. After one mile, turn left at the sign for the Owl Trail, which you find lined with ripe blueberries in late August and early September. Within a mile from the Hunt Trail, you pass huge boulders. About 0.2 mile below the summit, you emerge onto an open ledge with a great view down into the Katahdin Stream ravine and across it to Katahdin. Some hikers may want to turn around from here, because the trail grows increasingly difficult and exposed.

If you decide to persevere, scramble up rocks to a second ledge, where a boulder perches at the brink of a precipice. After another short scramble, you reach the level shoulder of the Owl. The trail follows the crest of that narrow ridge, ducking briefly through a subalpine forest and ascending slightly to the bare ledges at the summit, where there are sweeping views in every direction. An example of Baxter's famed striped forest is visible to the west. Katahdin dominates the skyline to the east; the Northwest Plateau lies to the northeast; the Brothers, Coe, and O-J-I to the west; and the wilderness lakes along the Appalachian Trail to the south. Descend along the same route.

User Groups

Hikers only. No wheelchair facilities. This trail should not be attempted in winter except by hikers experienced in mountaineering and prepared for severe winter weather, and is not suitable for skis. Bikes, dogs, horses, and hunting are prohibited.

Access and Fees

Baxter Park is open from May 15 to November 1 (no camping in the park after October 15) and from December 1 to March 31. An entrance fee of $12 per vehicle is charged at the gatehouse, but vehicles bearing Maine registration can enter at no charge. During the summer season, the park's Togue Pond Gate opens at 6 A.M. and closes at 10 P.M.—though it may open at 5 A.M. some summer days. The road is not maintained to the trailhead in winter, but it can be skied.

Maps

For a park trails map, get the *Baxter State Park and Katahdin* map for $7.95 from the DeLorme Publishing Company, 800/642-0970; or the

Rangeley–Stratton/Baxter State Park–Katahdin map, $7.95 in waterproof Tyvek, from the Appalachian Mountain Club, 800/262-4455, website: www.outdoors.org. For topographic area maps, request Doubletop Mountain and Mount Katahdin from USGS Map Sales, Federal Center, Box 25286, Denver, CO 80225, 888/ASK-USGS (888/275-8747), website: http://mapping.usgs.gov.

Directions
Take I-95 in Maine to Exit 56 for Medway/Millinocket. Drive on Route 157 west through East Millinocket to Millinocket. Follow signs for Baxter State Park; the park's Togue Pond gatehouse is 18 miles from Millinocket. Just beyond the gatehouse, take the gravel Tote Road's left fork and drive eight miles. Turn right into the Katahdin Stream Campground and continue 0.1 mile to the day-use parking area.

Contact
Baxter State Park, 64 Balsam Drive, Millinocket, ME 04462-2190, 207/ 723-5140, website: www.baxterstateparkauthority.com.

15 NORTH BROTHER
in southern Baxter State Park

Total distance: 8.5 miles round-trip   **Hiking time:** 6 hours

Difficulty: 9   **Rating:** 10

At 4,143 feet, Maine's seventh-highest mountain has a fairly extensive area above tree line around its summit, and the excellent views from the peak encompass Katahdin to the southeast, the remote Northwest Plateau and Basin to the east, Fort and Traveler Mountains to the north, Doubletop to the west, and the wild, trailless area known as the Klondike to the immediate south. The hike gains about 2,900 feet in elevation.

From the parking lot, pick up the Marston Trail. At 1.2 miles, the Mount Coe Trail branches right; bear left with the Marston Trail. At two miles the trail passes a small pond, and at 3.4 miles it reaches a second junction with the Mount Coe Trail. To reach the open summit of South Brother (3,930 feet), which has views comparable to North Brother for somewhat less effort, turn right at this junction and follow the Mount Coe Trail over fairly flat terrain for 0.7 mile to a side path leading left 0.3 mile to the top of South Brother. (South Brother adds two miles and more than 400 feet of climbing to this hike.) A good example of Baxter's famous striped forest is visible between South and North Brother. From the South

Brother summit trail junction, turn left and climb 0.8 mile to North Brother's summit. Return the same way you hiked up.

Special note: You can combine this hike with the hike up Mount Coe, and bag South Brother as well, in a loop of 9.4 miles. The best route is to ascend the Mount Coe slide, hitting Coe first, then continuing on the Mount Coe Trail to South Brother, and finally bagging North Brother, then descending the Marston Trail. See the Mount Coe hike description for more information.

User Groups

Hikers only. No wheelchair facilities. This trail should not be attempted in winter except by hikers experienced in mountaineering and prepared for severe winter weather, and is not suitable for skis. Bikes, dogs, horses, and hunting are prohibited.

Access and Fees

Baxter Park is open from May 15 to November 1 (no camping in the park after October 15) and from December 1 to March 31. An entrance fee of $12 per vehicle is charged at the gatehouse, but vehicles bearing Maine registration can enter at no charge. During the summer season, the park's Togue Pond Gate opens at 6 A.M. and closes at 10 P.M.—though it may open at 5 A.M. some summer days. The road is not maintained to the trailhead in winter, but it can be skied.

Maps

For a park trails map, get the *Baxter State Park and Katahdin* map for $7.95 from the DeLorme Publishing Company, 800/642-0970; or the *Rangeley-Stratton/Baxter State Park-Katahdin* map, $7.95 in waterproof Tyvek, from the Appalachian Mountain Club, 800/262-4455, website: www.outdoors.org. For topographic area maps, request Doubletop Mountain and Mount Katahdin from USGS Map Sales, Federal Center, Box 25286, Denver, CO 80225, 888/ASK-USGS (888/275-8747), website: http://mapping.usgs.gov.

Directions

Take I-95 in Maine to Exit 56 for Medway/Millinocket. Drive on Route 157 west through East Millinocket to Millinocket. Follow signs for Baxter State Park; the park's Togue Pond gatehouse is 18 miles from Millinocket. Just beyond the gatehouse, take the gravel Tote Road's left fork and drive 13.5 miles to a parking area on the right for the Marston Trail.

Contact

Baxter State Park, 64 Balsam Drive, Millinocket, ME 04462-2190, 207/723-5140, website: www.baxterstateparkauthority.com.

16 MOUNT COE

in southern Baxter State Park

Total distance: 6.6 miles round-trip

Hiking time: 6 hours

Difficulty: 9

Rating: 9

Mount Coe's 3,764-foot summit has a sweeping view of the southern end of Baxter State Park, including east over the Klondike and toward Katahdin and the Northwest Plateau. This 6.6-mile out-and-back hike ascends about 2,500 feet. From the parking area, follow the Marston Trail for 1.2 miles and then bear right onto the Mount Coe Trail. It ascends easily at first, reaching the foot of the Mount Coe rockslide, still in the forest, within a quarter of a mile. The trail emerges about a mile farther onto the open, broad scar of the slide, and for the next half mile climbs the slide's steep slabs and loose stone; this section becomes treacherous when wet, with the potential for injurious falls. Watch closely for the blazes and rock cairns, because the trail zigzags several times across the slide.

Near the top of the slide, a side trail—easy to overlook—branches right, leading 0.7 mile to the Mount O-J-I summit. This hike continues straight up the slide, enters the scrub forest, and reaches the Mount Coe summit 3.3 miles from the trailhead. It's possible to continue over Coe toward the Brothers (see the previous listing). This hike descends the same way you came.

User Groups

Hikers only. No wheelchair facilities. This trail should not be attempted in winter except by hikers experienced in mountaineering and prepared for severe winter weather, and is not suitable for skis. Bikes, dogs, horses, and hunting are prohibited.

Access and Fees

Baxter Park is open from May 15 to November 1 (no camping in the park after October 15) and from December 1 to March 31. An entrance fee of $12 per vehicle is charged at the gatehouse, but vehicles bearing Maine registration can enter at no charge. During the summer season, the park's Togue Pond Gate opens at 6 A.M. and closes at 10 P.M.—though it may open at 5 A.M. some summer days. The road is not maintained to the trailhead in winter, but it can be skied.

Maps

For a park trails map, get the *Baxter State Park and Katahdin* map for $7.95 from the DeLorme Publishing Company, 800/642-0970; or the *Rangeley-Stratton/Baxter State Park-Katahdin* map, $7.95 in waterproof

Tyvek, from the Appalachian Mountain Club, 800/262-4455, website: www.outdoors.org. For topographic area maps, request Doubletop Mountain and Mount Katahdin from USGS Map Sales, Federal Center, Box 25286, Denver, CO 80225, 888/ASK-USGS (888/275-8747), website: http://mapping.usgs.gov.

Directions
Take I-95 in Maine to Exit 56 for Medway/Millinocket. Drive on Route 157 west through East Millinocket to Millinocket. Follow signs for Baxter State Park; the park's Togue Pond gatehouse is 18 miles from Millinocket. Just beyond the gatehouse, take the gravel Tote Road's left fork and drive 13.5 miles to a parking area on the right for the Marston Trail.

Contact
Baxter State Park, 64 Balsam Drive, Millinocket, ME 04462-2190, 207/723-5140, website: www.baxterstateparkauthority.com.

17 MOUNT O-J-I
in southern Baxter State Park

Total distance: 6.2 miles round-trip   **Hiking time:** 6 hours

Difficulty: 8   **Rating:** 9

This 6.2-mile loop up 3,410-foot Mount O-J-I is one of the most arduous hikes in Baxter State Park, excluding Katahdin. It climbs about 2,300 feet, but more significantly, involves fairly serious scrambling. Traditionally, this hike ascended the mountain's north rockslide—the logical ascent route, being the more difficult of the two slides—and descended the south slide. But Baxter Park officials decided after the summer of 2000 to no longer maintain the north slide as a trail, though hikers may continue to use it as a bushwhacking route. The maintained trail up O-J-I ascends and descends the south slide. Both slides are steep, with lots of loose rock and slabs that are hazardous when wet. Hiking time can vary greatly depending upon your comfort level on exposed rock. But you enjoy extensive views from the slides to the west and south, and excellent views from points near the summit. By the way, O-J-I takes its name from the shapes of three slides when seen from the southwest, although the slides have expanded and the letters have become obscured in recent decades.

From the parking area, walk the road toward Foster Field for about 50 feet, and turn right onto the O-J-I Trail. For the first 0.4 mile, the terrain is flat, crossing wet areas. The junction where the former North Slide Trail and the South Slide Trail diverge is no longer marked as such, so you'll have to watch for the path of the former North Slide Trail if you want to take it. Otherwise, go up the South Slide. The North Slide Trail reaches an often-dry streambed at 1.1 miles; turn left and follow it upward for 0.1 mile to the base of the north slide. Follow the trail's cairns and blazes, snaking up the slide for about a mile. The trail then reenters the woods; at 2.5 miles, turn left onto the Old Jay Eye Rock Trail, which leads 0.4 mile down a ridge to Old Jay Eye Rock, a boulder perched on the crest of the open ridge where there are long views in every direction. (Skipping this side trail cuts 0.8 mile from this hike's distance.) Double back to the main trail and follow it another 0.2 mile to the largely wooded summit, where you get a view toward Mount Coe. Continuing over the summit, the ridge opens up more, with sweeping views of Coe, Katahdin, Doubletop Mountain, and the wilderness lakes to the south. Turn right and descend the south slide, which reenters the forest within a mile and reaches the junction with the North Slide Trail 2.5 miles below O-J-I's summit. Turn left for the flat walk of 0.4 mile back to the road.

User Groups
Hikers only. No wheelchair facilities. This trail should not be attempted in winter except by hikers experienced in mountaineering and prepared for severe winter weather, and is not suitable for skis. Bikes, dogs, horses, and hunting are prohibited.

Access and Fees
Baxter Park is open from May 15 to November 1 (no camping in the park after October 15) and from December 1 to March 31. An entrance fee of $12 per vehicle is charged at the gatehouse, but vehicles bearing Maine registration can enter at no charge. During the summer season, the park's Togue Pond Gate opens at 6 A.M. and closes at 10 P.M.—though it may open at 5 A.M. some summer days. The road is not maintained to the trailhead in winter, but it can be skied.

Maps
For a park trails map, get the *Baxter State Park and Katahdin* map for $7.95 from the DeLorme Publishing Company, 800/642-0970; or the *Rangeley-Stratton/Baxter State Park-Katahdin* map, $7.95 in waterproof Tyvek, from the Appalachian Mountain Club, 800/262-4455, website: www.outdoors.org. For topographic area maps, request Doubletop Mountain and Mount Katahdin from USGS Map Sales, Federal Center, Box 25286, Denver, CO 80225, 888/ASK-USGS (888/275-8747), website: http://mapping.usgs.gov.

Directions

Take I-95 in Maine to Exit 56 for Medway/Millinocket. Drive on Route 157 west through East Millinocket to Millinocket. Follow signs for Baxter State Park; the park's Togue Pond gatehouse is 18 miles from Millinocket. Just beyond the gatehouse, take the gravel Tote Road's left fork and drive 10.5 miles to a parking area on the right for the Mount O-J-I Loop, just before Foster Field.

Contact

Baxter State Park, 64 Balsam Drive, Millinocket, ME 04462-2190, 207/723-5140, website: www.baxterstateparkauthority.com.

18 DOUBLETOP MOUNTAIN

in southern Baxter State Park

Total distance: 6 miles round-trip   **Hiking time:** 5.5 hours

Difficulty: 8   **Rating:** 10

Measuring 3,488 feet, Doubletop Mountain's distinctive high ridge stands out prominently from various points around Baxter State Park's south end, rising like an upturned ax blade above the narrow valley of Nesowadnehunk Stream. Much of the quarter mile of ridge connecting the north and south peaks lies above tree line, affording some of the best views in the park, from Katahdin to the east, to the cluster of peaks immediately north that includes the Brothers, Coe, and O-J-I, and the wilderness lakes to the south. This six-mile hike ascends about 2,200 feet.

From the parking area, cross the road onto the campground road and follow it past campsites. At half a mile, the campground road ends at the start of the Doubletop Trail. The trail begins relatively flat, until crossing a stream at 1.2 miles, where it begins a very steep climb. It levels out briefly on the mountain's north shoulder and then ascends again. After climbing a short iron ladder, you emerge above the forest a few steps from the North Peak of Doubletop, which is marked by a sign, at 3.1 miles. The trail drops off that summit to the west, then turns south and follows the ridge for 0.2 mile to the South Peak. Return the same way you hiked up.

User Groups

Hikers only. No wheelchair facilities. This trail should not be attempted in winter except by hikers experienced in mountaineering and prepared for severe winter weather, and is not suitable for skis. Bikes, dogs, horses, and hunting are prohibited.

Access and Fees

Baxter Park is open from May 15 to November 1 (no camping in the park after October 15) and from December 1 to March 31. An entrance fee of $12 per vehicle is charged at the gatehouse, but vehicles bearing Maine registration can enter at no charge. During the summer season, the park's Togue Pond Gate opens at 6 A.M. and closes at 10 P.M.—though it may open at 5 A.M. some summer days. The road is not maintained to the trailhead in winter, but it can be skied.

Maps

For a park trails map, get the *Baxter State Park and Katahdin* map for $7.95 from the DeLorme Publishing Company, 800/642-0970; or the *Rangeley-Stratton/Baxter State Park-Katahdin* map, $7.95 in waterproof Tyvek, from the Appalachian Mountain Club, 800/262-4455, website: www.outdoors.org. For a topographic area map, request Doubletop Mountain from USGS Map Sales, Federal Center, Box 25286, Denver, CO 80225, 888/ASK-USGS (888/275-8747), website: http://mapping.usgs.gov.

Directions

Take I-95 in Maine to Exit 56 for Medway/Millinocket. Drive on Route 157 west through East Millinocket to Millinocket. Follow signs for Baxter State Park; the park's Togue Pond gatehouse is 18 miles from Millinocket. Just beyond the gatehouse, take the gravel Tote Road's left fork and drive 16.9 miles, then turn left into the Nesowadnehunk Field Campground. Drive 0.3 mile to the parking area on the right.

Contact

Baxter State Park, 64 Balsam Drive, Millinocket, ME 04462-2190, 207/723-5140, website: www.baxterstateparkauthority.com.

19 KIDNEY POND LOOP
in southern Baxter State Park

Total distance: 3.1 miles round-trip   **Hiking time:** 1.5 hours

Difficulty: 2   **Rating:** 8

This easy 3.1-mile loop around lovely Kidney Pond offers a chance at seeing moose or other wildlife, and good views across the pond toward Katahdin, Doubletop, and O-J-I. Side paths lead to such scenic lakeshore spots as Colt's Point, a peninsula jutting into the pond. Paths radiate outward from the loop trail like spokes from a wheel's hub, leading to Rocky Pond and other nearby ponds. You could spend hours exploring the various little water bodies in this corner of Baxter State Park.

This hike follows the loop trail around the pond. From the rear of the parking area, pick up the trail at a sign for the Kidney Pond Loop. The trail follows the pond's shore at first, then skirts wide of it into the woods at its southern end. Where a trail bears right toward Daicey Pond about halfway through the hike, go left, passing through woods, following and crossing a stream, and eventually reaching the campground road. Turn left on the road and walk the quarter mile back to the parking area.

User Groups
Hikers only. No wheelchair facilities. This trail should not be attempted in winter except by experienced skiers or snowshoers prepared for severe winter weather. Bikes, dogs, horses, and hunting are prohibited.

Access and Fees
Baxter Park is open from May 15 to November 1 (no camping in the park after October 15) and from December 1 to March 31. An entrance fee of $12 per vehicle is charged at the gatehouse, but vehicles bearing Maine registration can enter at no charge. During the summer season, the park's Togue Pond Gate opens at 6 A.M. and closes at 10 P.M.—though it may open at 5 A.M. some summer days. The road is not maintained to the trailhead in winter, but it can be skied.

Maps
For a park trails map, get the *Baxter State Park and Katahdin* map for $7.95 from the DeLorme Publishing Company, 800/642-0970; or the *Rangeley-Stratton/Baxter State Park-Katahdin* map, $7.95 in waterproof Tyvek, from the Appalachian Mountain Club, 800/262-4455, website: www.outdoors.org. For a topographic area map, request Doubletop Mountain from USGS Map Sales, Federal Center, Box 25286, Denver, CO 80225.

Directions
Take I-95 in Maine to Exit 56 for Medway/Millinocket. Drive on Route 157 west through East Millinocket to Millinocket. Follow signs for Baxter State Park; the park's Togue Pond gatehouse is 18 miles from Millinocket. Just beyond the gatehouse, take the dirt perimeter road's left fork and drive 10.6 miles, then turn left at a sign for Kidney Pond Camps. Drive 1.1 miles to the parking area.

Contact
Baxter State Park, 64 Balsam Drive, Millinocket, ME 04462-2190, 207/723-5140, website: www.baxterstateparkauthority.com.

20 POLLYWOG GORGE
southwest of Baxter State Park

Total distance: 3.8 miles round-trip   **Hiking time:** 2.5 hours

Difficulty: 3   **Rating:** 8

This hike makes a 3.8-mile loop mostly along the Appalachian Trail through scenic Pollywog Gorge, finishing on a 1.2-mile stretch of logging road. From a small ledge high above the stream, you peer down a precipitous cliff into the gorge. Day hikers could easily combine this with the Nesuntabunt Mountain hike (see next listing). Immediately before the bridge over Pollywog Stream, turn left (southbound) on the Appalachian Trail and follow it one mile to a side path leading about 150 feet to the gorge overlook. Continue south on the Appalachian Trail through woods and around Crescent Pond to the logging road, 2.6 miles from the hike's start. Turn left and follow the road 1.2 miles back to the bridge.

User Groups
Hikers only. No wheelchair facilities. Dogs are discouraged along the Appalachian Trail in Maine. This trail should not be attempted in winter except by hikers prepared for severe winter weather, and is not suitable for skis. Bikes, horses, and hunting are prohibited.

Access and Fees
A toll is charged on private Jo-Mary Road, which isn't passable at certain times of year due to snow or muddy conditions. The Rainbow Stream lean-to is located 2.4 miles north on the Appalachian Trail from the Pollywog Stream bridge (not along this hike). It's legal to camp anywhere along the Appalachian Trail in the 100-Mile Wilderness; low-impact camping is encouraged.

Maps
For a trail map, refer to map 1 in the *Map and Guide to the Appalachian Trail in Maine,* a set of seven maps and a guidebook for $24.95 from the Maine Appalachian Trail Club or the Appalachian Trail Conference. For a topographic area map, request Rainbow Lake West from USGS Map Sales, Federal Center, Box 25286, Denver, CO 80225.

Directions

From Route 11, 15.5 miles south of the junction of Routes 11 and 157 in Millinocket and near where Route 11 crosses over Bear Brook, turn west onto private, gravel Jo-Mary Road. In 0.2 mile, pass through a gate and pay a vehicle toll. Continue six miles from the gate and bear right at a sign for the Appalachian Trail. Follow that road another 20.2 miles (ignoring unimproved roads diverging from it) to where the Appalachian Trail crosses Pollywog Stream on a bridge, and park at the roadside.

Contact

Maine Appalachian Trail Club, P.O. Box 283, Augusta, ME 04332-0283, website: www.matc.org. Appalachian Trail Conference, 799 Washington Street, P.O. Box 807, Harpers Ferry, WV 25425-0807, 304/535-6331, website: www.appalachiantrail.org.

21 NESUNTABUNT MOUNTAIN
southwest of Baxter State Park

Total distance: 2.4 miles round-trip   **Hiking time:** 1.5 hours

Difficulty: 2   **Rating:** 8

At barely more than 1,500 feet, tiny Nesuntabunt Mountain merits notice only because the surrounding terrain is relatively flat and low here among the wilderness lakes along the Appalachian Trail's northern reaches. From an open ledge, down a short side path off the Appalachian Trail at Nesuntabunt's summit, hikers get a sweeping view of vast Nahmakanta Lake and Mount Katahdin, when clouds aren't smothering Maine's highest peak. You can turn this 2.4-mile hike into an overnight trip by pushing 1.9 miles beyond Nesuntabunt to the Wadleigh Stream lean-to and continuing south along Nahmakanta's isolated shore. (From Wadleigh Stream, it's 2.6 miles south along the Appalachian Trail to the lake's southern tip.) Or you might want to combine this hike with nearby Pollywog Gorge. From the logging road, walk southbound (to the right) along the white-blazed Appalachian Trail for 1.2 miles, climbing about 500 feet to Nesuntabunt's summit. Turn left onto a side path to the open ledge. Retrace your steps to the hike's beginning.

User Groups

Hikers only. No wheelchair facilities. Dogs are discouraged along the Appalachian Trail in Maine. This trail should not be attempted in winter except by hikers experienced in mountaineering and prepared for severe winter weather, and is not suitable for skis. Bikes, horses, and hunting are prohibited.

Access and Fees
A toll is charged on private Jo-Mary Road, which isn't passable at certain times of year due to snow or muddy conditions. The Wadleigh Stream lean-to is located 3.1 miles south on the Appalachian Trail from the access road and 1.9 miles south of the Nesuntabunt Mountain summit. It's legal to camp anywhere along the Appalachian Trail in the 100-Mile Wilderness; low-impact camping is encouraged.

Maps
For a trail map, refer to map 1 in the *Map and Guide to the Appalachian Trail in Maine,* a set of seven maps and a guidebook for $24.95 from the Maine Appalachian Trail Club or the Appalachian Trail Conference. For a topographic area map, request Rainbow Lake West from USGS Map Sales, Federal Center, Box 25286, Denver, CO 80225.

Directions
From Route 11, 15.5 miles south of the junction of Routes 11 and 157 in Millinocket and near where Route 11 crosses over Bear Brook, turn west onto the private, gravel Jo-Mary Road. In 0.2 mile, pass through a gate and pay a vehicle toll. Continue six miles from the gate and bear right at a sign for the Appalachian Trail. Follow that road another 19 miles (ignoring unimproved roads diverging from it) to the Appalachian Trail crossing, and park at the roadside.

Contact
Maine Appalachian Trail Club, P.O. Box 283, Augusta, ME 04332-0283, website: www.matc.org. Appalachian Trail Conference, 799 Washington Street, P.O. Box 807, Harpers Ferry, WV 25425-0807, 304/535-6331, website: www.appalachiantrail.org.

22 100-MILE WILDERNESS
between Monson and Baxter State Park

Total distance: 99.4 miles one-way   **Hiking time:** 9–10 days

Difficulty: 8   **Rating:** 10

The 100-Mile Wilderness is a stretch of the Appalachian Trail in northern Maine that runs for 99.4 miles without crossing a paved or public road. It starts just north of Monson on Route 15 and ends at the West Branch of the Penobscot River at Abol Bridge on the Golden Road, a private logging road just outside the Baxter State Park southern boundary. The trail, however, does cross a few logging roads that provide vehicle access to the Appalachian Trail in the 100-Mile Wilderness. Although it has grown more popular in recent years, the 100-Mile Wilderness still constitutes one of the most remote backpacking experiences possible in New England. On an August trip, my companions and I spent evenings by ourselves on the shores of vast wilderness lakes, listening to the hysterical song of loons, and enjoying wonderful sunsets and sunrises. We swam in chilly streams and walked hours at a time some days without encountering another hiker.

This stretch of trail is busiest in August and early September, when the weather is warm and drier, the mosquitoes have dissipated somewhat (though certainly not disappeared), and Appalachian Trail through-hikers are passing through on their way to Katahdin. This far north, the prime hiking season is short, usually commencing once the ground has dried out in July and lasting to early October, when the cooler temperatures start to feel like winter. The number of days spent on this trail can vary greatly. Generally, the southern half, below Crawford Pond, is more mountainous and rugged; and from Crawford north the trail covers easier, flatter terrain around several vast wilderness lakes. The trail is well marked with the white blazes of the Appalachian Trail, and there are signs at many junctions.

Because this is such a long hike, descriptions in mileage distances beginning at Route 15 and finishing at Abol Bridge are as follows:

From Route 15 (mile 0), the Appalachian Trail enters the woods at a trail sign; there is ample parking at a turnout. Traversing relatively easy terrain, the trail passes a series of ponds: the east shore of Spectacle Pond (mile 0.1), the south shore of Bell Pond (1.2), and then a short side path leading right to the west shore of Lily Pond (1.9). With relatively easy hiking from the highway, you reach the Leeman Brook lean-to (3.0), which sleeps six and sits above a small gorge and falls with reliable water. Continuing north, the trail crosses a gravel road (4.2) and then passes the west and north shores of Mud Pond (5.2). It crosses a gravel road (6.5) and then reaches the top of 60-foot Little Wilson Falls (6.6), one of the highest waterfalls along the Appalachian Trail. The trail turns sharply right, following the rim of the long, deep gorge below the falls, then descends steeply, eventually fording Little Wilson Stream (6.8) with a good view upstream into the gorge. Turn left onto a gravel road (7.2) and follow it for 100 yards, and then turn right into the woods. At mile 7.4, the trail reaches a 0.5-mile-long ridge of exposed slate with good views to the east. At the Big Wilson logging road (9.1), turn left, follow it for 0.6 mile; then turn right off the road (9.7) and ford Big Wilson Stream, which can be difficult in high water. A bridge across the stream is 1.5 miles downstream. At mile 10, cross the Canadian Pacific Railroad line.

Less than 0.5 mile from the railroad right-of-way, a short side path leads right to the Wilson Valley lean-to (10.4), which sleeps six; there is water at a nearby spring. At mile 11.6, cross open ledges with views of Barren Mountain. The trail fords Wilbur Brook (13.6) and Vaughn Stream (13.7) above a spectacular 20-foot waterfall that drops into a broad pool. At a logging road (14.2), turn right for 100 yards and then left again into the woods. (That road continues another 1.6 miles southwest to the old Bodfish Farm site, from which it's nearly 12 miles to Monson on Elliotsville Road.) Ford Long Pond Stream (14.3), walk alongside narrow pools and flumes of smooth rock, and then reach a short side path at 15 miles that leads left to Slugundy Gorge, a scenic gorge and falls. Just beyond, another side path leads left 150 yards to the Long Pond Stream lean-to, which sleeps eight; get water from the nearby brook.

Beyond the shelter, the Appalachian Trail begins the steep climb of Barren Mountain. At mile 16.2, a side path leads to the right about 250 feet to the top of the Barren Slide, from which there are excellent views south of Lake Onawa and Boarstone Mountain. Following the ridge, the trail reaches the 2,670-foot summit of Barren Mountain (18.2), which offers sweeping views, particularly south and west; also here is an abandoned fire tower, no longer open. Dropping back into the woods, you pass a side trail (19.1) leading right 0.3 mile to the beautiful tarn called Cloud Pond and the nearby lean-to, which sleeps six; water can be obtained from a spring or the pond.

Continuing along the Barren-Chairback Ridge, the trail bounces like a yo-yo over rugged terrain, passing over the wooded 2,383-foot summit of Fourth Mountain (21.2), cliffs on Third Mountain that offer some views (23.7), and a side path leading right 0.2 mile to West Chairback Pond (24.3). Just beyond that path, the Appalachian Trail crosses a good stream where you may want to load up on water if you're planning to stay at the Chairback Gap lean-to, where the spring may run dry in late summer. The trail climbs steeply over Columbus Mountain, then drops into Chairback Gap, passing in front of the lean-to there, which sleeps six; the spring is about 200 yards downhill along the trail. The trail then ascends to the top of 2,219-foot Chairback Mountain (26.5), traversing its long, open crest with excellent views west and north. At the end of the ridge, the trail descends a very steep slope (26.6) of loose talus, trending left near its bottom. It passes over open ledges (26.9) with views back to Chairback Mountain, then a side path (28.7)—the sign for which is easily overlooked—leading left 0.2 mile to East Chairback Pond. At mile 29.9, cross a wide logging road; half a mile to the right (east) is a parking area heavily used by day visitors to Gulf Hagas. The road continues east for 7.1 miles to the Katahdin Iron Works Museum.

Crossing the road, the Appalachian Trail passes through woods to the West Branch of the Pleasant River (30.4), a wide channel that was knee-deep during our August trip, but could be dangerous at high water. (Before fording the river, you will notice a blue-blazed trail leading back to the parking area on the logging road.) After crossing the river, the Appalachian Trail follows easy ground through a forest of tall white pines; a short side path (30.7) leads right to the Hermitage, a stand of white pines up to 130 feet tall. At mile 32, the Appalachian Trail hooks right, and a blue-blazed trail leads straight ahead to the 5.2-mile loop through Gulf Hagas, one of the most scenic areas along the Appalachian Trail corridor through Maine and a very worthwhile (and packless!) detour if you have the time (see the Gulf Hagas hike description). The Appalachian Trail ascends steadily northward for 4.2 miles, through dense forest where campsites are difficult to find, following Gulf Hagas Brook to the Carl A. Newhall lean-to and tent sites; the lean-to, accessed by a short side path off the Appalachian Trail (35.9), sleeps six, and water is available from the brook. Climbing steeply, the trail passes over the 2,683-foot summit of Gulf Hagas Mountain (36.8), where there are limited views to the west from just north of the true summit, and then descends to the Sidney Tappen campsite (37.7) for tents only; a nearby spring provides water. It continues north along the arduous ridge, over 3,178-foot West Peak (38.4), with limited views, and the wooded summit of 3,244-foot Hay Mountain (40.0).

At mile 40.6, the White Brook Trail departs to the right (east), descending 1.9 miles to logging roads that eventually link with the road to Katahdin Iron Works. The Appalachian Trail then climbs to the highest point on the ridge and one of the finest views along the 100-Mile Wilderness, the 3,654-foot summit of White Cap Mountain (41.7), where you get your first view on this hike of Mount Katahdin to the north. White Cap is the last big peak in the 100-Mile Wilderness. Descending north off White Cap and passing an open ledge with another good view toward Katahdin (42.5), the trail reaches the Logan Brook lean-to (43.1), which sleeps six and has marginal tent sites and a good stream nearby. Cross a gravel road (44.7) and then reach a lean-to (46.8), which opened in 1996 and sleeps at least six. The trail fords the East Branch of the Pleasant River (47.0), which could be difficult at high water, and then climbs over 2,017-foot Little Boardman Mountain (50.2); just 0.1 mile south of the summit are good views from open ledges.

Descending easily, the Appalachian Trail crosses the dirt Kokadjo-B Pond Road (51.6); to reach Route 11, you would turn right (east), continue 8.4 miles to Jo-Mary Road, then bear right, and continue another 6.2

miles to Route 11. The Appalachian Trail crosses Kokadjo-B Pond Road, enters the woods, and soon reaches the east shore of Crawford Pond (51.7). Then a side path (51.9), marked by a sign, leads left about 200 feet to Sand Beach, a beautiful little beach of crushed pebbles. Descending very slightly northward along an old woods road, the Appalachian Trail reaches a side path (54.8) leading 150 feet to the right to the Cooper Brook Falls lean-to and the spectacular cascades along Cooper Brook. Continuing along that flat woods road, the trail crosses the dirt Jo-Mary Road (58.5) beside a bridge over Cooper Brook. To reach Route 11, turn right (east) and follow Jo-Mary Road for 12 miles. To keep on the Appalachian Trail, cross the road and reenter the woods. The trail passes a side path (59.8) leading right 0.2 mile to the shore of Cooper Pond.

Continuing north on flat, easy terrain, the Appalachian Trail crosses a gravel road (61.4), fords several streams in succession (61.5), crosses another old logging road (62.0), and reaches a short side path (62.7), veering right to the Antlers campsite, a tenting area set amid red pines on a land point jutting into vast Lower Jo-Mary Lake. From that junction, the Appalachian Trail hooks left and swings around the lake's west shore to a junction with the Potaywadjo Ridge Trail (64.2), which leads left and ascends steadily for one mile to broad, open ledges on Potaywadjo Ridge, with sweeping views of the lakes and mountains to the south and east. This is one of the finest viewpoints in the northern half of the 100-Mile Wilderness and a great place for picking blueberries in late August. From that junction, the Appalachian Trail ascends the wooded end of the ridge and then drops to the Potaywadjo Spring lean-to (66.2), which sleeps six; nearby is a large, reliable spring. Following easy terrain again, the Appalachian Trail crosses Twitchell Brook (66.7) and passes a junction with a side path (66.8) leading a short distance to the right to the shore of Pemadumcook Lake, where you get an excellent view across the water to Katahdin. Cross Deer Brook (68.0), an old logging road (68.8) that leads 0.2 mile to the right to a cove on Pemadumcook, and then ford a tributary of Nahmakanta Stream (68.9). A high-water bypass trail 0.2 mile long diverges from the Appalachian Trail (69.3) and then rejoins it (69.4). At mile 70, you ford Tumbledown Dick Stream.

The Appalachian Trail parallels Nahmakanta Stream, where footing grows difficult over many rocks and roots, and then crosses a gravel road (73.4); to reach Route 11, you would turn left (southwest) and continue 24 miles on this gravel road to the Jo-Mary Road. The Appalachian Trail crosses the gravel road and reenters the woods. At mile 73.8, the Appalachian Trail reaches the south shore of Nahmakanta Lake near a short side path leading to a gravel beach. It follows the lakeshore, skirting into the woods and out onto the rocky shore to a short side path (76.0) leading right to a sandy beach; the path emerges at one end of the beach, near a small spring. From here, the Appalachian Trail crosses Wadleigh Stream (76.3) and then reaches the Wadleigh Stream lean-to (76.4), which sleeps six; the nearby stream provides water. The trail then makes a steep ascent up Nesuntabunt Mountain; from its north summit (78.3), a short side path leads to an open ledge with an excellent view from high above Nahmakanta Lake toward Katahdin. Descending somewhat more moderately off Nesuntabunt, the Appalachian Trail crosses a logging road (79.5); to the right (north), it's 1.2 miles to Pollywog Bridge, and to the left (south) it's 25.2 miles to Route 11. This hike crosses the logging road and reenters the woods.

After circling Crescent Pond (80.1), the Appalachian Trail passes a short side path (81.1) leading left to a rather exposed ledge high above Pollywog Gorge. It then parallels Pollywog Stream to a logging road (82.1); to reach Route 11, you would turn south and follow the road 26.4 miles. The Appalachian Trail turns left and crosses the stream on a bridge. Walk past a dirt road branching right and reenter the woods to the right. The trail follows a picturesque gorge along Rainbow Stream for about two miles and then reaches the Rainbow Stream lean-to (84.5), which sleeps six; water is available from the stream. After crossing the stream, the trail follows the Rainbow Deadwaters for 1.6 miles to the west end of Rainbow Lake (86.5). From here, easy terrain leads to a small clearing (89.8); to the right, a short path leads to tent sites at the Rainbow Spring Campsite, and to the left, it's just a short walk to the spring and the lakeshore. Continuing along the big lake's shore, the Appalachian Trail reaches the Rainbow Mountain Trail at mile 90, which bears right and climbs a fairly easy 1.1 miles to the bare summit of Rainbow Mountain and excellent views, especially toward Katahdin.

The Appalachian Trail continues to the east end of Rainbow Lake (91.7), passes a side path (91.8) leading right 0.1 mile to Little Beaver Pond and 0.4 mile to Big Beaver Pond, and then ascends to Rainbow Ledges (93.5); from various points along the ledges you get long views south and northeast to Katahdin. Descending easily, the Appalachian Trail fords Hurd Brook (96.0), which can be difficult when the water is high, and reaches the Hurd Brook lean-to on the other side of the brook; it sleeps six, and water is available from the brook. From here, the trail rolls through fairly easy terrain to Golden Road (99.3). Turn right and follow the road to Abol Bridge (99.4), the terminus of this memorable trek.

User Groups

Hikers only. No wheelchair facilities. Dogs are discouraged along the Appalachian Trail in Maine. This trail should not be attempted in winter except by hikers prepared for severe winter weather, and is not suitable for skis. Bikes, horses, and hunting are prohibited.

Access and Fees

A fee is charged for access to privately owned Golden Road; it has been $8 per vehicle in the past, but could change. There are numerous shelters along the Appalachian Trail, and it's legal to camp anywhere along the Appalachian Trail in the 100-Mile Wilderness; low-impact camping is encouraged. A fee-based shuttle to road crossings along the Appalachian Trail, as well as other hiker services, is offered by Shaw's Lodging, 17 Pleasant Street, P.O. Box 157, Monson, ME 04464, 207/997-3597, website: www.shawslodging.com. A hiker shuttle, free Kennebec River ferry service, and other hiker services along the Appalachian Trail in Maine are also provided by Steve Longley, P.O. Box 90, Route 201, The Forks, ME 04985, 207/663-4441 or (in Maine only) 888/FLOAT-ME, website: www.riversandtrails.com.

Maps

For a trail map, refer to maps 1, 2, and 3 in the *Map and Guide to the Appalachian Trail in Maine,* a set of seven maps and a guidebook for $24.95 from the Maine Appalachian Trail Club or the Appalachian Trail Conference. For topographic area maps, request Rainbow Lake East, Rainbow Lake West, Wadleigh Mountain, Nahmakanta Stream, Pemadumcook Lake, Jo-Mary Mountain, Big Shanty Mountain, Silver Lake, Barren Mountain East, Barren Mountain West, Monson East, and Monson West from USGS Map Sales, Federal Center, Box 25286, Denver, CO 80225.

Directions

You need to shuttle two vehicles for this trip. Take I-95 in Maine to Exit 56 for Medway/Millinocket. Drive on Route 157 west through East Millinocket to Millinocket. Follow signs for Baxter State Park. About a mile beyond the North Woods Trading Post (before the park entrance), bear left onto Golden Road, a private logging road where you pass through a gate and pay a toll. Continue about seven miles to the private campground at Abol Bridge. Drive over the bridge and park in the dirt lot on the left, about 0.1 mile east of where the Appalachian Trail emerges at the road. Drive a second vehicle to Monson, and pick up Route 15 north for 3.5 miles to a large turnout on the right and the trailhead for the Appalachian Trail.

Contact

Maine Appalachian Trail Club, P.O. Box 283, Augusta, ME 04332-0283, website: www.matc.org. Appalachian Trail Conference, 799 Washington Street, P.O. Box 807, Harpers Ferry, WV 25425-0807, 304/535-6331, website: www.appalachiantrail.org.

23 HALF A 100-MILE WILDERNESS
between Monson and Baxter State Park

Total distance: 47.8 or 51.6 miles one-way   **Hiking time:** 4–6 days

Difficulty: 8   **Rating:** 10

Backpackers seeking one of the most remote experiences possible in New England, but who don't have the time to hike the entire 100-Mile Wilderness—the stretch of the Appalachian Trail in northern Maine that crosses no paved or public road for 99.4 miles—can instead backpack "half a wilderness." The Appalachian Trail crosses the dirt Kokadjo-B Pond Road, identified on some maps as Johnson Pond Road, a logical place to begin or conclude a trek of either the northern or southern half of the 100-Mile Wilderness. The 51.6 trail miles from this logging road south to Route 15 are characterized by rugged hiking over a landscape dominated by low mountains boasting sporadic but long views of a forest expanse with few signs of civilization. The 47.8 miles of trail north to Golden Road at Abol Bridge have an entirely different personality, traversing mostly flat, low terrain around sprawling wilderness lakes. The southern portion can take five days or more; the northern is easier and can be done in four days by fit hikers. See the trail notes on the 100-Mile Wilderness hike (previous listing) for a detailed description of both options.

User Groups
Hikers only. No wheelchair facilities. Dogs are discouraged along the Appalachian Trail in Maine. This trail should not be attempted in winter except by hikers experienced in mountaineering and prepared for severe winter weather, and is not suitable for skis. Bikes, horses, and hunting are prohibited.

Access and Fees
A vehicle toll (most recently $8) is charged for access to privately owned Golden Road and Jo-Mary Road, which aren't passable at certain times of year due to snow or muddy conditions. There are numerous shelters along the Appalachian Trail, and it's legal to camp anywhere along the Appalachian Trail in the 100-Mile Wilderness; low-impact camping is encouraged. A fee-based shuttle to road crossings along the Appalachian Trail, as well as other hiker services, is offered by Shaw's Lodging, 17 Pleasant Street, P.O. Box 157, Monson, ME 04464, 207/997-3597, website: www.shawslodging.com. A hiker shuttle, free Kennebec River ferry service, and other hiker services along the Appalachian Trail in Maine are also provided by Steve Longley, P.O. Box 90, Route 201, The Forks, ME 04985, 207/663-4441 or (in Maine only) 888/FLOAT-ME, website: www.riversandtrails.com.

Maps

For a trail map, refer to maps 1, 2, and 3 in the *Map and Guide to the Appalachian Trail in Maine,* a set of seven maps and a guidebook for $24.95 from the Maine Appalachian Trail Club or the Appalachian Trail Conference. For topographic area maps, request Rainbow Lake East, Rainbow Lake West, Wadleigh Mountain, Nahmakanta Stream, Pemadumcook Lake, Jo-Mary Mountain, Big Shanty Mountain, Silver Lake, Barren Mountain East, Barren Mountain West, Monson East, and Monson West from USGS Map Sales, Federal Center, Box 25286, Denver, CO 80225.

Directions

You need to shuttle two vehicles for this trip. To backpack the northern half of the 100-Mile Wilderness, take I-95 in Maine to Exit 56 for Medway/Millinocket. Drive on Route 157 west through East Millinocket to Millinocket. Follow signs for Baxter State Park. About a mile beyond the North Woods Trading Post (before the park entrance), bear left onto Golden Road, a private logging road where you pass through a gate and pay a toll. Continue about seven miles to the private campground at the Abol Bridge over the West Branch of the Penobscot River. Drive over the bridge and park in the dirt lot on the left, about 0.1 mile east of where the Appalachian Trail emerges at the road. Drive a second vehicle back to Millinocket. From the junction of Routes 11 and 157, go south on Route 11 for 15.5 miles and turn right (west) onto gravel Jo-Mary Road. Continue 0.2 mile and pass through a gate where a vehicle toll is collected. Proceed another six miles and bear left at a fork, following the sign for Gauntlet Falls/B-Pond (ignore the sign for the Appalachian Trail, which is also reached via the right fork). Continuing another 2.6 miles, bear right where the B-Pond Road branches left. At 14.6 miles from Route 11, the Appalachian Trail crosses the road 0.1 mile south of Crawford Pond; park off the road.

To backpack the southern half of the 100-Mile Wilderness, leave one car at the Appalachian Trail crossing of the above-mentioned logging road near Crawford Pond, then return to Route 11 and drive south to Monson. Pick up Route 15 north for 3.5 miles to a large turnout on the right and the trailhead for the Appalachian Trail at the 100-Mile Wilderness's southern end.

Contact

Maine Appalachian Trail Club, P.O. Box 283, Augusta, ME 04332-0283, website: www.matc.org. Appalachian Trail Conference, 799 Washington Street, P.O. Box 807, Harpers Ferry, WV 25425-0807, 304/535-6331, website: www.appalachiantrail.org.

24 WHITE CAP MOUNTAIN

between Monson and Baxter State Park

Total distance: 23 miles round-trip   **Hiking time:** 2–3 days

Difficulty: 8   **Rating:** 10

At 3,654 feet, White Cap Mountain is the tallest peak in the 100-Mile Wilderness, the 99.4-mile stretch of the Appalachian Trail through northern Maine that isn't crossed by a paved or public road. White Cap is also the last big peak in the Wilderness for northbound hikers and offers excellent views, especially toward Katahdin. A remote summit, White Cap can be reached on a two- or three-day trek via the logging road that accesses the Appalachian Trail near Gulf Hagas.

From the parking area, follow the blue-blazed trail 0.2 mile to the white-blazed Appalachian Trail at the West Branch of the Pleasant River, a normally knee-deep channel about 80 feet across, which you must ford (bring a pair of sandals or old sneakers for this stony crossing). Continue along the wide, flat Appalachian Trail, past a side trail 0.2 mile from the river, which leads to campsites at Hay Brook. At 0.3 mile, another side path leads about 200 feet into the Hermitage, a grove of ancient white pine trees, some as tall as 130 feet. The Appalachian Trail continues over easy ground among other giant pines to the junction with the Gulf Hagas Trail, 1.3 miles from the river (a worthwhile detour from this hike; see the Gulf Hagas hike description, next listing). The Appalachian Trail turns sharply right and ascends steadily northward for 4.2 miles, following Gulf Hagas Brook through dense forest to the Carl A. Newhall lean-to and tent sites, reached by a short side path off the Appalachian Trail; the lean-to sleeps six, and water is available from the brook.

Climbing steeply, the trail passes over the 2,683-foot summit of Gulf Hagas Mountain 6.6 miles from the road, where there are limited views to the west from just north of the true summit. After descending to the Sidney Tappen campsite, the Appalachian Trail yo-yos north along the arduous ridge, over 3,178-foot West Peak (8.2 miles), with limited views, and the wooded summit of 3,244-foot Hay Mountain (9.8 miles). The trail dips again, passing a junction at 10.4 miles with the White Brook Trail (which descends east 1.9 miles to logging roads that eventually link with the road to Katahdin Iron Works). The Appalachian Trail then climbs to the White Cap summit. Return the way you came.

User Groups

Hikers only. No wheelchair facilities. Dogs are discouraged along the Appalachian Trail in Maine. This trail should not be attempted in winter except by hikers experienced in mountaineering and prepared for severe winter weather, and is not suitable for skis. Bikes, horses, and hunting are prohibited.

Access and Fees
This section of the Appalachian Trail is reached via a private logging road, and a nominal per-person toll is collected; children under 15 enter free. The access road isn't passable at certain times of year due to snow or muddy conditions. The Carl A. Newhall lean-to, with tent sites, is located 5.7 miles north on the Appalachian Trail from the parking area, and the Sidney Tappen campsite, for tents only, lies 1.8 miles farther north. It's legal to camp anywhere along the Appalachian Trail in the 100-Mile Wilderness; low-impact camping is encouraged.

Maps
For a trail map, refer to map 2 in the *Map and Guide to the Appalachian Trail in Maine,* a set of seven maps and a guidebook for $24.95 available from the Maine Appalachian Trail Club or the Appalachian Trail Conference. For topographic area maps, request Hay Mountain, Big Shanty Mountain, Barren Mountain East, and Silver Lake from USGS Map Sales, Federal Center, Box 25286, Denver, CO 80225.

Directions
From Route 11, 5.5 miles north of Brownville Junction and 25.6 miles south of Millinocket, turn west onto a gravel road at a sign for Katahdin Iron Works. Follow it nearly seven miles to a gate where an entrance fee is collected. Beyond the gate, cross the bridge and turn right. Drive three miles, bear left at a fork, and then continue another 3.7 miles to a parking area (half a mile before the road's crossing of the Appalachian Trail).

Contact
Maine Appalachian Trail Club, P.O. Box 283, Augusta, ME 04332-0283, website: www.matc.org. Appalachian Trail Conference, 799 Washington Street, P.O. Box 807, Harpers Ferry, WV 25425-0807, 304/535-6331, website: www.appalachiantrail.org.

25 GULF HAGAS
between Monson and Baxter State Park

Total distance: 8 miles round-trip

Hiking time: 5.5 hours

Difficulty: 6

Rating: 10

Known as Maine's Little Grand Canyon, Gulf Hagas is a deep, narrow canyon along the West Branch of the Pleasant River that inspired a friend and me to ooh and aah nonstop throughout our hike along its rim. At every turn we'd think we had seen a view without comparison in New England, then we'd reach another lookout that completely blew us away again. Admiring its sheer walls that drop right into a boulder-choked, impassable river, it's easy to understand why the Abenaki gave it the name "hagas," their word for "evil place." The blue-blazed loop trail through the gulf is a 5.2-mile detour off the Appalachian Trail in the 100-Mile Wilderness, but the round-trip hike from the parking area is eight miles. This trail goes through very little elevation gain or loss, but runs constantly up and down over rugged, rocky terrain; your hike could easily take more than the estimated 5.5 hours, especially when you start hanging out at the many waterfalls and clifftop viewpoints. Be forewarned: This is a very popular hike in summer, so expect crowds.

From the parking area, follow the blue-blazed trail 0.2 mile to the white-blazed Appalachian Trail at the West Branch of the Pleasant River, a normally knee-deep channel about 80 feet across, which you must ford (bringing a pair of sandals or old sneakers for this stony crossing makes it much easier on the feet). Continuing along the wide, flat Appalachian Trail, pass a side trail 0.2 mile from the river that leads to campsites at Hay Brook. At 0.3 mile, another side path leads about 200 feet into the Hermitage, a grove of ancient white pine trees, some as tall as 130 feet. The Appalachian Trail continues over easy ground among other giant pines to the junction with the Gulf Hagas Trail, 1.3 miles from the river. The Appalachian Trail turns sharply right, but continue straight onto the blue-blazed trail, immediately crossing Gulf Hagas Brook. Bear left onto the loop trail. At 0.1 mile, a side path leads left to beautiful Screw Auger Falls on Gulf Hagas Brook. At 0.2 mile, another side path leads to the bottom of Screw Auger. (The brook continues down through a series of cascades and pools, including some spots ideal for swimming.)

The Gulf Hagas Trail continues down to the canyon rim, weaving in and out of the forest to views from the canyon rim and dropping down to the riverbank in places. Significant features along the rim include Hammond Street Pitch, a view high above the river, reached on a short path at 0.7 mile; the Jaws Cascades (seen from side paths or views at 1.2, 1.4, and 1.5

miles); Buttermilk Falls at 1.8 miles; Stair Falls at 1.9 miles; Billings Falls at 2.7 miles; and a view down the gulf from its head at 2.9 miles. Three miles into the loop, turn right onto the Pleasant River Road, an old logging road that is at first a footpath but widens over the 2.2 miles back to the start of this loop. The logging road provides much easier walking and a faster return route than doubling back along the gulf rim.

User Groups
Hikers only. No wheelchair facilities. Dogs are discouraged along the Appalachian Trail in Maine. Portions of this trail are difficult to ski or snowshoe. Bikes, horses, and hunting are prohibited.

Access and Fees
Gulf Hagas is reached via a private logging road, and a nominal per-person toll is collected; children under 15 enter free. The access roads are not passable at certain times of year due to snow or muddy conditions.

Maps
For a trail map, refer to map 2 in the *Map and Guide to the Appalachian Trail in Maine,* a set of seven maps and a guidebook for $24.95 available from the Maine Appalachian Trail Club or the Appalachian Trail Conference. For topographic area maps, request Barren Mountain East and Silver Lake from USGS Map Sales, Federal Center, Box 25286, Denver, CO 80225.

Directions
From Route 11, 5.5 miles north of Brownville Junction and 25.6 miles south of Millinocket, turn west onto a gravel road at a sign for Katahdin Iron Works. Follow it nearly seven miles to a gate where an entrance fee is collected. Beyond the gate, cross the bridge and turn right. Drive three miles, bear left at a fork, and then continue another 3.7 miles to a parking area (half a mile before the road crosses the Appalachian Trail).

Contact
Maine Appalachian Trail Club, P.O. Box 283, Augusta, ME 04332-0283, website: www.matc.org. Appalachian Trail Conference, 799 Washington Street, P.O. Box 807, Harpers Ferry, WV 25425-0807, 304/535-6331, website: www.appalachiantrail.org.

26 BARREN MOUNTAIN AND SLUGUNDY GORGE

northeast of Monson

Total distance: 8 miles round-trip

Difficulty: 8

Hiking time: 6 hours

Rating: 10

By employing dirt logging roads to access this stretch of the Appalachian Trail, you can make a one-day or an overnight hike into this picturesque and varied area of the 100-Mile Wilderness (see listing in this chapter). The round-trip hike to the summit of Barren Mountain entails eight demanding miles round-trip and 2,000 feet of climbing, but it's just 1.6 miles round-trip to Slugundy Gorge. Barren and Slugundy are reached by walking north on the Appalachian Trail, but just half a mile south on the trail lies a broad, 20-foot-high waterfall along Vaughn Stream (an easy detour not figured into this hike's distance). The one caveat about this hike is that Long Pond Stream can be very difficult to cross, so it's best to go in late summer or early fall, when water levels are down.

From the dirt road, turn right (north) onto the Appalachian Trail. Within 0.1 mile, ford Long Pond Stream. The trail parallels pools and flumes in the stream for more than half a mile; after it turns uphill, a short side path leads left to Slugundy Gorge, a scenic gorge and falls. Just beyond, another side path leads left 150 yards to the Long Pond Stream lean-to. Beyond the shelter, the Appalachian Trail begins the steep Barren Mountain climb. At two miles, a side path leads right about 250 feet to the top of the Barren Slide, from which there are excellent views south of Lake Onawa and Boarstone Mountain. Following the ridge, the trail reaches the aptly named, 2,670-foot summit of Barren Mountain two miles beyond the slide, where there are sweeping views, particularly south and west; an abandoned fire tower stands at the summit. Continuing north on the Appalachian Trail for 0.9 mile brings you to a side trail leading right 0.3 mile to the beautiful tarn called Cloud Pond and the nearby lean-to, but to finish this hike, turn around and hike back the way you came.

User Groups

Hikers only. No wheelchair facilities. Dogs are discouraged along the Appalachian Trail in Maine. Portions of this trail are difficult to ski or snowshoe. Bikes, horses, and hunting are prohibited.

Access and Fees

Parking and access are free. The dirt roads from Monson aren't passable at certain times of year due to snow or muddy conditions. The Long Pond

Stream lean-to is along the Appalachian Trail 0.9 mile into this hike, and the Cloud Pond lean-to lies 1.2 miles beyond the summit of Barren Mountain. It's legal to camp anywhere along the Appalachian Trail in the 100-Mile Wilderness; low-impact camping is encouraged.

Maps

For a trail map, refer to map 3 in the *Map and Guide to the Appalachian Trail in Maine,* a set of seven maps and a guidebook for $24.95 from the Maine Appalachian Trail Club or the Appalachian Trail Conference. For topographic area maps, request Monson East, Barren Mountain West, and Barren Mountain East from USGS Map Sales, Federal Center, Box 25286, Denver, CO 80225.

Directions

From the center of Monson, drive half a mile north on Route 15 and turn right onto Elliottsville Road. Continue 7.8 miles to Big Wilson Stream, cross the bridge, and then turn left onto a dirt road. Drive another 2.8 miles to the Bodfish Farm, bear left at a fork and go 2.9 miles farther to where the white-blazed Appalachian Trail crosses the dirt road, known as the Bodfish Farm–Long Pond Tote Road; park at the roadside.

Contact

Maine Appalachian Trail Club, P.O. Box 283, Augusta, ME 04332-0283, website: www.matc.org. Appalachian Trail Conference, 799 Washington Street, P.O. Box 807, Harpers Ferry, WV 25425-0807, 304/535-6331, website: www.appalachiantrail.org.

Chapter 2

COURTESY OF THE MAINE OFFICE OF TOURISM

Down East

Down East Maine harbors some of the best coastal hiking you'll find anywhere. This chapter's 26 hikes are all within in Acadia National Park and Camden Hills State Park.

Occupying 47,633 acres of granite-domed mountains, woodlands, lakes, ponds, and ocean shoreline, mostly on Mount Desert Island, Acadia is one of the country's smallest, yet most popular, national parks. Glaciers carved a unique landscape here of mountains rising as high as 1,500 feet virtually out of the ocean—most of them thrusting bare summits into the sky—and innumerable islands, bays, and coves that collaborate to create a hiking environment unlike any other in New England.

Acadia boasts more than 120 miles of hiking trails and 45 miles of carriage roads ideal for hiking, running, mountain biking, snowshoeing, or cross-country skiing. Many of the hikes described in this chapter are relatively short but lead to spectacular views of mountains, ocean, and islands. Although some trails are steep and rugged, most of these hikes are suitable for young children.

July and August are crowded months on Mount Desert Island. May, June, September, and October are much less crowded; spring tends to be cool and sometimes rainy, while fall is drier, with its share of both warm and cool days. Snowfall is rare in winter.

From May 1 to October 31, the park entrance fee is $20 per vehicle—or $5 for walkers, bicyclists, or motorcyclists—for a seven-day pass. A one-year vehicle pass costs $40. From late June to mid-October, the Island Explorer shuttle bus provides free transportation from local lodges and campgrounds to points within the park and across Mount Desert Island; contact Downeast Transportation, 207/667-5796, website: www.exploreacadia.com/index.html. Camping reservations can be made by calling 800/365-CAMP or through the park's website. There are two campgrounds in Acadia: Blackwoods Campground, off Route 3 just south of Cadillac Mountain and east of Seal Harbor, is open year-round; Seawall Campground, off Route 102A east of Bass Harbor, opens in late June and closes after Labor Day.

Isle au Haut, the outermost island in Penobscot Bay, harbors a remote outpost of Acadia National Park. Reached by a mail boat/ferry from Stonington (contact the Isle au Haut Boat Company, 207/367-5193, website: www.isleauhaut.com), Isle au Haut (pronounced "eyel a ho" locally) has 18 miles of hiking trails on rocky coastline and low hills, a couple of dirt roads, and a campground with five lean-to shelters and a water pump less than a quarter of a mile from the boat landing at Duck Harbor. Isle au Haut can be visited on a day trip or for overnight stays.

Isle au Haut's lean-to shelters can be reserved from May 15 to October 15 by contacting the park; reservations are required. Reservations requests cannot be postmarked or made in person at park headquarters before April 1. Camping reservations cost $25 per site, regardless of the number of nights. Camping is limited to three nights from mid-June to mid-September, and five nights the rest of the year. You can pitch a tent inside the lean-to only (which is advised in early summer, when the mosquitoes are vicious). Park rangers discourage bikes because of the limited roads, and bikes are prohibited from hiking trails. No wheelchair facilities are available.

Across the 5,500 acres of Camden Hills State Park, 25 miles of hiking trails follow the coast and weave through the Megunticook Mountain range above the town of Camden, where the hills rise from near sea level to 1,380 feet. The trails offer a variety of hiking experiences, from coastal walks to quiet, forested heights and dramatic cliff-top views. Because these hikes are nearby and similar in character to the hikes in Acadia, hikers planning a trip to Acadia or Camden should consider linking up the two places. The park also has a campground and picnic area.

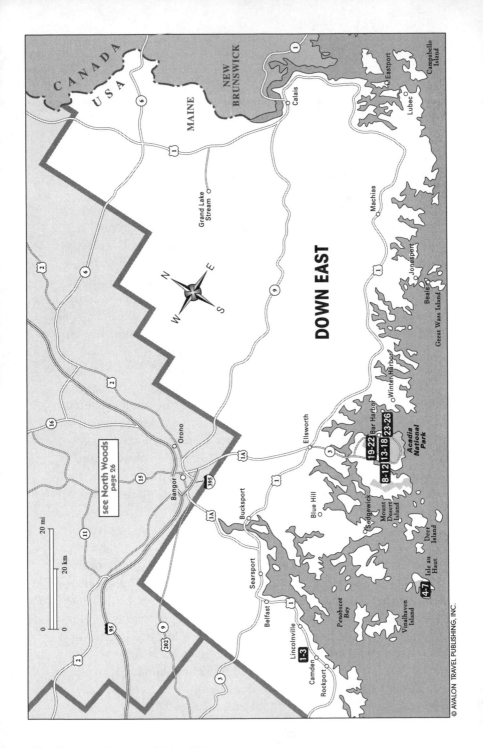

© AVALON TRAVEL PUBLISHING, INC.

Contents

1 MAIDEN CLIFF
in Camden Hills State Park

Total distance: 2 miles round-trip   **Hiking time:** 1.5 hours

Difficulty: 3   **Rating:** 9

This is my favorite hike in Camden Hills State Park. The Scenic Trail follows the open clifftops high above sprawling Megunticook Lake, with extensive views of the hills to the west. It is a great hike for late in the day, when the sun is sinking toward those hills and sparkling off the lake.

From the parking lot, follow the wide Maiden Cliff Trail, which ascends steadily through the woods for 0.5 mile. Bear right on the Ridge Trail, reaching an open area and the junction with the Scenic Trail in 0.3 mile. Turn left (northwest) on the Scenic Trail, following the clifftops with outstanding views for 0.25 mile and then descending into the woods again to reach the junction with the Maiden Cliff Trail (marked by a sign) 0.5 mile from the Ridge Trail. Before descending the Maiden Cliff Trail back to your car, continue ahead 100 feet to the Maiden Cliff; here a large wooden cross marks the spot where a young girl named Elenora French fell to her death in 1864. The cliffs seem to drop almost straight down into the lake. Double back and descend the Maiden Cliff Trail for nearly a mile to the parking lot.

User Groups
Hikers, snowshoers, and dogs. Dogs must be leashed. No wheelchair facilities. This trail is not suitable for skis. Bikes and horses are prohibited. Hunting is allowed in season.

Access and Fees
Parking and access are free at the Maiden Cliff Trailhead. A fee of $2 per person (age 12 and over) is charged at the state park entrance. It's 50 cents for children age 5–12, and children under 5 and adults over 65 are free. The park season is May 15 to October 15, although this trail is accessible year-round. No staff is on duty and no fee is collected off-season.

Maps
A basic trail system map is available at the state park entrance on U.S. 1, two miles north of the Route 52 junction in Camden. Or get the *Camden-Pleasant-Weld/Mahoosuc-Evans map,* $7.95 in waterproof Tyvek, from the Appalachian Mountain Club, 800/262-4455, website: www.outdoors.org. For topographic area maps, request Camden and Lincolnville from USGS Map Sales, Federal Center, Box 25286, Denver, CO 80225, 888/ASK-USGS (888/275-8747), website: http://mapping.usgs.gov.

Directions

From the junction of Route 52 and U.S. 1 in Camden, drive west on Route 52 for three miles to a parking area on the right (just before Megunticook Lake). The Maiden Cliff Trail begins at the back of the lot.

Contact

Camden Hills State Park, 280 Belfast Road, Camden, ME 04843, 207/236-3109 in season, 207/236-0849 off-season. Maine Department of Conservation, Bureau of Parks and Lands, 286 Water Street, Key Bank Plaza, 3rd and 5th floors, Augusta, ME 04333-0022, 207/287-3821, website: www.state.me.us/doc/parks/.

2 MOUNT MEGUNTICOOK TRAVERSE
in Camden Hills State Park

Total distance: 5.3 miles one-way   **Hiking time:** 3 hours

Difficulty: 3   **Rating:** 9

This fairly easy traverse of the highest mountain in Camden Hills State Park combines the good views of the Maiden Cliff (see previous listing) and Ocean Lookout (see next listing) hikes with a pleasant walk along the mostly wooded ridge—though this ridge has its own views as well.

From the parking area on Mount Battie Road, follow the Mount Megunticook Trail for a mile to Ocean Lookout, where you get terrific views south and east of the Camden area and the Penobscot Bay islands. Continue northwest on the Ridge Trail, passing over the wooded 1,380-foot summit of Megunticook, 0.5 mile beyond Ocean Lookout. A mile past the summit, stay left on the Ridge Trail where Zeke's Trail branches right; then 0.5 mile farther, stay right where the Jack Williams Trail enters from the left. Two miles past the summit, walk straight onto the Scenic Trail, following the open clifftops with views of Megunticook Lake and the hills to the west. Descending into the woods again, you reach the Maiden Cliff Trail (marked by a sign) 0.5 mile from the Ridge Trail. Before heading down, though, continue ahead 100 feet to the Maiden Cliff; here a large wooden cross marks the spot where a young girl named Elenora French fell to her death in 1864. The cliffs seem to drop almost straight down into the lake. Double back and descend the Maiden Cliff Trail for nearly a mile to the parking lot on Route 52.

User Groups

Hikers, snowshoers, and dogs. Dogs must be leashed. No wheelchair facilities.

This trail is not suitable for skis. Bikes and horses are prohibited. Hunting is allowed in season.

Access and Fees

Parking and access are free at the Maiden Cliff Trailhead. A fee of $2 per person (age 12 and over) is charged at the state park entrance. It's 50 cents for children age 5–12, and children under 5 and adults over 65 are free. The park season is May 15 to October 15, although this trail is accessible year-round. No staff is on duty and no fee is collected off-season.

Maps

A basic trail system map is available at the state park entrance. Or get the *Camden-Pleasant-Weld/Mahoosuc-Evans map,* $7.95 in waterproof Tyvek, from the Appalachian Mountain Club, 800/262-4455, website: www.outdoors.org. For topographic area maps, request Camden and Lincolnville from USGS Map Sales, Federal Center, Box 25286, Denver, CO 80225, 888/ASK-USGS (888/275-8747), website: http://mapping.usgs.gov.

Directions

Two vehicles must be shuttled at either end of this hike. From the junction of Route 52 and U.S. 1 in Camden, drive west on Route 52 for three miles to a parking area on the right (just before Megunticook Lake). The Maiden Cliff Trail begins at the back of the lot. Leave one vehicle there. Drive back to Camden and head north on U.S. 1 for two miles to the state park entrance on the left. Past the entrance gate, turn left on the Mount Battie Road and then right into a parking lot marked with a sign reading "Hikers Parking." The Mount Megunticook Trail begins at the back of the lot.

Contact

Camden Hills State Park, 280 Belfast Road, Camden, ME 04843, 207/236-3109 in season, 207/236-0849 off-season. Maine Department of Conservation, Bureau of Parks and Lands, 286 Water Street, Key Bank Plaza, 3rd and 5th floors, Augusta, ME 04333-0022, 207/287-3821, website: www.state.me.us/doc/parks/.

🄵 OCEAN LOOKOUT
in Camden Hills State Park

Total distance: 2 miles round-trip

Difficulty: 2

Hiking time: 1.5 hours

Rating: 8

This relatively easy hike to the best viewpoint on Mount Megunticook—which is the biggest hill in Camden Hills State Park—is very popular because it offers a wide view of the Camden area and the Penobscot Bay islands. My wife and I hiked up here on a weekday afternoon and had the view to ourselves for a little while: Mount Battie was visible below us, and a cloud bank rolling in off the ocean crested like a wave over Camden.

Follow the Mount Megunticook Trail for one mile to Ocean Lookout, 1,300 feet above the sea. The wooded summit of 1,380-foot Mount Megunticook lies 0.5 mile farther north on the Ridge Trail (see the previous listing for descriptions of the Mount Megunticook Traverse hike), but this hike ends at the lookout. After you've looked out, return the same way you came.

User Groups
Hikers, snowshoers, and dogs. Dogs must be leashed. No wheelchair facilities. This trail is not suitable for skis. Bikes and horses are prohibited. Hunting is allowed in season.

Access and Fees
A fee of $2 per person (age 12 and over) is charged at the state park entrance; it's 50 cents for children age 5 to 12, and children under 5 and adults over 65 are free. The park season is May 15 to –October 15. No staff is on duty and no fee is collected off-season.

Maps
A basic trail system map is available at the state park entrance. Or get the *Camden-Pleasant-Weld/Mahoosuc-Evans map,* $7.95 in waterproof Tyvek, from the Appalachian Mountain Club, 800/262-4455, website: www.outdoors.org. For topographic area maps, request Camden and Lincolnville from USGS Map Sales, Federal Center, Box 25286, Denver, CO 80225, 888/ASK-USGS (888/275-8747), website: http://mapping.usgs.gov.

Directions
The entrance to Camden Hills State Park is along U.S. 1, two miles north of the Route 52 junction in Camden. After passing through the entrance gate, turn left on Mount Battie Road and then right into a parking lot

marked with a sign reading "Hikers Parking." The Mount Megunticook Trail begins at the back of the lot.

Contact
Camden Hills State Park, 280 Belfast Road, Camden, ME 04843, 207/236-3109 in season, 207/236-0849 off-season. Maine Department of Conservation, Bureau of Parks and Lands, 286 Water Street, Key Bank Plaza, 3rd and 5th floors, Augusta, ME 04333-0022, 207/287-3821, website: www.state.me.us/doc/parks/.

4 ISLE AU HAUT: EBEN'S HEAD
in Acadia National Park on Isle au Haut

Total distance: 1 mile round-trip   **Hiking time:** 0.75 hour

Difficulty: 1   **Rating:** 8

Eben's Head is the rocky bluff jutting into the ocean at the mouth of Duck Harbor opposite the boat landing. I watched the sunset behind Eben's Head two nights straight before getting up early one morning and walking the trail out onto the head. There, I stood atop cliffs above the pounding surf, watching morning fog slowly lift off the ocean. I also spent some time exploring the cove on the other side of Eben's Head before returning the same way I hiked in. I highly recommend the short walk out here to catch the sunset or sunrise—or on any foggy morning or evening.

From the boat landing at Duck Harbor, turn left on the trail toward the water pump. Pass the trail branching right for the campground and continue straight onto Western Head Road. Follow it past the water pump and out to the main road. Turn left and follow the dirt main road around Duck Harbor. About 0.1 mile after the main road turns inland, you'll pass the Duck Harbor Trail on the right; then turn left onto the Eben's Head Trail, which leads through woods out to that rocky bluff visible from the boat landing.

User Groups
Hikers and dogs. Dogs must be leashed in the park and are prohibited in the campground. No wheelchair facilities. The island rarely gets enough snow for winter activities. Bikes, horses, and hunting are prohibited.

Access and Fees
Isle au Haut is reached by mail boat/ferry from Stonington, Maine, to Duck Harbor, the starting point for the four Isle au Haut hikes described

in this chapter. The round-trip cost in 2004 was $32 for adults and $16 for children under age 12. For information, contact the Isle au Haut Boat Company, P.O. Box 709, Sea Breeze Avenue, Stonington, ME 04651, 207/367-5193, website: www.isleauhaut.com. The ferry is a small boat and does not transport motor vehicles. The Duck Harbor Campground has five lean-to shelters that can sleep up to six people each, and each lean-to site has a fire ring and picnic table. The lean-to shelters can be reserved from May 15 to October 15 by contacting the park; reservations are required. Reservations requests cannot be postmarked or made in person at park headquarters before April 1. Camping reservations cost $25 per site, regardless of the number of nights.

Maps

A basic map of island trails and roads is issued free to visitors arriving on the ferry or to those with camping reservations. The park website has a map of Isle au Haut. Good trail maps of the area are the waterproof *Acadia National Park* (map 212) for $9.95 from Trails Illustrated, 800/962-1643, website: http://maps.nationalgeographic.com/trails/; and the *Hiking and Biking Map to Acadia National Park and Mount Desert Island*, $7.95 in waterproof Tyvek, from the Appalachian Mountain Club, 800/262-4455, website: www.outdoors.org. For topographic island maps, request Isle au Haut West and Isle au Haut East from USGS Map Sales, Federal Center, Box 25286, Denver, CO 80225, 888/ASK-USGS (888/275-8747), website: http://mapping.usgs.gov.

Directions

To reach the dock where the ferry departs for Isle au Haut, take Route 15 to Main Street in Stonington and turn left at Bartlett's Market; the ferry landing is past the firehouse, at the end of the pier.

Contact

Acadia National Park, P.O. Box 177, Eagle Lake Road, Bar Harbor, ME 04609-0177, 207/288-3338, website: www.nps.gov/acad. Friends of Acadia, P.O. Box 45, 43 Cottage Street, Bar Harbor, ME 04609, 207/288-3340 or 800/625-0321, website: www.friendsofacadia.org.

5 ISLE AU HAUT: WESTERN HEAD LOOP

in Acadia National Park on Isle au Haut

Total distance: 5 miles round-trip

Hiking time: 3 hours

Difficulty: 3

Rating: 9

If you have time for just one hike on Isle au Haut, this is the one to take. It follows the stunning rocky coast around Western Head, offers the opportunity at low tide to wander onto the tiny island known as Western Ear, and climbs over 314-foot Duck Harbor Mountain, which boasts the most sweeping views on the island. Although much of the hike is relatively flat, the trail is fairly rugged in places. My companions on this hike ranged in age from 11 to 71, and we all equally enjoyed exploring the shore and woods—as well as receiving a surprise visit from a seal.

From the boat landing at Duck Harbor, follow the trail leading left toward the water pump. Pass the trail branching right for the campground and continue straight until reaching Western Head Road. Bearing left along the road, it's about 200 yards to the water pump (if you need water). For this hike, take the grassy road to the right and follow it for less than a mile. Turn right onto the Western Head Trail, which reaches the coast within about a half mile. The trail turns left (south) and follows the rugged coast out to the point at Western Head, where that trail ends and the Cliff Trail begins. (At low tide, you can walk across the narrow channel out to Western Ear. Be careful not to get trapped out there, or you'll have to wait hours for the tide to go out again.)

The Cliff Trail heads northward into the woods, alternately following more rugged coastline and turning back into the forest to skirt steep cliffs. It reaches the end of Western Head Road in less than a mile. Turn left and follow the road about a quarter mile. When you see a cove on your right, turn right (watch for the trail sign, which is somewhat hidden) onto the Goat Trail. (The Western Head Road leads directly back to the Duck Harbor landing, a hike of less than two miles, and is a good option for hikers who want to avoid the steep rock scrambling on Duck Harbor Mountain.) Follow the Goat Trail along the coast for less than a half mile. At scenic Squeaker Cove, turn left onto the Duck Harbor Mountain Trail; from here it's a bit more than a mile back to the Duck Harbor landing. The trail grows steep, involving somewhat exposed scrambling up rock slabs, and traverses several open ledges on Duck Harbor Mountain, with terrific long views of Isle au Haut Bay to the west (including Vinalhaven Island, the nearest piece of land across Isle au Haut Bay) and the Penobscot Bay islands and peninsulas to the north. The trail then descends to Western Head Road; turn right for Duck Harbor.

User Groups

Hikers and dogs. Dogs must be leashed in the park and are prohibited from the campground. No wheelchair facilities. The island rarely gets enough snow for winter activities. Bikes, horses, and hunting are prohibited.

Access and Fees

Isle au Haut is reached by mail boat/ferry from Stonington, Maine, to Duck Harbor, the starting point for the four Isle au Haut hikes described in this chapter. The round-trip cost in 2004 was $32 for adults and $16 for children under age 12. For information, contact the Isle au Haut Boat Company, P.O. Box 709, Sea Breeze Avenue, Stonington, ME 04651, 207/367-5193, website: www.isleauhaut.com. The ferry is a small boat and does not transport motor vehicles. The Duck Harbor Campground has five lean-to shelters that can sleep up to six people each, and each lean-to site has a fire ring and picnic table. The lean-to shelters can be reserved from May 15 to October 15 by contacting the park; reservations are required. Reservations requests cannot be postmarked or made in person at park headquarters before April 1. Camping reservations cost $25 per site, regardless of the number of nights.

Maps

A basic map of island trails and roads is issued free to visitors arriving on the ferry or to those with camping reservations. The park website has a map of Isle au Haut. Good trail maps of the area are the waterproof *Acadia National Park* (map 212) for $9.95 from Trails Illustrated, 800/962-1643, website: http://maps.nationalgeographic.com/trails/; and the *Hiking and Biking Map to Acadia National Park and Mount Desert Island,* $7.95 in waterproof Tyvek, from the Appalachian Mountain Club, 800/262-4455, website: www.outdoors.org. For topographic island maps, request Isle au Haut West and Isle au Haut East from USGS Map Sales, Federal Center, Box 25286, Denver, CO 80225, 888/ASK-USGS (888/275-8747), website: http://mapping.usgs.gov.

Directions

To reach the dock where the ferry departs for Isle au Haut, drive Route 15 to Main Street in Stonington and turn left at Bartlett's Market; the ferry landing is past the firehouse, at the end of the pier.

Contact

Acadia National Park, P.O. Box 177, Eagle Lake Road, Bar Harbor, ME 04609-0177, 207/288-3338, website: www.nps.gov/acad. Friends of Acadia, P.O. Box 45, 43 Cottage Street, Bar Harbor, ME 04609, 207/288-3340 or 800/625-0321, website: www.friendsofacadia.org.

6 ISLE AU HAUT: DUCK HARBOR MOUNTAIN/MERCHANT POINT LOOP

in Acadia National Park on Isle au Haut

Total distance: 4.5 miles round-trip

Hiking time: 2.5 hours

Difficulty: 3

Rating: 9

This loop offers another way of hiking Duck Harbor Mountain and takes you out to rugged coastline, scenic coves, and Merchant Point. My companions and I saw few other people on these trails one June day—but we did see a seal, ducks, and cormorants, and we explored a wonderful cove strewn with smooth stones. This hike traverses the mountain in the opposite direction from the Western Head Loop (see previous listing). It's easier going up the mountain from this side, so hikers squeamish about the rock scrambling on the other side can hike up this way for the views, then just double back to Duck Harbor.

From the boat landing at Duck Harbor, turn left on the trail toward the water pump. Pass the trail branching right for the campground, and continue straight until you reach Western Head Road. Bearing left along the road, it's about 200 yards to the water pump (if you need water). For this hike, take the grassy road to the right and follow it about a quarter mile, then turn left onto the Duck Harbor Mountain Trail. Follow it a little more than a mile over several open ledges with commanding views of the Isle au Haut's southern end. Reaching the trail's terminus at Squeaker Cove, turn left onto the Goat Trail, which moves in and out between woods and the coast. In less than a mile you reach a trail junction; left leads back to the dirt main road (where you would turn left for Duck Harbor), but bear right on a trail out to the rocky protrusion of Merchant Point (a great lunch spot). From the point, the trail turns back into the forest, crosses a marshy area, and reaches the main road. Turn left and follow the road a bit more than a mile to the head of Duck Harbor. Turn left onto Western Head Road, passing the water pump on the way back to the landing.

User Groups

Hikers and dogs. Dogs must be leashed in the park and are prohibited from the campground. No wheelchair facilities. The island rarely gets enough snow for winter activities. Bikes, horses, and hunting are prohibited.

Access and Fees

Isle au Haut is reached by mail boat/ferry from Stonington, Maine, to Duck Harbor, the starting point for the four Isle au Haut hikes described

in this chapter. The round-trip cost in 2004 was $32 for adults and $16 for children under age 12. For information, contact the Isle au Haut Boat Company, P.O. Box 709, Sea Breeze Avenue, Stonington, ME 04651, 207/367-5193, website: www.isleauhaut.com. The ferry is a small boat and does not transport motor vehicles. The Duck Harbor Campground has five lean-to shelters that can sleep up to six people each, and each lean-to site has a fire ring and picnic table. The lean-to shelters can be reserved from May 15 to October 15 by contacting the park; reservations are required. Reservations requests cannot be postmarked or made in person at park headquarters before April 1. Camping reservations cost $25 per site, regardless of the number of nights.

Maps
A basic map of island trails and roads is issued free to visitors arriving on the ferry or to those with camping reservations. The park website has a map of Isle au Haut. Good trail maps of the area are the waterproof *Acadia National Park* (map 212) for $9.95 from Trails Illustrated, 800/962-1643, website: http://maps.nationalgeographic.com/trails/; and the *Hiking and Biking Map to Acadia National Park and Mount Desert Island,* $7.95 in waterproof Tyvek, from the Appalachian Mountain Club, 800/262-4455, website: www.outdoors.org. For topographic island maps, request Isle au Haut West and Isle au Haut East from USGS Map Sales, Federal Center, Box 25286, Denver, CO 80225, 888/ASK-USGS (888/275-8747), website: http://mapping.usgs.gov.

Directions
To reach the dock where the ferry departs for Isle au Haut, take Route 15 to Main Street in Stonington and turn left at Bartlett's Market; the ferry landing is past the firehouse, at the end of the pier.

Contact
Acadia National Park, P.O. Box 177, Eagle Lake Road, Bar Harbor, ME 04609-0177, 207/288-3338, website: www.nps.gov/acad. Friends of Acadia, P.O. Box 45, 43 Cottage Street, Bar Harbor, ME 04609, 207/288-3340 or 800/625-0321, website: www.friendsofacadia.org.

7 ISLE AU HAUT: EASTERN HEAD
in Acadia National Park on Isle au Haut

Total distance: 6.5 miles round-trip   **Hiking time:** 3.5 hours

Difficulty: 6   **Rating:** 9

The Eastern Head of Isle au Haut attracts few hikers, probably for a variety of reasons, none of which reflect how nice a spot this is. It is not connected to the rest of the national parkland on the island, it is fairly distant from Duck Harbor, and the trail out to Eastern Head is not marked or easy to find—all of which help explain why my wife and I had this stretch of battered shoreline to ourselves for an entire afternoon. The trail to Eastern Head, however, was virtually obliterated by a December 2000 storm, but the trail has since reopened.

The best way to take this hike is to combine it with the Duck Harbor Mountain/Merchant Point Loop (see previous listing), but what follows is the most direct route to Eastern Head. This hike is fairly flat. From the boat landing at Duck Harbor, turn left on the trail toward the water pump. Upon reaching Western Head Road, continue straight, passing the water pump, out to the main road. Turn right and follow the dirt main road for more than two miles (passing the trail coming from Merchant Point on the right) to a cove on Head Harbor where there are several small homes. Respect the fact that this is private land along the town road. The road bends to the left and becomes pavement. Less than 0.1 mile after the pavement begins, turn right onto an unmarked dirt road; a yellow house lies a short distance down this road on the left. Follow the road for about a half mile to its end, where it becomes a little-used, grassy lane and terminates at a red house. An old car sits in the yard, as a ranger described it to me, "melting into the ground." The unmarked but obvious trail begins here and continues nearly a mile out to the coast at Thunder Gulch, a deep chop reaching about 100 feet back into the oceanside cliffs. You can wander around the clifftops here and enjoy a view of the ocean and a tiny island called Eastern Ear (which cannot be reached on foot). Return the way you came.

User Groups
Hikers and dogs. Dogs must be leashed in the park and are prohibited in the campground. No wheelchair facilities. The island rarely gets enough snow for winter activities. Bikes, horses, and hunting are prohibited.

Access and Fees
Isle au Haut is reached by mail boat/ferry from Stonington, Maine, to Duck Harbor, the starting point for the four Isle au Haut hikes described

in this chapter. The round-trip cost in 2004 was $32 for adults and $16 for children under age 12. For information, contact the Isle au Haut Boat Company, P.O. Box 709, Sea Breeze Avenue, Stonington, ME 04651, 207/367-5193, website: www.isleauhaut.com. The ferry is a small boat and does not transport motor vehicles. The Duck Harbor Campground has five lean-to shelters that can sleep up to six people each, and each lean-to site has a fire ring and picnic table. The lean-to shelters can be reserved from May 15 to October 15 by contacting the park; reservations are required. Reservations requests cannot be postmarked or made in person at park headquarters before April 1. Camping reservations cost $25 per site, regardless of the number of nights.

Maps
A basic map of island trails and roads is issued free to visitors arriving on the ferry or to those with camping reservations. The park website has a map of Isle au Haut. Good trail maps of the area are the waterproof *Acadia National Park* (map 212) for $9.95 from Trails Illustrated, 800/962-1643, website: http://maps.nationalgeographic.com/trails/; and the *Hiking and Biking Map to Acadia National Park and Mount Desert Island,* $7.95 in waterproof Tyvek, from the Appalachian Mountain Club, 800/262-4455, website: www.outdoors.org. For topographic island maps, request Isle au Haut West and Isle au Haut East from USGS Map Sales, Federal Center, Box 25286, Denver, CO 80225, 888/ASK-USGS (888/275-8747), website: http://mapping.usgs.gov.

Directions
To reach the dock where the ferry departs for Isle au Haut, drive on Route 15 to Main Street in Stonington and turn left at Bartlett's Market; the ferry landing is past the firehouse, at the end of the pier.

Contact
Acadia National Park, P.O. Box 177, Eagle Lake Road, Bar Harbor, ME 04609-0177, 207/288-3338, website: www.nps.gov/acad. Friends of Acadia, P.O. Box 45, 43 Cottage Street, Bar Harbor, ME 04609, 207/288-3340 or 800/625-0321, website: www.friendsofacadia.org.

8 BERNARD AND MANSELL MOUNTAINS
in Acadia National Park

Total distance: 3.7 miles round-trip   **Hiking time:** 2.5 hours

Difficulty: 4   **Rating:** 7

While Bernard (1,071 feet) and Mansell (949 feet) are the two highest mountains on Mount Desert Island's west side, their summits are wooded, so these trails lack the spectacular views of other peaks in Acadia National Park. Still, this loop offers a scenic walk through the woods, is fairly challenging, and does take you past a few good views of the bays and Long Pond. The cumulative elevation gain on this 3.7-mile hike is about 1,200 feet.

From the parking area, hike west on the Long Pond Trail, soon bearing left onto the Cold Brook Trail. In less than a half mile, cross Gilley Field and follow a road a short distance to the Sluiceway Trail on the right. It climbs fairly steeply to the South Face Trail, where you turn left for the Bernard Mountain summit, a few minutes' walk away. Backtrack and follow the trail down into Great Notch and straight ahead to the summit of Mansell Mountain. Continue over the summit, picking up the Perpendicular Trail, which descends the rugged east face of Mansell, often passing below low cliffs, to the Long Pond Trail. Turn right for the parking area.

User Groups
Hikers, snowshoers, and dogs. Dogs must be leashed. No wheelchair facilities. This trail is not suitable for skis. Bikes, horses, and hunting are prohibited.

Access and Fees
Parking and access are free.

Maps
A basic park map is available at the visitors center, and the park website has maps showing roads, trails, and carriage roads. Good trail maps of the area are the waterproof *Acadia National Park* (map 212) for $9.95 from Trails Illustrated, 800/962-1643, website: http://maps.nationalgeographic.com/trails/ and the *Hiking and Biking Map to Acadia National Park and Mount Desert Island,* $7.95 in waterproof Tyvek, from the Appalachian Mountain Club, 800/262-4455, website: www.outdoors.org. For a topographic area map, request Southwest Harbor from USGS Map Sales, Federal Center, Box 25286, Denver, CO 80225, 888/ASK-USGS (888/275-8747), website: http://mapping.usgs.gov.

Directions

From Route 102 in Southwest Harbor, turn west onto Seal Cove Road. Take a right onto Long Pond Road and follow it to the parking area at the south end of Long Pond (and a great view of the pond). The park visitors center is located north of Bar Harbor at the junction of Route 3 and the start of the Park Loop Road.

Contact

Acadia National Park, P.O. Box 177, Eagle Lake Road, Bar Harbor, ME 04609-0177, 207/288-3338, website: www.nps.gov/acad. Friends of Acadia, P.O. Box 45, 43 Cottage Street, Bar Harbor, ME 04609, 207/288-3340 or 800/625-0321, website: www.friendsofacadia.org.

9 BEECH MOUNTAIN

in Acadia National Park

Total distance: 1.2 miles round-trip   **Hiking time:** 1 hour

Difficulty: 2   **Rating:** 9

Want a scenic hike with long views that avoids the crowds common on the east side of Acadia? This is the one, and it entails just a bit more than a mile of hiking and a few hundred feet of elevation gain. Soon after leaving the parking lot, the trail forks; the loop can be hiked in either direction, but I recommend bearing left. You soon emerge onto an open ledge with a terrific view east and north: from the islands south of Mount Desert to Acadia, Sargent, and Penobscot mountains and the myriad waterways to the north. A short distance farther up the trail is the summit, where trees block any view, but you can climb one flight of stairs on the closed fire tower for a 360-degree view. Beyond the summit, bear right onto the descent trail, which offers magnificent views over Long Pond and all the way to Camden Hills.

User Groups

Hikers, snowshoers, and dogs. Dogs must be leashed. No wheelchair facilities. This trail is not suitable for skis. Bikes, horses, and hunting are prohibited.

Access and Fees

Parking and access are free.

Maps

A basic park map is available at the visitors center, and the park website has maps showing roads, trails, and carriage roads. Good trail maps of the

area are the waterproof *Acadia National Park* (map 212) for $9.95 from
Trails Illustrated, 800/962-1643, website: http://maps.nationalgeographic
.com/trails/ and the *Hiking and Biking Map to Acadia National Park and
Mount Desert Island,* $7.95 in waterproof Tyvek, from the Appalachian
Mountain Club, 800/262-4455, website: www.outdoors.org. For a topographic area map, request Southwest Harbor from USGS Map Sales, Federal Center, Box 25286, Denver, CO 80225, 888/ASK-USGS (888/275-
8747), website: http://mapping.usgs.gov.

Directions
From the junction of Routes 198 and 102 in Somesville, drive south on
Route 102 for 0.8 mile and turn right onto Pretty Marsh Road at the sign
for Beech Mountain and the Beech Cliffs. Drive 0.2 mile, turn left onto
Beech Hill Road, and then drive 3.1 miles to the parking lot at the end of
the road. The trailhead is on the right as you enter. The park visitors center is located north of Bar Harbor at the junction of Route 3 and the start
of the Park Loop Road.

Contact
Acadia National Park, P.O. Box 177, Eagle Lake Road, Bar Harbor, ME
04609-0177, 207/288-3338, website: www.nps.gov/acad. Friends of Acadia,
P.O. Box 45, 43 Cottage Street, Bar Harbor, ME 04609, 207/288-3340 or
800/625-0321, website: www.friendsofacadia.org.

10 BEECH AND CANADA CLIFFS
in Acadia National Park

Total distance: 0.7 miles round-trip   **Hiking time:** 0.75 hour

Difficulty: 1   **Rating:** 8

From the parking lot, this almost flat, short hike leads to the crest of cliffs
high above Echo Lake. A quarter mile up the trail you reach a junction: to
the right is the trail to the Canada Cliffs, to the left the trail to the Beech
Cliffs. Both entail a short walk to worthwhile views, but the Beech Cliffs
may be closed in late spring and early summer to protect nesting peregrine
falcons. The Canada Cliffs should be open all year.

User Groups
Hikers, snowshoers, and dogs. Dogs must be leashed. No wheelchair facilities.
This trail is not suitable for skis. Bikes, horses, and hunting are prohibited.

Access and Fees
Parking and access are free.

Maps
A basic park map is available at the visitors center, and the park website has maps showing roads, trails, and carriage roads. Good trail maps of the area are the waterproof *Acadia National Park* (map 212) for $9.95 from Trails Illustrated, 800/962-1643, website: http://maps.nationalgeographic .com/trails/ and the *Hiking and Biking Map to Acadia National Park and Mount Desert Island,* $7.95 in waterproof Tyvek, from the Appalachian Mountain Club, 800/262-4455, website: www.outdoors.org. For a topographic area map, request Southwest Harbor from USGS Map Sales, Federal Center, Box 25286, Denver, CO 80225, 888/ASK-USGS (888/275-8747), website: http://mapping.usgs.gov.

Directions
From the junction of Routes 198 and 102 in Somesville, drive south on Route 102 for 0.8 mile and turn right onto Pretty Marsh Road at the sign for Beech Mountain and the Beech Cliffs. Continue 0.2 mile, turn left onto Beech Hill Road, and then drive 3.1 miles to the parking lot at the end of the road; the trailhead is on the left as you enter. The park visitors center is located north of Bar Harbor at the junction of Route 3 and the start of the Park Loop Road.

Contact
Acadia National Park, P.O. Box 177, Eagle Lake Road, Bar Harbor, ME 04609-0177, 207/288-3338, website: www.nps.gov/acad. Friends of Acadia, P.O. Box 45, 43 Cottage Street, Bar Harbor, ME 04609, 207/288-3340 or 800/625-0321, website: www.friendsofacadia.org.

11 ACADIA MOUNTAIN
in Acadia National Park

Total distance: 2.5 miles round-trip   **Hiking time:** 1.5 hours

Difficulty: 2   **Rating:** 9

At 681 feet, Acadia Mountain is the biggest hill on the west side of Somes Sound—the only true fjord in the eastern United States—and offers excellent views of the sound, the towns of Northeast Harbor and Southwest Harbor, and the islands south of Mount Desert. Although you scramble a little up rocks on the way up, climbing about 500 feet, this easy hike is a good one for young children.

From the turnout, cross the highway to the trail. It soon branches; stay left, cross a fire road (your route of descent), and proceed to the open ledges at the summit. The trail continues past the summit to even better views from ledges atop the mountain's east face. The trail then turns right, descending steep ledges with good views, and reaches a junction with the fire road (which resembles a trail here). Turn right, and the road soon widens. Just before reaching the highway, turn left onto the Acadia Mountain Trail, which leads back to the start.

User Groups

Hikers, snowshoers, and dogs. Dogs must be leashed. No wheelchair facilities. This trail is not suitable for skis. Bikes, horses, and hunting are prohibited.

Access and Fees

Parking and access are free.

Maps

A basic park map is available at the visitors center, and the park website has maps showing roads, trails, and carriage roads. Good trail maps of the area are the waterproof *Acadia National Park* (map 212) for $9.95 from Trails Illustrated, 800/962-1643, website: http://maps.nationalgeographic .com/trails/ and the *Hiking and Biking Map to Acadia National Park and Mount Desert Island,* $7.95 in waterproof Tyvek, from the Appalachian Mountain Club, 800/262-4455, website: www.outdoors.org. For a topographic area map, request Southwest Harbor from USGS Map Sales, Federal Center, Box 25286, Denver, CO 80225, 888/ASK-USGS (888/275-8747), website: http://mapping.usgs.gov.

Directions

From the junction of Routes 198 and 102 in Somesville, drive south on Route 102 for 3.4 miles to a turnout on the right (there is a sign) at the trailhead for Acadia Mountain. The park visitors center is located north of Bar Harbor at the junction of Route 3 and the start of the Park Loop Road.

Contact

Acadia National Park, P.O. Box 177, Eagle Lake Road, Bar Harbor, ME 04609-0177, 207/288-3338, website: www.nps.gov/acad. Friends of Acadia, P.O. Box 45, 43 Cottage Street, Bar Harbor, ME 04609, 207/288-3340 or 800/625-0321, website: www.friendsofacadia.org.

12 FLYING MOUNTAIN
in Acadia National Park

Total distance: 0.6 miles round-trip

Hiking time: 0.5 hour

Difficulty: 2

Rating: 8

This is a short hike up a hill that rises just 284 feet above Somes Sound, but that offers views of the fjord from open ledges. The trail begins at the parking area and ascends steadily; the last stretch is a bit steep. Once on the ledges, be sure to continue over them to the true summit, marked by a signpost, where the views are even better than those you see when you first reach the ledges.

User Groups
Hikers, snowshoers, and dogs. Dogs must be leashed. No wheelchair facilities. This trail is not suitable for skis. Bikes, horses, and hunting are prohibited.

Access and Fees
Parking and access are free.

Maps
A basic park map is available at the visitors center, and the park website has maps showing roads, trails, and carriage roads. Good trail maps of the area are the waterproof *Acadia National Park* (map 212) for $9.95 from Trails Illustrated, 800/962-1643, website: http://maps.nationalgeographic .com/trails/ and the *Hiking and Biking Map to Acadia National Park and Mount Desert Island,* $7.95 in waterproof Tyvek, from the Appalachian Mountain Club, 800/262-4455, website: www.outdoors.org. For a topographic area map, request Southwest Harbor from USGS Map Sales, Federal Center, Box 25286, Denver, CO 80225, 888/ASK-USGS (888/275-8747), website: http://mapping.usgs.gov.

Directions
From the junction of Routes 198 and 102 in Somesville, go south on Route 102 for 5.4 miles and turn left on Fernald Point Road. Drive one mile to parking on the left at Valley Road. The park visitors center is north of Bar Harbor, at the junction of Route 3 and Park Loop Road.

Contact
Acadia National Park, P.O. Box 177, Eagle Lake Road, Bar Harbor, ME 04609-0177, 207/288-3338, website: www.nps.gov/acad. Friends of Acadia, P.O. Box 45, 43 Cottage Street, Bar Harbor, ME 04609, 207/288-3340 or 800/625-0321, website: www.friendsofacadia.org.

13 PENOBSCOT AND SARGENT MOUNTAINS
in Acadia National Park

Total distance: 4.5 miles round-trip

Hiking time: 3 hours

Difficulty: 5

Rating: 10

While nearly everyone who comes to Acadia National Park knows of Cadillac Mountain, few have heard of—and even fewer will actually hike—Penobscot and Sargent Mountains, which rise abruptly to the west of Jordan Pond. Yet the elevations of Sargent at 1,373 feet and Penobscot at 1,194 feet rank them as the second- and fifth-highest peaks on Mount Desert Island. And the ridge connecting them pushes nearly as much area above the trees as Cadillac's scenic South Ridge. For much of this 4.5-mile hike, which climbs more than 1,200 feet in elevation, you enjoy long views east to the Pemetic and Cadillac Mountains, south to the many offshore islands, and west across Somes Sound and Penobscot Bay to the Camden Hills.

From the parking area, head down the dirt access road toward Jordan Pond and turn left onto a trail leading to the Jordan Pond House. The Penobscot Mountain Trail begins behind the Jordan Pond House, soon ascending steep ledges that require some scrambling. Up on the ridge the hiking gets much easier. Beyond Penobscot's summit, the trail dips into a small saddle between the mountains. Turn left onto the Sargent Pond Trail, passing the small pond in the woods. Turn right onto the Sargent Mountain South Ridge Trail, ascending the long slope to the summit, marked by a pile of rocks. Just beyond the summit, turn right onto the Jordan Cliffs Trail, which traverses above the cliffs visible from Jordan Pond. Cross a carriage road and turn left onto the Penobscot Mountain Trail to return.

User Groups
Hikers, snowshoers, and dogs. Dogs must be leashed. No wheelchair facilities. This trail is not suitable for skis. Bikes, horses, and hunting are prohibited.

Access and Fees
Parking and access are free.

Maps
A basic park map is available at the visitors center, and the park website has maps showing roads, trails, and carriage roads. Good trail maps of the area are the waterproof *Acadia National Park* (map 212) for $9.95 from Trails Illustrated, 800/962-1643, website: http://maps.nationalgeographic.com/trails/ and the *Hiking and Biking Map to Acadia National Park and*

Mount Desert Island, $7.95 in waterproof Tyvek, from the Appalachian Mountain Club, 800/262-4455, website: www.outdoors.org. For a topographic area map, request Southwest Harbor from USGS Map Sales, Federal Center, Box 25286, Denver, CO 80225, 888/ASK-USGS (888/275-8747), website: http://mapping.usgs.gov.

Directions
Take Route 3 south from Bar Harbor to Seal Harbor. Turn right at the Acadia National Park entrance and left on the Park Loop Road, following it to the Jordan Pond parking area. Or from the park visitors center, follow the Park Loop Road south. Where it splits, turn right and continue to the Jordan Pond parking area. The park visitors center is located north of Bar Harbor, at the junction of Route 3 and the start of the Park Loop Road.

Contact
Acadia National Park, P.O. Box 177, Eagle Lake Road, Bar Harbor, ME 04609-0177, 207/288-3338, website: www.nps.gov/acad. Friends of Acadia, P.O. Box 45, 43 Cottage Street, Bar Harbor, ME 04609, 207/288-3340 or 800/625-0321, website: www.friendsofacadia.org.

14 JORDAN POND/SARGENT MOUNTAIN CARRIAGE ROAD LOOP
in Acadia National Park

Total distance: 16 miles round-trip   **Hiking time:** 8 hours

Difficulty: 6   **Rating:** 9

While the Jordan Pond area is popular with bicyclists, the farther you wander from the pond, the fewer people you see on the carriage roads. This moderately hilly loop makes for a pleasant ride over the gravel roadways traveled by the country's upper crust decades ago. As with the Jordan Pond/Eagle Lake/Bubble Pond Carriage Road Loop (see listing in this chapter), I recommend doing this on a bike or skis rather than hiking; on a bike, it will take about three hours.

From the Jordan Pond parking area, go south on the Park Loop Road a short distance and turn right onto a carriage road. Stay right, soon ascending a gradual slope above Jordan Pond. Turn right, then left, and follow the northwest shoreline of Eagle Lake. At the lake's northwest corner, turn left. After passing Aunt Betty Pond—where there's a view across the pond toward Sargent Mountain—turn right and contour around Sargent. After passing Upper Hadlock Pond on the right, the carriage road makes a U-turn; take the first right after that. Stay left all the way back to Jordan Pond.

User Groups
Hikers, bikers, dogs, horses, skiers, and snowshoers. Dogs must be leashed. No wheelchair facilities. Hunting is prohibited.

Access and Fees
Parking and access are free.

Maps
A basic park map is available at the visitors center, and the park website has maps showing roads, trails, and carriage roads. A map of the carriage roads, showing the intersection signpost numbers—which other maps do not show—is available at the park website. Good trail maps of the area are the waterproof *Acadia National Park* (map 212) for $9.95 from Trails Illustrated, 800/962-1643, website: http://maps.nationalgeographic.com/trails/ and the *Hiking and Biking Map to Acadia National Park and Mount Desert Island,* $7.95 in waterproof Tyvek, from the Appalachian Mountain Club, 800/262-4455, website: www.outdoors.org. For topographic area maps, request Seal Harbor and Southwest Harbor from USGS Map Sales, Federal Center, Box 25286, Denver, CO 80225, 888/ASK-USGS (888/275-8747), website: http://mapping.usgs.gov.

Directions
Drive Route 3 south from Bar Harbor to Seal Harbor. Turn right at the Acadia National Park entrance and left on the Park Loop Road, following it to the Jordan Pond parking area. You can bike to the start from Blackwoods Campground, adding about seven miles round-trip: Bike Route 3 toward Seal Harbor, and where the highway crosses a bridge over the Park Loop Road, carry your bike down a footpath to the Loop Road; then follow it north and turn left onto a carriage path just before the Jordan Pond House. The park visitors center is located north of Bar Harbor at the junction of Route 3 and the start of the Park Loop Road.

Contact
Acadia National Park, P.O. Box 177, Eagle Lake Road, Bar Harbor, ME 04609-0177, 207/288-3338, website: www.nps.gov/acad. Friends of Acadia, P.O. Box 45, 43 Cottage Street, Bar Harbor, ME 04609, 207/288-3340 or 800/625-0321, website: www.friendsofacadia.org.

15 THE BUBBLES/EAGLE LAKE LOOP
in Acadia National Park

Total distance: 4.2 miles round-trip

Hiking time: 2 hours

Difficulty: 4

Rating: 10

If the view of The Bubbles from the south end of Jordan Pond is one of Acadia's most famous, then the views of Jordan Pond and the steep hills enclosing it from the open ledges atop North and South Bubble rival any in the national park. Best of all, they are reached with little effort, ascending just a few hundred feet.

This loop takes in Conners Nubble—a commanding overlook of Eagle Lake—and finishes with a walk along the rocky shore of Eagle Lake. For a shorter walk, the round-trip hike to the summit of North Bubble alone is 1.2 miles. From the Bubble Rock parking area, the Bubble-Pemetic Trail heads west, then northwest through the woods, then turns sharply left, and climbs to the saddle between North and South Bubble. Turn left to reach the summit of South Bubble. Backtrack and ascend the North Bubble Trail to that summit, which is higher than the South Bubble sum-

mit. Continue over North Bubble, crossing a carriage road, to Conners Nubble. Descend and turn right onto the Eagle Lake Trail, right again on the Jordan Pond Carry Trail, and left on the Bubble-Pemetic Trail to return to the parking area.

a hiker on The Bubbles, above Jordan Pond, Acadia National Park

User Groups
Hikers, dogs, skiers, and snowshoers. Dogs must be leashed. No wheelchair facilities. Bikes, horses, and hunting are prohibited.

Access and Fees
Parking and access are free.

Maps
A basic park map is available at the visitors center, and the

park website has maps showing roads, trails, and carriage roads. Good trail maps of the area are the waterproof *Acadia National Park* (map 212) for $9.95 from Trails Illustrated, 800/962-1643, website: http://maps.nationalgeographic.com/trails/ and the *Hiking and Biking Map to Acadia National Park and Mount Desert Island,* $7.95 in waterproof Tyvek, from the Appalachian Mountain Club, 800/262-4455, website: www.outdoors.org. For topographic area maps, request Seal Harbor and Southwest Harbor from USGS Map Sales, Federal Center, Box 25286, Denver, CO 80225, 888/ASK-USGS (888/275-8747), website: http://mapping.usgs.gov.

Directions
Drive on Route 3 south from Bar Harbor to Seal Harbor. Turn right at the Acadia National Park entrance and left on the Park Loop Road, following it to the Bubble Rock parking area, 1.6 miles past the Jordan Pond parking area. Or from the park visitors center, follow the Park Loop Road south. Where it splits, turn right for the Bubble Rock parking area. The park visitors center is located north of Bar Harbor, at the junction of Route 3 and the start of the Park Loop Road.

Contact
Acadia National Park, P.O. Box 177, Eagle Lake Road, Bar Harbor, ME 04609-0177, 207/288-3338, website: www.nps.gov/acad. Friends of Acadia, P.O. Box 45, 43 Cottage Street, Bar Harbor, ME 04609, 207/288-3340 or 800/625-0321, website: www.friendsofacadia.org.

16 JORDAN POND LOOP
in Acadia National Park

Total distance: 3.3 miles round-trip   **Hiking time:** 1.5 hours

Difficulty: 2   **Rating:** 8

This fairly easy, flat trail loops around scenic Jordan Pond. You're constantly gazing across the water to the steep mountainsides surrounding it— from the cliffs and rounded humps of The Bubbles to the wooded slopes of Penobscot and Pemetic Mountains. The easiest walking is along the pond's east shore; on the northeast and especially the northwest shores, the trail crosses areas of boulders that require some scrambling and rock-hopping. Although these patches are not too difficult to navigate, you can avoid them altogether by hiking in a counterclockwise direction and turning back upon reaching these sections.

From the Jordan Pond parking area, continue down the dirt road to the shore and turn right onto the wide gravel path of the Jordan Pond Shore Trail. At the pond's southwest corner, the trail reaches a carriage road; turn left over a bridge, then immediately left onto the trail again, soon reaching the famous view of The Bubbles from the pond's south end. Just beyond that, the trail completes the loop at the dirt access road. Turn right for the parking lot.

User Groups

Hikers, dogs, skiers, and snowshoers. Dogs must be leashed. No wheelchair facilities. Bikes, horses, and hunting are prohibited.

Access and Fees

Parking and access are free.

Maps

A basic park map is available at the visitors center, and the park website has maps showing roads, trails, and carriage roads. Good trail maps of the area are the waterproof *Acadia National Park* (map 212) for $9.95 from Trails Illustrated, 800/962-1643, website: http://maps.nationalgeographic .com/trails/ and the *Hiking and Biking Map to Acadia National Park and Mount Desert Island,* $7.95 in waterproof Tyvek, from the Appalachian Mountain Club, 800/262-4455, website: www.outdoors.org. For topographic area maps, request Seal Harbor and Southwest Harbor from USGS Map Sales, Federal Center, Box 25286, Denver, CO 80225, 888/ASK-USGS (888/275-8747), website: http://mapping.usgs.gov.

Directions

Take Route 3 south from Bar Harbor to Seal Harbor. Turn right at the Acadia National Park entrance and left on the Park Loop Road, following it to the Jordan Pond parking area. Or from the park visitors center, follow the Park Loop Road south. Where it splits, turn right for the Jordan Pond parking area. The park visitors center is located north of Bar Harbor at the junction of Route 3 and the start of the Park Loop Road.

Contact

Acadia National Park, P.O. Box 177, Eagle Lake Road, Bar Harbor, ME 04609-0177, 207/288-3338, website: www.nps.gov/acad. Friends of Acadia, P.O. Box 45, 43 Cottage Street, Bar Harbor, ME 04609, 207/288-3340 or 800/625-0321, website: www.friendsofacadia.org.

17 JORDAN POND/EAGLE LAKE/ BUBBLE POND CARRIAGE ROAD LOOP

in Acadia National Park

Total distance: 11.5 miles round-trip   **Hiking time:** 6 hours

Difficulty: 6   **Rating:** 9

This moderately hilly loop is one of the best carriage road trails in the park, passing high above Jordan Pond, circling Eagle Lake, and cruising along the western shore of Bubble Pond. Although hiking is permitted, it's more interesting on a bike—or cross-country skis in winter when there's enough snow.

From the Bubble Pond parking area, follow the carriage road north along Eagle Lake. At the lake's northwest corner, turn left and follow the carriage road along the lake's western shore. After angling away from the lake (around Conners Nubble), turn right, then left, soon passing above Jordan Pond. At the pond's south end, turn left and cross the Park Loop Road. Follow this carriage road all the way back to Bubble Pond. Along the way, you pass a carriage road leading to the right across a bridge over the Loop Road; the loop beginning across the bridge climbs Day Mountain, a fun if challenging ride up and a fast ride down for mountain bikers who have the time and energy to add a few miles to this trail's distance.

User Groups

Hikers, bikers, dogs, skiers, and snowshoers. Dogs must be leashed. No wheelchair facilities. Horses and hunting are prohibited.

Access and Fees

Parking and access are free.

Maps

A basic park map is available at the visitors center, and the park website has maps showing roads, trails, and carriage roads. A map of the carriage roads, showing the intersection signpost numbers—which other maps do not show—is available at the park website. Good trail maps of the area are the waterproof *Acadia National Park* (map 212) for $9.95 from Trails Illustrated, 800/962-1643, website: http://maps.nationalgeographic.com/trails/ and the *Hiking and Biking Map to Acadia National Park and Mount Desert Island,* $7.95 in waterproof Tyvek, from the Appalachian Mountain Club, 800/262-4455, website: www.outdoors.org. For a topographic area map, request Seal Harbor and Southwest Harbor from USGS Map Sales, Federal Center, Box 25286, Denver, CO 80225, 888/ASK-USGS (888/275-8747), website: http://mapping.usgs.gov.

Directions

Take Route 3 south from Bar Harbor to Seal Harbor. Turn right at the Acadia National Park entrance and left on the Park Loop Road, following it 2.6 miles past the Jordan Pond parking area to the Bubble Pond parking area. From the park visitors center, follow the Park Loop Road south. Where it splits, turn right for the Bubble Pond parking area. You can bike to the start from Blackwoods Campground, adding about seven miles round-trip: Bike Route 3 toward Seal Harbor and where the highway crosses a bridge over the Park Loop Road, carry your bike down a footpath to the Loop Road and follow it north. Just before the Jordan Pond House, turn right onto this carriage road loop. The park visitors center is north of Bar Harbor at the junction of Route 3 and Park Loop Road.

Contact

Acadia National Park, P.O. Box 177, Eagle Lake Road, Bar Harbor, ME 04609-0177, 207/288-3338, website: www.nps.gov/acad. Friends of Acadia, P.O. Box 45, 43 Cottage Street, Bar Harbor, ME 04609, 207/288-3340 or 800/625-0321, website: www.friendsofacadia.org.

18 PEMETIC MOUNTAIN
in Acadia National Park

Total distance: 3.3 miles round-trip   **Hiking time:** 2.5 hours

Difficulty: 3   **Rating:** 10

Pemetic Mountain, situated between Jordan Pond to the west and Bubble Pond and Cadillac Mountain to the east, thrusts a long, open ridge of rock into the sky. Its summit, at 1,284 feet, offers one of the most sweeping views—but it's the walk along the ridge that makes this hike memorable. The views take in Cadillac, Penobscot, and Sargent Mountains, the islands south of Mount Desert, and Jordan Pond, and offer a unique perspective on The Bubbles. The elevation gain is a bit less than 1,000 feet.

From the Jordan Pond parking area, follow the dirt access road to the southeast shore of Jordan Pond. Turn left, follow the Jordan Pond Shore Trail a short distance, and then turn left onto the Pond Trail. Cross the Park Loop Road and in less than a half mile, turn left onto the Pemetic Mountain West Cliff Trail, ascending the ridge. At the junction with the Pemetic Mountain Trail, turn left (north) and proceed to the summit.

Double back and follow the Pemetic Mountain Trail all the way to the Pond Trail, then turn right to go back the way you came.

User Groups
Hikers, dogs, skiers, and snowshoers. Dogs must be leashed. No wheelchair facilities. Bikes, horses, and hunting are prohibited.

Access and Fees
Parking and access are free.

Maps
A basic park map is available at the visitors center, and the park website has maps showing roads, trails, and carriage roads. Good trail maps of the area are the waterproof *Acadia National Park* (map 212) for $9.95 from Trails Illustrated, 800/962-1643, website: http://maps.nationalgeographic.com/trails/ and the *Hiking and Biking Map to Acadia National Park and Mount Desert Island,* $7.95 in waterproof Tyvek, from the Appalachian Mountain Club, 800/262-4455, website: www.outdoors.org. For topographic area maps, request Seal Harbor and Southwest Harbor from USGS Map Sales, Federal Center, Box 25286, Denver, CO 80225, 888/ASK-USGS (888/275-8747), website: http://mapping.usgs.gov.

Directions
Take Route 3 south from Bar Harbor to Seal Harbor. Turn right at the Acadia National Park entrance and left on the Park Loop Road, following it to the Jordan Pond parking area. Or from the park visitors center, follow the Park Loop Road south. Where it splits, turn right and continue to the Jordan Pond parking area. The park visitors center is located north of Bar Harbor at the junction of Route 3 and the start of the Park Loop Road.

Contact
Acadia National Park, P.O. Box 177, Eagle Lake Road, Bar Harbor, ME 04609-0177, 207/288-3338, website: www.nps.gov/acad. Friends of Acadia, P.O. Box 45, 43 Cottage Street, Bar Harbor, ME 04609, 207/288-3340 or 800/625-0321, website: www.friendsofacadia.org.

19 CADILLAC MOUNTAIN: WEST FACE TRAIL
in Acadia National Park

Total distance: 2.8 miles round-trip   **Hiking time:** 2.5 hours

Difficulty: 4   **Rating:** 9

This trail offers the most direct and difficult route up Mount Desert Island's highest peak, 1,530-foot Cadillac Mountain. It involves a great deal of scrambling over steep slabs of open rock, relentlessly strenuous hiking, and about 1,200 feet of elevation gain. Descending may be more difficult than ascending. Much of the trail lies in the woods, but the occasional views—which become more frequent as you climb higher—down to Bubble Pond and of the deep cleft separating Cadillac and Pemetic Mountains are spectacular. I like this trail for its challenge and relatively light hiker traffic.

From the parking area, cross the carriage road and pick up the Cadillac Mountain West Face Trail at the north end of Bubble Pond. In just under a mile of steep climbing, you top out on the mountain's South Ridge. Turn left onto the Cadillac Mountain South Ridge Trail and follow it to the summit. Head back along the same route.

User Groups

Hikers and dogs. Dogs must be leashed. No wheelchair facilities. This trail is not suitable for skis or snowshoes. Bikes, horses, and hunting are prohibited.

Access and Fees

Parking and access are free.

Maps

A basic park map is available at the visitors center, and the park website has maps showing roads, trails, and carriage roads. Good trail maps of the area are the waterproof *Acadia National Park* (map 212) for $9.95 from Trails Illustrated, 800/962-1643, website: http://maps.nationalgeographic .com/trails/ and the *Hiking and Biking Map to Acadia National Park and Mount Desert Island,* $7.95 in waterproof Tyvek, from the Appalachian Mountain Club, 800/262-4455, website: www.outdoors.org. For topographic area maps, request Seal Harbor and Southwest Harbor from USGS Map Sales, Federal Center, Box 25286, Denver, CO 80225, 888/ASK-USGS (888/275-8747), website: http://mapping.usgs.gov.

Directions

Take Route 3 south from Bar Harbor to Seal Harbor. Turn right at the Acadia National Park entrance and left on the Park Loop Road, following it 2.6 miles past the Jordan Pond parking area to the Bubble Pond parking area. Or from the park visitors center, follow the Park Loop Road south. Where it splits, turn right for the Bubble Pond parking area. The park visitors center is located north of Bar Harbor at the junction of Route 3 and Park Loop Road.

Contact
Acadia National Park, P.O. Box 177, Eagle Lake Road, Bar Harbor, ME 04609-0177, 207/288-3338, website: www.nps.gov/acad. Friends of Acadia, P.O. Box 45, 43 Cottage Street, Bar Harbor, ME 04609, 207/288-3340 or 800/625-0321, website: www.friendsofacadia.org.

20 CADILLAC MOUNTAIN: SOUTH RIDGE TRAIL
in Acadia National Park

Total distance: 7 miles round-trip

Hiking time: 4 hours

Difficulty: 6

Rating: 10

The long, spectacular, wide-open South Ridge of the highest peak on Mount Desert Island—1,530-foot Cadillac Mountain—affords one of the longest and most scenic hikes in Acadia National Park. How many mountain ridges offer views not only of surrounding hills, but also of the ocean and a profusion of islands? This seven-mile round-tripper climbs about 1,300 feet, making it one of the most challenging outings in the park.

One of my first hikes ever in Acadia, it remains one of my favorites. A relatively short and somewhat steep hike through the woods brings you onto the broad ridge; then you have an easy walk and sweeping views all the way to the summit. About a mile from Route 3, take the loop trail out to Eagle Crag, which offers views to the east; the loop trail rejoins the South Ridge Trail in 0.2 mile. Continuing up the South Ridge, you break out above the trees to views west to Pemetic and Sargent Mountains, and east and south to Frenchman Bay and numerous islands. At three miles, the trail passes a junction with the Cadillac Mountain West Face Trail (which descends left, or west), reaches a switchback in the paved summit road, and veers right, winding another half mile to the summit. Return the same way you came.

User Groups
Hikers, snowshoers, and dogs. Dogs must be leashed. No wheelchair facilities. This trail is not suitable for skis. Bikes, horses, and hunting are prohibited.

Access and Fees

Parking and access are free.

Maps

A basic park map is available at the visitors center, and the park website has maps showing roads, trails, and carriage roads. Good trail maps of the area are the waterproof *Acadia National Park* (map 212) for $9.95 from Trails Illustrated, 800/962-1643, website: http://maps.nationalgeographic .com/trails/ and the *Hiking and Biking Map to Acadia National Park and Mount Desert Island,* $7.95 in waterproof Tyvek, from the Appalachian Mountain Club, 800/262-4455, website: www.outdoors.org. For a topographic area map, request Seal Harbor from USGS Map Sales, Federal Center, Box 25286, Denver, CO 80225, 888/ASK-USGS (888/275-8747), website: http://mapping.usgs.gov.

Directions

Drive Route 3 south from Bar Harbor to the Blackwoods Campground entrance. The Cadillac Mountain South Ridge Trail enters the woods on the right about 50 yards past the campground entrance road; there is parking at the roadside. Campers in Blackwoods can pick up the trail at the west end of the campground's south loop (adding 1.4 miles to the hike's round-trip distance). The park visitors center is located north of Bar Harbor, at the junction of Route 3 and the start of the Park Loop Road.

Contact

Acadia National Park, P.O. Box 177, Eagle Lake Road, Bar Harbor, ME 04609-0177, 207/288-3338, website: www.nps.gov/acad. Friends of Acadia, P.O. Box 45, 43 Cottage Street, Bar Harbor, ME 04609, 207/288-3340 or 800/625-0321, website: www.friendsofacadia.org.

21 DORR AND CADILLAC MOUNTAINS
in Acadia National Park

Total distance: 3 miles round-trip   **Hiking time:** 2 hours

Difficulty: 7   **Rating:** 10

This moderate hike combines the highest peak on Mount Desert Island, 1,530-foot Cadillac Mountain, with its neighbor to the east, 1,270-foot Dorr, a mountain just as scenic and far less crowded. For much of this hike, you enjoy continuous views that take in Champlain Mountain, the islands of Frenchman Bay, and the rugged terrain atop Dorr and Cadillac.

While just three miles long, this hike's cumulative elevation gain exceeds 1,500 feet.

From the parking area, turn left onto the Jessup Path and right onto the Dorr Mountain East Face Trail, which ascends numerous switchbacks up the steep flank of the mountain. Turn left onto the Dorr Mountain Trail; the trail actually passes just north of Dorr's true summit, which is reached by walking a nearly flat 0.1 mile south on the Dorr Mountain South Ridge Trail. Double back and turn left (west) onto the Dorr Mountain Notch Trail, which drops into the rugged—though not very deep—notch between Dorr and Cadillac. (This distinctive notch is visible from Route 3 south of the Tarn.) Follow the trail up the open east slope of Cadillac to the summit. Descend the way you came, but instead of turning right onto the Dorr Mountain East Face Trail, continue straight on the somewhat more forgiving Dorr Mountain Trail and then turn right onto the Jessup Path for the parking area.

User Groups
Hikers and dogs. Dogs must be leashed. No wheelchair facilities. The trail would be very difficult to snowshoe and is not suitable for skis. Bikes, horses, and hunting are prohibited.

Access and Fees
Parking and access are free.

Maps
A basic park map is available at the visitors center, and the park website has maps showing roads, trails, and carriage roads. Good trail maps of the area are the waterproof *Acadia National Park* (map 212) for $9.95 from Trails Illustrated, 800/962-1643, website: http://maps.nationalgeographic .com/trails/ and the *Hiking and Biking Map to Acadia National Park and Mount Desert Island,* $7.95 in waterproof Tyvek, from the Appalachian Mountain Club, 800/262-4455, website: www.outdoors.org. For a topographic area map, request Seal Harbor from USGS Map Sales, Federal Center, Box 25286, Denver, CO 80225, 888/ASK-USGS (888/275-8747), website: http://mapping.usgs.gov.

Directions
Take Route 3 south from Bar Harbor or north from Blackwoods Campground, and turn into the parking area at the Tarn, just south of the Sieur de Monts entrance to the Park Loop Road. The park visitors center is located north of Bar Harbor, at the junction of Route 3 and the start of the Park Loop Road.

Contact

Acadia National Park, P.O. Box 177, Eagle Lake Road, Bar Harbor, ME 04609-0177, 207/288-3338, website: www.nps.gov/acad. Friends of Acadia, P.O. Box 45, 43 Cottage Street, Bar Harbor, ME 04609, 207/288-3340 or 800/625-0321, website: www.friendsofacadia.org.

22 ACADIA TRAVERSE
in Acadia National Park

Total distance: 13.5 miles one-way   **Hiking time:** 10 hours

Difficulty: 10   **Rating:** 10

While poring over my maps of Acadia National Park one evening (my idea of a wild night), I noticed that I could link trails and create a traverse of Mount Desert Island's east side—hitting the park's six major peaks and using no roads (though crossing a few). At roughly 13 miles, the traverse would be an ambitious but feasible day hike. So I recruited five guinea pigs—um, fellow intrepid adventurers—including my wife's 13-year-old nephew, Brendan, and we embarked on a hike that far exceeded our expectations.

On this Acadia Traverse, you hit the national park's tallest hills and spend much of the day above the trees, with sweeping views from a succession of long, open ridges. And it's a long day: Including time spent on short rest stops (but not including time spent shuttling vehicles), we were out for 10 hours, finishing just before sunset. The cumulative elevation gain is about 4,700 feet—more than hiking up Mount Washington. And many of these trails—particularly the Beechcroft, the Cadillac Mountain West Face, and a section of the Penobscot Mountain Trail—are very steep. There are water sources on top of Cadillac Mountain and at the Jordan Pond House for refilling bottles. An exciting alternative start would be on the Precipice Trail of Champlain Mountain (which is often closed in late spring and early summer to protect nesting peregrine falcons).

Follow the Bear Brook Trail south to the summit of Champlain Mountain; within minutes of setting out, you enjoy views of the Frenchman Bay islands. Turn right (west) and descend the Beechcroft Trail 0.8 mile to the small pond called the Tarn (crossing Route 3). Ascend the Dorr Mountain East Face Trail, then turn left (south) onto the Dorr Mountain Trail, and take it to the top of Dorr Mountain, one mile from the Tarn. (To reach the true summit, turn left, or south, on the Dorr Mountain South Ridge Trail for a flat 0.1 mile, then double back.) The Dorr Mountain Notch Trail dips 0.4 mile into the shallow but spectacular notch between Dorr and Cadillac, and then climbs the open slope for half a mile to the Cadillac Mountain summit.

Descend the Cadillac Mountain South Ridge Trail for half a mile to the Cadillac Mountain West Face Trail, which drops very steeply for nearly a mile to a parking lot at the north end of Bubble Pond. Follow the carriage road south roughly 0.1 mile; then turn right onto the Pemetic Mountain Trail and take it over Pemetic's summit, 1.3 miles from Bubble Pond. Continue south over the long, rocky ridge for just over half a mile and then bear right onto the Pemetic West Cliff Trail. That trail descends 0.6 mile to the Pond Trail; turn right, and descend easily another 0.4 mile to the Park Loop Road. Cross the road, enter the woods, and turn left on a trail to the Jordan Pond House. The Penobscot Mountain Trail begins behind the Jordan Pond House and leads 1.5 miles to the summit of Penobscot, at one point going straight up steep, rocky terrain. Pick up the Sargent Pond Trail north and west—passing the tiny alpine pond nestled in conifers—then turn right (north) onto the Sargent Mountain South Ridge Trail, gradually climbing the long ridge to the 1,373-foot summit, a mile beyond Penobscot's, for the final panoramic view of this hike.

Descend west on the Grandgent Trail (be careful not to confuse it with the Sargent Mountain North Ridge Trail, which will add mileage to your hike at a time when you don't want it) for just over a mile to the top of little Parkman Mountain. Turn left onto the Parkman Mountain Trail, descending southward. You cross two carriage roads; at the second crossing, turn right and follow that carriage road a short distance to a connector leading left to the parking area on Route 198, a mile from the Parkman summit. Then take off your boots and vigorously massage your feet.

User Groups

Hikers and dogs. Dogs must be leashed. No wheelchair facilities. The trail would be very difficult to snowshoe or ski. Bikes, horses, and hunting are prohibited.

Access and Fees

From May 1 to October 31, the park charges an entrance fee of $20 per vehicle for a seven-day pass or $5 for walkers, bicyclists, or motorcycles for a seven-day pass, at an entrance station beyond the Sieur de Monts entrance on the one-way Park Loop Road, through which you must pass after this hike. A one-year vehicle pass costs $40.

Maps

A basic park map is available at the visitors center, and the park website has maps showing roads, trails, and carriage roads. Good trail maps of the

area are the waterproof *Acadia National Park* (map 212) for $9.95 from
Trails Illustrated, 800/962-1643, website: http://maps.nationalgeographic
.com/trails/ and the *Hiking and Biking Map to Acadia National Park and
Mount Desert Island,* $7.95 in waterproof Tyvek, from the Appalachian
Mountain Club, 800/262-4455, website: www.outdoors.org. For a topo-
graphic area map, request Seal Harbor from USGS Map Sales, Federal
Center, Box 25286, Denver, CO 80225, 888/ASK-USGS (888/275-8747),
website: http://mapping.usgs.gov.

Directions

Two vehicles are needed for this traverse. Leave one vehicle at the northernmost of the two parking areas north of Upper Hadlock Pond along
Route 198 in Northeast Harbor. Then drive to the hike's start, a turnout
on the Park Loop Road at the Bear Brook Trail, 0.2 mile past a picnic
area. If you're traveling with a group of friends, you might leave a third vehicle roughly halfway through the hike, at either the Bubble Pond or Jordan Pond parking areas, in case you can't finish the hike. The park visitors
center is located north of Bar Harbor at the junction of Route 3 and the
start of the Park Loop Road.

Contact

Acadia National Park, P.O. Box 177, Eagle Lake Road, Bar Harbor, ME
04609-0177, 207/288-3338, website: www.nps.gov/acad. Friends of Acadia,
P.O. Box 45, 43 Cottage Street, Bar Harbor, ME 04609, 207/288-3340 or
800/625-0321, website: www.friendsofacadia.org.

23 THE BEEHIVE
in Acadia National Park

Total distance: 1.3 miles round-trip   **Hiking time:** 1.5 hours

Difficulty: 4   **Rating:** 10

The climb up the cliffs on the Beehive's east face looks as if it's strictly
for technical rock climbers when you stare up at it from the Sand
Beach parking lot. The trail zigs and zags up ledges on the nearly vertical face, requiring hand-and-foot scrambling and the use of iron ladder
rungs drilled into the rock. Though it's a fairly short climb, and just a
0.5-mile walk some 400 feet uphill, this trail is not for anyone in poor
physical condition or uncomfortable with exposure and heights. On
the other hand, it's a wonderful trail for hikers looking for a little adventure—and for children old enough to know not to wander off a

hikers ascending the Beehive, Acadia National Park

precipice. All the way up, you're treated to unimpeded views over Frenchman Bay and the coast, from Sand Beach and Great Head south to Otter Cliffs. On the summit, you look north to Champlain Mountain and northwest to Dorr and Cadillac Mountains.

From the parking area, cross the Loop Road and walk a few steps to the right, to the Bowl Trail. You will soon turn onto the Beehive Trail and follow it to the summit. Continuing over the summit, turn left onto the Bowl Trail and make the easy descent back to the Loop Road. A very scenic and popular 3.7-mile loop links this with the Gorham Mountain Trail (see next listing) and Ocean Path (see listing in this chapter).

User Groups

Hikers and dogs. Dogs must be leashed. No wheelchair facilities. The trail would be very difficult to snowshoe and is not suitable for skis. Bikes, horses, and hunting are prohibited.

Access and Fees

From May 1 to October 31, the park charges an entrance fee of $20 per vehicle for a seven-day pass or $5 for walkers, bicyclists, or motorcycles for a seven-day pass, at an entrance station beyond the Sieur de Monts entrance on the one-way Park Loop Road, through which you must pass after this hike. A one-year vehicle pass costs $40.

Maps

A basic park map is available at the visitors center, and the park website has maps showing roads, trails, and carriage roads. Good trail maps of the area are the waterproof *Acadia National Park* (map 212) for $9.95 from Trails Illustrated, 800/962-1643, website: http://maps.nationalgeographic .com/trails/ and the *Hiking and Biking Map to Acadia National Park and Mount Desert Island,* $7.95 in waterproof Tyvek, from the Appalachian

Mountain Club, 800/262-4455, website: www.outdoors.org. For a topographic area map, request Seal Harbor from USGS Map Sales, Federal Center, Box 25286, Denver, CO 80225, 888/ASK-USGS (888/275-8747), website: http://mapping.usgs.gov.

Directions
Drive the Park Loop Road to the east side of Mount Desert Island and the large parking area at Sand Beach, half a mile south of the entrance station. The park visitors center is located north of Bar Harbor, at the junction of Route 3 and the start of the Park Loop Road.

Contact
Acadia National Park, P.O. Box 177, Eagle Lake Road, Bar Harbor, ME 04609-0177, 207/288-3338, website: www.nps.gov/acad. Friends of Acadia, P.O. Box 45, 43 Cottage Street, Bar Harbor, ME 04609, 207/288-3340 or 800/625-0321, website: www.friendsofacadia.org.

24 GORHAM MOUNTAIN/CADILLAC CLIFFS
in Acadia National Park

Total distance: 2 miles round-trip   **Hiking time:** 1.5 hours

Difficulty: 2   **Rating:** 10

I hiked over Gorham Mountain after making the climb of the Beehive and thinking nothing could match that experience. But I had to change my mind after walking along Gorham's long, open ridge, enjoying views of Acadia's coast and countless islands. At just 525 feet high, Gorham's rocky crown is easily reached. Only the Cadillac Cliffs Trail requires some scrambling, and that can be avoided. From the parking area, follow the Gorham Mountain Trail, then turn right onto the Cadillac Cliffs Trail, which passes below the cliffs and rejoins the Gorham Mountain Trail just below the summit. Descend the Gorham Mountain Trail. A 3.7-mile loop links this with the Beehive (see previous listing) and Ocean Path (see listing in this chapter) trails.

User Groups
Hikers, dogs, skiers, and snowshoers. Dogs must be leashed. No wheelchair facilities. Bikes, horses, and hunting are prohibited.

Access and Fees
From May 1 to October 31, the park charges an entrance fee of $20 per vehicle for a seven-day pass or $5 for walkers, bicyclists, or motorcycles for

a seven-day pass, at an entrance station beyond the Sieur de Monts entrance on the one-way Park Loop Road, through which you must pass after this hike. A one-year vehicle pass costs $40.

Maps
A basic park map is available at the visitors center, and the park website has maps showing roads, trails, and carriage roads. Good trail maps of the area are the waterproof *Acadia National Park* (map 212) for $9.95 from Trails Illustrated, 800/962-1643, website: http://maps.nationalgeographic .com/trails/ and the *Hiking and Biking Map to Acadia National Park and Mount Desert Island,* $7.95 in waterproof Tyvek, from the Appalachian Mountain Club, 800/262-4455, website: www.outdoors.org. For a topographic area map, request Seal Harbor from USGS Map Sales, Federal Center, Box 25286, Denver, CO 80225, 888/ASK-USGS (888/275-8747), website: http://mapping.usgs.gov.

Directions
Take the Park Loop Road to the east side of Mount Desert Island and the parking area at the Gorham Mountain Trail and Monument Cove, south of Sand Beach and north of Otter Cliffs. The park visitors center is located north of Bar Harbor at the junction of Route 3 and the start of the Park Loop Road.

Contact
Acadia National Park, P.O. Box 177, Eagle Lake Road, Bar Harbor, ME 04609-0177, 207/288-3338, website: www.nps.gov/acad. Friends of Acadia, P.O. Box 45, 43 Cottage Street, Bar Harbor, ME 04609, 207/288-3340 or 800/625-0321, website: www.friendsofacadia.org.

25 GREAT HEAD
in Acadia National Park

Total distance: 1.6 miles round-trip

Difficulty: 1

Hiking time: 1 hour

Rating: 9

This short, easy walk leads out to the top of tall cliffs rising virtually out of the ocean, offering spectacular views that stretch from the islands of Frenchman Bay to Otter Cliffs. It's a popular hike, but like many popular hikes, it tends to attract most folks during the day. Two friends and I found solitude out here one sunny late afternoon in early June.

From the parking area, follow the wide gravel path into the woods, soon reaching a trail entering from the left—the way this loop returns. Continue straight ahead, passing above Sand Beach (a trail leads down to the beach) and then ascending slightly. Where the trail forks, be sure to stay to the right (the left fork cuts off the walk along the cliffs), soon emerging at the cliffs. To return, follow the blue blazes north back to the gravel path and then turn right to head back to the parking area.

User Groups
Hikers, dogs, skiers, and snowshoers. Dogs must be leashed. No wheelchair facilities. Bikes, horses, and hunting are prohibited.

Access and Fees
From May 1 to October 31, the park charges an entrance fee of $20 per vehicle for a seven-day pass or $5 for walkers, bicyclists, or motorcycles for a seven-day pass, at an entrance station beyond the Sieur de Monts entrance on the one-way Park Loop Road, through which you must pass after this hike. A one-year vehicle pass costs $40.

Maps
A basic park map is available at the visitors center, and the park website has maps showing roads, trails, and carriage roads. Good trail maps of the area are the waterproof *Acadia National Park* (map 212) for $9.95 from Trails Illustrated, 800/962-1643, website: http://maps.nationalgeographic.com/trails/ and the *Hiking and Biking Map to Acadia National Park and Mount Desert Island,* $7.95 in waterproof Tyvek, from the Appalachian Mountain Club, 800/262-4455, website: www.outdoors.org. For a topographic area map, request Seal Harbor from USGS Map Sales, Federal Center, Box 25286, Denver, CO 80225, 888/ASK-USGS (888/275-8747), website: http://mapping.usgs.gov.

Directions
Drive on the Park Loop Road to the east side of Mount Desert Island, past the Precipice parking area. Immediately before the Loop Road entrance station (fee charged), turn left onto an unmarked road. Drive 0.2 mile, turn right, drive another 0.4 mile, and pull into a parking area on the left. The park visitors center is located north of Bar Harbor at the junction of Route 3 and the start of Park Loop Road.

Contact
Acadia National Park, P.O. Box 177, Eagle Lake Road, Bar Harbor, ME 04609-0177, 207/288-3338, website: www.nps.gov/acad. Friends of Acadia, P.O. Box 45, 43 Cottage Street, Bar Harbor, ME 04609, 207/288-3340 or 800/625-0321, website: www.friendsofacadia.org.

26 OCEAN PATH

in Acadia National Park

Total distance: 3.6 miles round-trip   **Hiking time:** 2 hours

Difficulty: 2   **Rating:** 10

This is one of the most popular hikes in the national park—and for good reason. The Ocean Path follows the rugged shoreline from Sand Beach to Otter Point, passing over the top of Otter Cliffs—the island's tallest cliffs, popular with rock climbers. About midway along this trail is the famous Thunder Hole, where incoming waves crash into a channel-like pocket in the rocks, trapping air to create a loud and deep popping noise; it's most impressive around high tide.

From the parking area, the trail veers right. The shore here is mostly rocky, but constantly changes character over the course of this trail—some beaches are covered exclusively with small, round stones, others only with large rocks. As it approaches Otter Cliffs, the trail enters a small woods (across the road from another parking lot) and emerges atop Otter Cliffs. The trail continues beyond the cliffs to Otter Point, where it was extended a short distance in recent years to include a particularly scenic section right along the shore at Otter Point. Hike back along the same route.

User Groups

Hikers and dogs. Dogs must be leashed. No wheelchair facilities. This trail rarely receives enough snow for skis or snowshoes. Bikes, horses, and hunting are prohibited.

Access and Fees

From May 1 to October 31, the park charges an entrance fee of $20 per vehicle for a seven-day pass or $5 for walkers, bicyclists, or motorcycles for a seven-day pass, at an entrance station beyond the Sieur de Monts entrance on the one-way Park Loop Road, through which you must pass after this hike. A one-year vehicle pass costs $40.

Maps

A basic park map is available at the visitors center, and the park website has maps showing roads, trails, and carriage roads. Good trail maps of the area are the waterproof *Acadia National Park* (map 212) for $9.95 from Trails Illustrated, 800/962-1643, website: http://maps.nationalgeographic.com/trails/ and the *Hiking and Biking Map to Acadia National Park and Mount Desert Island,* $7.95 in waterproof Tyvek, from the Appalachian Mountain Club, 800/262-4455, website: www.outdoors.org. For a topographic area map, request Seal Harbor from USGS Map Sales, Federal Center, Box 25286, Denver, CO 80225, 888/ASK-USGS (888/275-8747), website: http://mapping.usgs.gov.

Directions

Drive on the Park Loop Road to Mount Desert Island's east side and the large parking area at Sand Beach, half a mile south of the entrance station. The park visitors center is located north of Bar Harbor at the junction of Route 3 and the start of the Park Loop Road.

Contact

Acadia National Park, P.O. Box 177, Eagle Lake Road, Bar Harbor, ME 04609-0177, 207/288-3338, website: www.nps.gov/acad. Friends of Acadia, P.O. Box 45, 43 Cottage Street, Bar Harbor, ME 04609, 207/288-3340 or 800/625-0321, website: www.friendsofacadia.org.

Chapter 3

© MICHAEL LANZA

Western and Southern Mountains and Hills

Western and Southern Mountains and Hills

The 32 hikes in this chapter include some of the state's biggest and most popular hiking destinations, like Bigelow Mountain and the Saddleback Range; some of New England's most rugged backcountry in the Mahoosuc Range; some of the finest small-mountain hiking in New England, such as Tumbledown Mountain and Pleasant Mountain; and some of the region's most wonderfully obscure trails, like the hikes of Evans Notch.

Fifteen of this chapter's hikes lie on or very near the Appalachian Trail, and several lead to beautiful cascades and waterfalls, like Screw Auger Falls and Step Falls in Grafton Notch. Although the neighboring White Mountains draw all the limelight, this part of Maine remains quietly spectacular.

Winter access gets trickier on many of these hikes. Some roads, such as Route 113 through Evans Notch, are not maintained in winter, and others simply are often covered with ice and snow. Many of the trails in this chapter see little or no visitors in winter, meaning you'll probably be breaking trail through snow, without the security of knowing other people might come along to help you out in case of an emergency. That can be exciting, but it's certainly riskier.

A few hikes are on private land left open to public use in keeping with a long-standing tradition in Maine—a state where more than 90 percent of the total land area is privately held. Consequently, some hikes' descriptions do not list any contact agency for additional information; in other words, you explore these places with the understanding that you alone are responsible for yourself. Bear in mind that while most of these private-land trails have been open to public use for many years, access can be restricted or denied at any time. Respect private property when on it, obey "No Trespassing" signs, and assume that hunting is allowed in season unless posted otherwise.

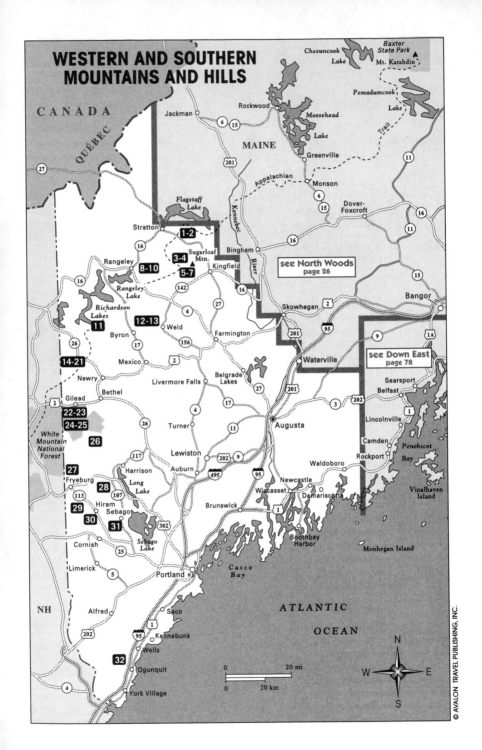

WESTERN AND SOUTHERN MOUNTAINS AND HILLS

CANADA

QUÉBEC

Chesuncook Lake

Baxter State Park
Mt. Katahdin

Pemadumcook Lake

Rockwood

Jackman

6
15

MAINE

Moosehead Lake

Greenville

201

Appalachian

Monson

6
15

Dover-Foxcroft

11

16

11

Flagstaff Lake

Stratton

1-2

16

3-4

Sugarloaf Mtn.

Bingham

see North Woods
page 26

Bangor

Rangeley

8-10

5-7

Kingfield

Kennebec River

15

Rangeley Lake

142

16

Richardson Lakes

11

12-13

Weld

4

27

Farmington

Skowhegan

2

95

1A

Byron

26

17

156

Mexico

2

Livermore Falls

Belgrade Lakes

27

Waterville

9

see Down East
page 78

14-21

Newry

Bethel

Gilead

2

22-23

24-25

26

Turner

4

17

11

201

Augusta

202

3

Searsport

Belfast

Lincolnville

1

White Mountain National Forest

27

117

Lewiston

202
9

Auburn

495

95

Waldoboro

Camden

Rockport

Penobscot Bay

Harrison

Long Lake

Newcastle

Wiscasset

Damariscotta

Fryeburg

28

113

107

29

Hiram
Sebago

30

31

302

Brunswick

1

Boothbay Harbor

Vinalhaven Island

Cornish

25

Sebago Lake

Monhegan Island

Limerick

5

Portland

Casco Bay

NH

Alfred

Saco

ATLANTIC

202

1

95

Kennebunk

OCEAN

Wells

32

Ogunquit

4

York Village

0   20 mi

0   20 km

N
W   E
S

© AVALON TRAVEL PUBLISHING, INC.

Contents

1 BIGELOW RANGE
east of Stratton

Total distance: 16.7 miles one-way

Hiking time: 2 days

Difficulty: 9

Rating: 10

A darling of Maine hikers, Bigelow Mountain is unquestionably one of the two or three most spectacular peaks in the state; only Katahdin and Bigelow's neighbor to the south, the Saddleback Range, warrant comparison. Reflecting the state's affection for this range, Maine voters supported a grassroots movement and in 1976 created the Bigelow Preserve, a 35,000-acre park encompassing the entire Bigelow Range—including about 17 miles of the Appalachian Trail—and 21 miles of shoreline on sprawling Flagstaff Lake. Both of Bigelow's summits rise well above tree line, affording long views in every direction. Perhaps the best view is north to Flagstaff Lake and the vast wilderness of Maine's North Woods (though a few logging clear-cuts tarnish that view). On rare clear days, you can see north to Katahdin and southwest to Mount Washington.

This 16.7-mile, two-day backpacking trip traverses the entire Bigelow Mountain range along the Appalachian Trail. The distance is moderate for two days, but don't underestimate the trail's ruggedness. From East Flagstaff Road, follow the white blazes of the Appalachian Trail southbound, passing a blue-blazed side trail at 1.4 miles that leads 0.1 mile to the Little Bigelow lean-to, where there is a good spring and tent space. From there, the Appalachian Trail climbs steadily until cresting the eastern end of the long, low ridge of Little Bigelow Mountain three miles from the road. There are excellent views from open ledges west toward Bigelow Mountain and the ski area at Sugarloaf Mountain, across the Carrabassett Valley. The trail follows the relatively flat, wooded ridge top, passing another open ledge with a view of Bigelow and Flagstaff Lake at 4.5 miles. It then descends about 1,000 feet over less than two miles into Safford Notch, where the forested floor is littered with giant boulders, some of them stacked dramatically atop one another.

At 6.3 miles from East Flagstaff Road, a side trail leads left (southwest) 0.3 mile to tent platforms at the Safford Notch campsite. Just 0.1 mile farther down the Appalachian Trail, the Safford Brook Trail exits right (north), leading 2.2 miles to East Flagstaff Road (and 2.5 miles to Flagstaff Lake). The Appalachian Trail climbs steeply out of Safford Notch, over and around boulders, gaining about 2,000 feet in elevation over two miles to Bigelow's east summit, 4,088-foot Avery Peak. On the way up Avery, the trail passes a side path at 7.5 miles that leads 0.1 mile to an excellent view east and north from atop the cliff called the "Old Man's

Head." Beyond that side path, the Appalachian Trail ascends the crest of a narrow, wooded ridge, breaking out of the trees for the final 0.1 mile up Avery Peak. Passing over Avery, the trail descends into the wooded col between the summits, reaching the Avery tenting area at 8.7 miles, where I once found the lone water source, a spring, dried up in early September.

The ascent grows fairly steep up West Peak, the true summit at 4,145 feet, 0.7 mile from Avery Peak. The Appalachian Trail descends to and follows the up-and-down ridge connecting Bigelow to the 3,805-foot summit of South Horn, where you get a good view to the west from directly above Horns Pond. Just 0.1 mile farther, a side trail leads 0.2 mile to the summit of North Horn (3,792 feet). Continue steeply downhill on the Appalachian Trail, reaching the Horns Pond lean-tos and tent sites at 11.6 miles from East Flagstaff Road and half a mile from South Horn. Horns Pond is a scenic tarn nestled in a tiny bowl at about 3,200 feet on Bigelow's west slope. From here, the Appalachian Trail climbs slightly out of the bowl, passing the junction with the Horns Pond Trail 0.2 mile south of Horns Pond and a short side path to a pond overlook at 0.3 mile. The trail then descends steadily, swinging south and passing the Bigelow Range Trail junction nearly two miles from Horns Pond, to the Cranberry Stream campsite at 14.8 miles (3.2 miles south of Horns Pond and 1.9 miles north of Route 27/16). At 15.8 miles, the Appalachian Trail crosses Stratton Brook on a bridge before reaching Route 27/16 at mile 16.7 of this trip, 5.1 miles from Horns Pond.

Special note: The traverse of this range ranks among the most popular backpacking treks in New England. Especially during the warmer months, the campsites and shelters fill quickly, even during the week. Bringing a tent is recommended. Also take care to walk only on the trail above tree line, where fragile alpine vegetation is easily trampled.

User Groups

Hikers only. No wheelchair facilities. Dogs are discouraged along the Appalachian Trail in Maine. Bikes and horses are prohibited. Hunting is allowed in season in the Bigelow Preserve, but not on or near trails. This trail should not be attempted in winter except by hikers experienced in mountaineering and prepared for severe winter weather, and is not suitable for skis.

Access and Fees

Parking and access are free. Camp at existing camping areas and shelters: Little Bigelow lean-to at 1.4 miles south of East Flagstaff Road, Safford Notch campsite at 6.3 miles, Avery tenting area at 8.7 miles, Horns Pond lean-tos and tent sites at 11.6 miles, and the Cranberry Stream campsite at

14.8 miles. Stephen Martelli of Stratton runs a fee-based hiker shuttle service to road crossings along the Appalachian Trail between Grafton Notch and Monson; call 207/246-4642. For information about a hiker shuttle, free Kennebec River ferry service, and other hiker services along the Appalachian Trail in Maine, contact Steve Longley, P.O. Box 90, Route 201, The Forks, ME 04985, 207/663-4441 or 888/FLOAT-ME (in Maine only), website: www.riversandtrails.com.

Maps
A free contour map of trails in the Bigelow Preserve is available at some trailheads and from the Maine Bureau of Public Lands. For a trail map, refer to map 5 in the *Map and Guide to the Appalachian Trail in Maine,* a set of seven maps and a guidebook for $24.95 from the Maine Appalachian Trail Club or the Appalachian Trail Conference. Also available is the *Rangeley-Stratton/Baxter State Park-Katahdin* map, $7.95 in waterproof Tyvek, which is available in many stores and from the Appalachian Mountain Club, 800/262-4455, website: www.outdoors.org. For topographic area maps, request Little Bigelow Mountain, the Horns, Sugarloaf Mountain, and Poplar Mountain from USGS Map Sales, Federal Center, Box 25286, Denver, CO 80225, 888/ASK-USGS (888/275-8747), website: http://mapping.usgs.gov.

Directions
You need to shuttle two vehicles for this trip. To do the hike from north to south, as described here, leave one vehicle at the junction of the Appalachian Trail and Routes 27 and 16, 5.3 miles south of where Routes 27 and 16 split in Stratton and 16 miles north of where Routes 27 and 16 split in Kingfield. Then drive on Route 16 east to North New Portland. Turn left (north) in front of the country store onto Long Falls Dam Road and follow it for 17.4 miles. Bear left onto the dirt Bog Brook Road. Drive 0.7 mile, bear left onto the dirt East Flagstaff Road, and drive 0.1 mile. Park either in the gravel pit on the right, or at the roadside where the Appalachian Trail crosses the road just beyond the pit.

Contact
Maine Department of Conservation, Bureau of Parks and Lands, 286 Water Street, Key Bank Plaza, 3rd and 5th floors, Augusta, ME 04333-0022, 207/287-3821, website: www.state.me.us/doc/parks/. Maine Appalachian Trail Club, P.O. Box 283, Augusta, ME 04332-0283, website: www.matc.org. Appalachian Trail Conference, 799 Washington Street, P.O. Box 807, Harpers Ferry, WV 25425-0807, 304/535-6331, website: www.appalachiantrail.org.

2 BIGELOW MOUNTAIN
east of Stratton

Total distance: 13.8 miles

Hiking time: 10.5 hours or 1–2 days

Difficulty: 9

Rating: 10

This hike up one of Maine's most spectacular and popular mountains, Bigelow, can be accomplished in a single long day by fit hikers getting an early start. But there are two camping areas along the trail that offer the option of a two-day trip, leaving your heavy pack behind for the day hike to Bigelow's summits. The cumulative elevation gained by hitting both of Bigelow's summits is nearly 4,000 feet. (To make a loop hike of about 12.5 miles instead of this route over Bigelow's two summits, go up the Fire Warden's Trail, which begins a little more than a half mile beyond the Appalachian Trail crossing of Stratton Brook Pond Road. Climb the Fire Warden's Trail for 3.5 miles to Avery col, turn right, or northbound, on the Appalachian Trail for 0.4 mile to Avery Peak, then turn around and descend the Appalachian Trail southbound for nearly eight miles to Stratton Brook Road. Turn left and walk the road for 0.5 mile to complete the loop. The upper half mile of the Fire Warden's Trail is very steep and severely eroded.)

© MICHAEL LANZA

a backpacker on Bigelow Mountain

For the Bigelow summit hike, begin at Stratton Brook Pond Road and follow the white blazes of the Appalachian Trail northbound into the woods. Within 0.25 mile you will cross a logging road and Stratton Brook on a bridge. The Appalachian Trail ascends steadily, passing the Cranberry Stream campsite at 1.1 miles and a junction with the Bigelow Range Trail at 2.4 miles. Stay on the Appalachian Trail, which swings east and climbs past a short side trail out to ledges above Horns Pond at four miles, and then passes the Horns Pond Trail junction 0.1 mile farther. The trail drops slightly into the bowl, home to the tiny mountain tarn called Horns Pond and a camping area with two lean-tos and tent sites, at 4.3 miles.

The Appalachian Trail climbs steeply for the next half mile, passing a side trail leading 0.2 mile to North Horn (3,792 feet) at 4.7 miles and reaching the 3,805-foot South Horn summit at 4.8 miles, with a good view over Horns Pond and north to Flagstaff Lake. Descending steeply off South Horn, you follow an up-and-down ridge for more than a mile, then climb steeply to West Peak, Bigelow's true summit at 4,145 feet, 6.9 miles in. The rocky, open summit affords views in every direction: north over Flagstaff Lake and the wilderness of the North Woods, all the way to Katahdin on a clear day, and southwest to Washington when conditions are right. For this hike, turn around and descend the same way you came. To reach 4,088-foot Avery Peak, continue northbound on the Appalachian Trail, dropping into the saddle between Bigelow's two summits, passing the Avery tenting area at 7.2 miles, and then climbing to the open summit of Avery Peak. Hiking to Avery and back adds 1.4 miles and an hour (possibly more) to this hike's distance.

Special note: Bigelow Mountain ranks among the most popular peaks in New England. Especially during the warmer months, the campsites and shelters fill quickly, even during the week. Bringing a tent is recommended. Also take care to walk only on the trail above tree line, where fragile alpine vegetation is easily trampled.

User Groups

Hikers only. No wheelchair facilities. Dogs are discouraged along the Appalachian Trail in Maine. This trail should not be attempted in winter except by hikers experienced in mountaineering and prepared for severe winter weather, and is not suitable for skis. Bikes and horses are prohibited. Hunting is allowed in season in the Bigelow Preserve, but not on or near trails.

Access and Fees

Parking and access are free. Camp at existing camping areas and shelters, which along this route include the Cranberry Stream campsite 1.1 miles from Stratton Brook Pond Road, the Horns Pond lean-tos and tent sites at 4.3 miles, and the Avery tenting area at 7.2 miles.

Maps

A free contour map of trails in the Bigelow Preserve is available at some trailheads and from the Maine Bureau of Public Lands. For a trail map, refer to map 5 in the *Map and Guide to the Appalachian Trail in Maine,* a set of seven maps and a guidebook for $24.95 from the Maine Appalachian

Trail Club or the Appalachian Trail Conference. Also available is the *Rangeley-Stratton/Baxter State Park-Katahdin* map, $7.95 in waterproof Tyvek, which is available in many stores and from the Appalachian Mountain Club, 800/262-4455, website: www.outdoors.org. For topographic area maps, request Horns and Sugarloaf Mountain from USGS Map Sales, Federal Center, Box 25286, Denver, CO 80225, 888/ASK-USGS (888/275-8747), website: http://mapping.usgs.gov.

Directions
From Route 27/16, turn north onto Stratton Brook Pond Road, five miles east of where Routes 27 and 16 split in Stratton and about 16.3 miles west of where Routes 27 and 16 split in Kingfield (and about 0.3 mile west of where the Appalachian Trail crosses Route 27/16). Drive 1.4 miles to where the Appalachian Trail crosses the dirt road and park at the roadside.

Contact
Maine Department of Conservation, Bureau of Parks and Lands, 286 Water Street, Key Bank Plaza, 3rd and 5th floors, Augusta, ME 04333-0022, 207/287-3821, website: www.state.me.us/doc/parks/. Maine Appalachian Trail Club, P.O. Box 283, Augusta, ME 04332-0283, website: www.matc.org. Appalachian Trail Conference, 799 Washington Street, P.O. Box 807, Harpers Ferry, WV 25425-0807, 304/535-6331, website: www.appalachiantrail.org.

3 NORTH CROCKER MOUNTAIN
south of Stratton

Total distance: 10.4 miles round-trip   **Hiking time:** 7 hours

Difficulty: 9   **Rating:** 7

Despite North Crocker Mountain's 4,168-foot elevation, Maine's fifth-highest summit does little to distinguish itself in the area of visual spectacle. The low spruce trees that grow right to the top of the peak obscure the views; I tried standing on the summit cairn to see over the trees, but it didn't help much. There is actually a decent view toward Sugarloaf Mountain and Mount Abraham just beyond the summit, heading south on the Appalachian Trail. But for someone looking to tick off a 4,000-footer or for a quiet and moderate hike up a wooded ridge, this 10.4-mile trip is a fine day's outing. In winter, with a snowpack at the summit, you might actually be able to see over the trees; but bear in mind that this could be a very long hike if you have to break trail in snowshoes all the way. The North and South Crocker Mountain hike (see next listing) provides a shorter route over both Crocker peaks.

From Route 16/27, follow the white blazes of the Appalachian Trail southbound. It rises gently at first and never grows more than moderately steep before reaching the wooded North Crocker summit, 5.2 miles and 2,700 vertical feet from the highway. Continuing south on the Appalachian Trail to the South Crocker summit (4,010 feet) adds two miles round-trip to this hike's distance. Retrace your steps to return to your car.

User Groups
Hikers and snowshoers. No wheelchair facilities. Dogs are discouraged along the Appalachian Trail in Maine. This trail is not suitable for skis. Bikes, horses, and hunting are prohibited.

Access and Fees
Parking and access are free.

Maps
For a trail map, refer to map 6 in the *Map and Guide to the Appalachian Trail in Maine,* a set of seven maps and a guidebook for $24.95 available from the Maine Appalachian Trail Club or the Appalachian Trail Conference. Also available is the *Rangeley–Stratton/Baxter State Park–Katahdin* map, $7.95 in waterproof Tyvek, which is available in many stores and from the Appalachian Mountain Club, 800/262-4455, website: www.outdoors.org. For topographic area maps, request Sugarloaf Mountain and Black Nubble from USGS Map Sales, Federal Center, Box 25286, Denver, CO 80225, 888/ASK-USGS (888/275-8747), website: http://mapping.usgs.gov.

Directions
Park where the Appalachian Trail crosses Route 27/16, 5.3 miles south of where Routes 27 and 16 split in Stratton and 16 miles north of where Routes 27 and 16 split in Kingfield.

Contact
Maine Appalachian Trail Club, P.O. Box 283, Augusta, ME 04332-0283, website: www.matc.org. Appalachian Trail Conference, 799 Washington Street, P.O. Box 807, Harpers Ferry, WV 25425-0807, 304/535-6331, website: www.appalachiantrail.org.

4 NORTH AND SOUTH CROCKER MOUNTAIN
south of Stratton

Total distance: 6.2 miles round-trip **Hiking time:** 4.5 hours

Difficulty: 8 **Rating:** 7

This 6.2-mile hike offers the most direct route up Maine's 5th- and 12th-highest peaks, the 4,000-footers North and South Crocker. Their wooded summits, unfortunately, offer only very limited views. South Crocker has the better view of the two, toward Sugarloaf Mountain and Mount Abraham from a small ledge. The best view on North Crocker is from the trail just shy of the actual summit, but it essentially mirrors the perspective from the south summit. The hike up South Crocker, however, does cross open slopes with nice views to the north and east. The cumulative elevation gained by hitting both summits is about 2,800 feet.

From Caribou Valley Road, turn right onto the Appalachian Trail northbound. It climbs steadily, and in one mile reaches a side path leading 0.1 mile to the Crocker Cirque campsite. Above the campsite, the Appalachian Trail heads straight up a very steep and loose slope of broken slate, which can be treacherous when wet and very difficult to descend even when dry; there are views from here of Crocker Cirque. The trail enters the woods again, then traverses an old rock slide, with views out toward the Bigelow Range. Climbing steadily from there, the Appalachian Trail reaches a side path 2.1 miles from Caribou Valley Road that leads about 150 feet to the South Crocker summit ledge. Continuing north, the Appalachian Trail drops down into the saddle between the two summits and then climbs to the higher of the two mountains, North Crocker, 3.1 miles from the road. Head back the same way you hiked up.

User Groups

Hikers only. No wheelchair facilities. Dogs are discouraged along the Appalachian Trail in Maine. Access to this trail by car during the winter may be limited since Caribou Valley Road may not be plowed; however, it could be skied as far as the Appalachian Trail crossing. Winter attempts on North and South Crocker Mountain should be made only by people experienced in mountaineering and prepared for severe weather. Bikes, horses, and hunting are prohibited.

Access and Fees

Parking and access are free. The dirt Caribou Valley Road was improved in recent years all the way to the Appalachian Trail crossing and is now usually passable for cars during the warm months. The Crocker Cirque campsite, with three tent platforms, lies 0.1 mile down a side path off the Appalachian Trail, one mile north of Caribou Valley Road.

Maps

For a trail map, refer to map 6 in the *Map and Guide to the Appalachian Trail in Maine,* a set of seven maps and a guidebook for $24.95 from the Maine Appalachian Trail Club or the Appalachian Trail Conference. Also available is the *Rangeley–Stratton/Baxter State Park–Katahdin* map, $7.95 in waterproof Tyvek, which is available in many stores and from the Appalachian Mountain Club, 800/262-4455, website: www.outdoors.org. For a topographic area map, request Sugarloaf Mountain from USGS Map Sales, Federal Center, Box 25286, Denver, CO 80225, 888/ASK-USGS (888/275-8747), website: http://mapping.usgs.gov.

Directions

From Route 27/16, about a mile west of the entrance to the Sugarloaf USA ski resort in Carrabassett, turn south onto the dirt Caribou Valley Road. Drive 4.3 miles to the Appalachian Trail crossing and park at the roadside.

Contact

Maine Appalachian Trail Club, P.O. Box 283, Augusta, ME 04332-0283, website: www.matc.org. Appalachian Trail Conference, 799 Washington Street, P.O. Box 807, Harpers Ferry, WV 25425-0807, 304/535-6331, website: www.appalachiantrail.org.

5 SUGARLOAF MOUNTAIN
south of Stratton

Total distance: 5.8 miles round-trip   **Hiking time:** 4.5 hours

Difficulty: 8   **Rating:** 9

Maine's third-highest peak at 4,237 feet, Sugarloaf's barren summit offers long views in every direction. On a clear day, you can see Mount Washington in New Hampshire to the southwest and all the way to Katahdin in the far north. Like any high, exposed peak, this can be a rough place in foul weather: I trucked up here while on a four-day traverse of the Saddleback Range only to be greeted by swirling fog and a biting wind—in August—although those conditions made for some interesting views into the Carrabassett Valley. When Caribou Valley Road is passable by car, it makes a day hike of Sugarloaf via the Appalachian Trail feasible by this rugged, 5.8-mile route, which ascends about 2,000 feet.

From Caribou Valley Road, follow the white-blazed Appalachian Trail to the left (south), immediately crossing the South Branch of the Carrabassett River, which can be dangerous at times of high water. The Appalachian Trail then climbs very steeply up Sugarloaf Mountain, involving short stretches of tricky scrambling up a heavily eroded trail. The trail emerges from the woods high on the north slope of Sugarloaf, with views to South and North Crocker across the valley. It reenters the woods and then reaches a junction with the Sugarloaf Mountain Trail 2.3 miles from Caribou Valley Road. Turn left onto that trail and follow its rocky path steeply uphill for 0.6 mile to the exposed Sugarloaf summit, where there are ski area buildings and long views in every direction. Descend the same route back to the road.

Special note: Sugarloaf can be linked with Spaulding Mountain by continuing on the Appalachian Trail southbound, a 10.2-mile round-trip from Caribou Valley Road. An ambitious hiker can continue on to Mount Abraham, making a 17.4-mile day hike or two-day backpacking trip. See the listings for those hikes for more details.

User Groups

Hikers only. No wheelchair facilities. Dogs are discouraged along the Appalachian Trail in Maine. Access to this trail by car during the winter may be limited since Caribou Valley Road may not be plowed; however, it could be skied as far as the Appalachian Trail crossing. Winter attempts on Sugarloaf should be made only by people experienced in mountaineering and prepared for severe weather. Bikes, horses, and hunting are prohibited.

Access and Fees

Parking and access are free. The dirt Caribou Valley Road was improved in recent years all the way to the Appalachian Trail crossing and is now usually passable for cars during the warm months.

Maps

For a trail map, refer to map 6 in the *Map and Guide to the Appalachian Trail in Maine,* a set of seven maps and a guidebook for $24.95 from the Maine Appalachian Trail Club or the Appalachian Trail Conference. Also available is the *Rangeley–Stratton/Baxter State Park–Katahdin* map, $7.95 in waterproof Tyvek, which is available in many stores and from the Appalachian Mountain Club, 800/262-4455, website: www.outdoors.org. For a topographic area map, request Sugarloaf Mountain from USGS Map Sales, Federal Center, Box 25286, Denver, CO 80225, 888/ASK-USGS (888/275-8747), website: http://mapping.usgs.gov.

Directions

From Route 27/16, about a mile west of the entrance to the Sugarloaf USA ski resort in Carrabassett, turn south onto the dirt Caribou Valley Road. Drive 4.3 miles to the Appalachian Trail crossing and park at the roadside.

Contact

Maine Appalachian Trail Club, P.O. Box 283, Augusta, ME 04332-0283, website: www.matc.org. Appalachian Trail Conference, 799 Washington Street, P.O. Box 807, Harpers Ferry, WV 25425-0807, 304/535-6331, website: www.appalachiantrail.org.

6 SPAULDING MOUNTAIN
south of Stratton

Total distance: 9 miles round-trip

Hiking time: 7 hours

Difficulty: 8

Rating: 8

Spaulding was previously thought to be "just 12 feet short of 4,000 feet high," but since a recent measure of its height put it at 4,010 feet, Spaulding is sure to enjoy a slight boost in popularity—at least among peak-baggers. (At the same time, Mount Redington, immediately west of Spaulding, saw its height adjusted from 3,984 feet to 4,010 feet, tying it with Spaulding and increasing Maine's tally of 4,000-footers from 12 to 14.) It offers better—if not spectacular—views than a pair of 4,000-footers to the north, the Crockers. Just a 0.2-mile detour off the Appalachian Trail, its summit has three short side paths that lead to views toward Sugarloaf Mountain and Mount Abraham. The total elevation gained by hiking Spaulding alone is about 2,000 feet. One of the features I enjoy most about this hike is walking the fairly flat ridge from Sugarloaf to Spaulding, a quiet stretch of trail through a lush forest of hemlock, ferns, and moss. Keep quiet and watch for wildlife—prolific hiker Ed Hawkins, of New Hampshire, tells me he ran into a bull moose with a 26-point rack on Spaulding's summit in the fall of 1999. He and his companions estimated the antlers spanned nearly six feet.

From Caribou Valley Road, turn left (south) on the Appalachian Trail, immediately crossing the South Branch of the Carrabassett River, which can be dangerous at times of high water. The trail climbs very steeply up Sugarloaf Mountain, involving short stretches of tricky scrambling on a heavily eroded trail. It breaks out of the woods high on the Sugarloaf north slope, with views to South and North Crocker across the valley. It reenters the woods and then reaches a junction with the Sugarloaf Mountain Trail, 2.3 miles from Caribou Valley Road (see the special note below). From the Sugarloaf Mountain Trail junction, follow the Appalachian Trail along the fairly flat ridge from Sugarloaf to Spaulding. About 0.1 mile south of the Sugarloaf Mountain Trail junction, a side path leads about 40 feet to a good view. The Appalachian Trail continues along the wooded ridge to a junction with the Spaulding Mountain Trail, 4.4 miles from Caribou Valley Road. That trail leads 0.1 mile uphill to Spaulding's summit. Return the way you came.

Special note: Spaulding can be linked with Sugarloaf Mountain—Maine's third-highest peak, with views in every direction—for a 10.2-mile round-trip from Caribou Valley Road. An ambitious hiker can continue on to Mount Abraham—making a 17.4-mile day hike or two-day backpacking trip. See the listings for those hikes for more details.

User Groups

Hikers only. No wheelchair facilities. Dogs are discouraged along the Appalachian Trail in Maine. This trail may be difficult to snowshoe and is not suitable for skis. Bikes, horses, and hunting are prohibited.

Access and Fees

Parking and access are free. The dirt Caribou Valley Road was improved in recent years all the way to the Appalachian Trail crossing. The Spaulding Mountain lean-to is located down a short side path off the Appalachian Trail, 5.2 miles south of Caribou Valley Road and 0.8 mile south of the Spaulding Mountain Trail/Appalachian Trail junction.

Maps

For a trail map, refer to map 6 in the *Map and Guide to the Appalachian Trail in Maine,* a set of seven maps and a guidebook for $24.95 from the Maine Appalachian Trail Club or the Appalachian Trail Conference. Also available is the *Rangeley–Stratton/Baxter State Park–Katahdin* map, $7.95 in waterproof Tyvek, which is available in many stores and from the Appalachian Mountain Club, 800/262-4455, website: www.outdoors.org. For a topographic area map, request Sugarloaf Mountain from USGS Map Sales, Federal Center, Box 25286, Denver, CO 80225, 888/ASK-USGS (888/275-8747), website: http://mapping.usgs.gov.

Directions

From Route 27/16, about a mile west of the entrance to the Sugarloaf USA ski resort in Carrabassett, turn south onto the dirt Caribou Valley Road. Drive 4.3 miles to the Appalachian Trail crossing and park at the roadside.

Contact

Maine Appalachian Trail Club, P.O. Box 283, Augusta, ME 04332-0283, website: www.matc.org. Appalachian Trail Conference, 799 Washington Street, P.O. Box 807, Harpers Ferry, WV 25425-0807, 304/535-6331, website: www.appalachiantrail.org.

7 MOUNT ABRAHAM
south of Stratton

Total distance: 16 miles round-trip   **Hiking time:** 12 hours or 1–2 days

Difficulty: 9   **Rating:** 10

Mount Abraham boasts one of the largest alpine areas in Maine, with more than four miles of ridge above tree line featuring excellent panoramic views. But because Appalachian Trail hikers have to make a 3.4-mile detour to climb Abraham, it attracts fewer visitors than some peaks in western Maine, such as neighboring Saddleback Mountain. I actually stood alone on this rocky summit one August morning on a trip where I saw at least several other hikers every day. This 16-mile hike to bag one of Maine's 14 4,000-footers is difficult and long—a conceivable one-day goal for fit hikers getting an early start at a time of year that affords lots of daylight, but it also makes for a satisfying two-day trip. The cumulative elevation gain on the round-trip is about 3,200 feet.

From Caribou Valley Road, turn left (southbound) on the Appalachian Trail, immediately crossing the South Branch of the Carrabassett River, which can be dangerous at times of high water. The trail then climbs very steeply up Sugarloaf Mountain, involving short stretches of tricky scrambling up a heavily eroded trail. The trail emerges from the woods high on the north slope of Sugarloaf, with views to South and North Crocker across the valley. It reenters the woods and then reaches a junction with the Sugarloaf Mountain Trail 2.3 miles from Caribou Valley Road. (For a scenic 1.2-mile detour off this hike, follow that rocky trail steeply uphill to the exposed 4,237-foot Sugarloaf summit, Maine's third-highest peak, where there are ski area buildings and long views in every direction.) From the Sugarloaf Mountain Trail junction, follow the Appalachian Trail along the fairly flat ridge connecting Sugarloaf to Spaulding Mountain—a quiet stretch through a lush forest of hemlock, ferns, and moss. About 0.1 mile south of the Sugarloaf Mountain Trail junction, a side path leads some 40 feet to a good view. The Appalachian Trail continues along the wooded ridge to a junction with the Spaulding Mountain Trail, 4.4 miles from Caribou Valley Road. (That trail, which is not included in this hike's distance, leads 0.1 mile uphill to Spaulding's 4,010-foot summit, where three short side paths lead to limited views toward Sugarloaf and Abraham—see the previous listing for the Spaulding Mountain hike.) From the Spaulding Mountain Trail junction, the Appalachian Trail descends 0.8 mile to a side path leading 150 feet to the Spaulding Mountain lean-to, where there is space for tents.

The Appalachian Trail follows moderate terrain southward, reaching the Mount Abraham Trail 1.1 miles from the Spaulding lean-to. On this blue-blazed trail, it's 1.7 miles one-way to Abraham's 4,043-foot summit. Although it's relatively flat for the first half mile, after emerging from the woods the trail climbs over three bumps on a ridge, crossing rough talus slopes. From the summit, marked by the rusting remains of an old fire tower, The Horn and Saddleback Mountain are visible to the southwest, and the Bigelow Range can be seen to the north. About 30 feet from the tower, along the Fire Warden's Trail, there is a primitive stone shelter with a shingled roof and enough space under its very low ceiling for a few people to crawl inside (not a place I'd want to spend a night). About 100 feet beyond the summit stand several tall cairns. For this hike, return to Caribou Valley Road via the same route you took up.

Special note: Abraham can be linked with Sugarloaf and Spaulding Mountains on a marathon 17.4-mile day hike or a more moderate two-day backpacking trip, adding just 1.4 miles to this hike.

User Groups

Hikers only. No wheelchair facilities. Dogs are discouraged along the Appalachian Trail in Maine. The Caribou Valley Road may not be plowed in winter to provide access to this trail, though it could be skied as far as the Appalachian Trail crossing. Winter attempts on Abraham should be made only by people experienced in mountaineering and prepared for severe weather. Bikes, horses, and hunting are prohibited.

Access and Fees

Parking and access are free. The dirt Caribou Valley Road was improved in recent years all the way to the Appalachian Trail crossing and is now usually passable for cars during the warm months. The Spaulding Mountain lean-to is located down a short side path off the Appalachian Trail, 5.2 miles south of Caribou Valley Road.

Maps

For a trail map, refer to map 6 in the *Map and Guide to the Appalachian Trail in Maine,* a set of seven maps and a guidebook for $24.95 from the Maine Appalachian Trail Club or the Appalachian Trail Conference. Also

available is the *Rangeley–Stratton/Baxter State Park–Katahdin* map, $7.95
in waterproof Tyvek, which is available in many stores and from the Appalachian Mountain Club, 800/262-4455, website: www.outdoors.org. For
topographic area maps, request Sugarloaf Mountain and Mount Abraham
from USGS Map Sales, Federal Center, Box 25286, Denver, CO 80225,
888/ASK-USGS (888/275-8747), website: http://mapping.usgs.gov.

Directions
From Route 27/16, about a mile west of the entrance to the Sugarloaf USA
ski resort in Carrabassett, turn south onto the dirt Caribou Valley Road.
Drive 4.3 miles to the Appalachian Trail crossing and park at the roadside.

Contact
Maine Appalachian Trail Club, P.O. Box 283, Augusta, ME 04332-0283,
website: www.matc.org. Appalachian Trail Conference, 799 Washington
Street, P.O. Box 807, Harpers Ferry, WV 25425-0807, 304/535-6331, website: www.appalachiantrail.org.

8 SADDLEBACK RANGE
east of Rangeley

Total distance: 32.2 miles one-way   **Hiking time:** 3–4 days

Difficulty: 10   **Rating:** 10

The Saddleback Range stands out as one of the three premier mountain
ranges in Maine—the other two being the greater Katahdin region and the
Bigelow Range—and a multiday traverse of its peaks is as rugged, varied,
and scenic a mountain experience as can be had anywhere in New England. Seven of the eight summits rise above 4,000 feet, and four of them
thrust extensive areas above tree line, offering long, panoramic views.
Three miles of ridge above the trees extend from Saddleback Mountain to
the Horn. Wintry storms with dangerously high winds occur year-round,
so avoid this exposed ground if bad weather threatens. (On my own traverse of this range, I had overcast weather until my final day, hiking over
Saddleback Junior, the Horn, and Saddleback.) This traverse could be accomplished in three days but I took four, allowing time to make the side
trips to Sugarloaf Mountain and Mount Abraham at a moderate pace.
Both side trips add to this hike's 32.2-mile distance.

From Route 16/27, follow the white blazes of the Appalachian Trail
southbound. It rises gently at first and never grows more than moderately
steep before reaching the wooded North Crocker Mountain summit (4,168

feet), 5.2 miles from the highway. There are limited views over the tops of low spruce trees. A better view is along the Appalachian Trail just south of the summit, looking toward Sugarloaf Mountain and Mount Abraham. Continuing south on the Appalachian Trail, you drop into the shallow col between the two summits of Crocker, then climb to the top of South Crocker (4,010 feet), a mile away from North Crocker. The actual summit is reached via a 100-foot side path off the Appalachian Trail. An open ledge there affords a limited view toward Sugarloaf and Abraham.

Descending south, the Appalachian Trail crosses an open slope of loose, broken rocks with views north and east toward the Bigelow Range. Footing becomes difficult descending the steep and very loose final half mile to Crocker Cirque campsite, just over a mile from South Crocker's summit and 7.3 miles from Route 27/16. One mile farther south, the Appalachian Trail crosses the dirt Caribou Valley Road (which was improved in recent years all the way to the Appalachian Trail crossing, providing another access to the Appalachian Trail; Route 27/16 is 4.3 miles down Caribou Valley Road). From the road, the Appalachian Trail immediately crosses the South Branch of the Carrabassett River—which can be dangerous at times of high water—then climbs very steeply up Sugarloaf Mountain, involving short stretches of tricky scrambling. The trail emerges from the woods high on Sugarloaf's north slope, with views of the Crockers across the valley. It reenters the woods and then reaches a junction with the Sugarloaf Mountain Trail 3.3 miles south of Crocker Cirque campsite (and 2.3 miles from Caribou Valley Road); this rocky trail leads steeply uphill 0.6 mile to the exposed 4,237-foot Sugarloaf summit, Maine's third-highest peak, where there are ski area buildings and long views in every direction. From the Sugarloaf Mountain Trail junction, the Appalachian Trail follows the fairly flat ridge connecting Sugarloaf to Spaulding Mountain—a quiet trail stretch through a lush forest of hemlock, ferns, and moss. About 0.1 mile south of the Sugarloaf Mountain Trail junction, a side path leads about 40 feet to a good view. The Appalachian Trail continues along the wooded ridge to a junction with the Spaulding Mountain Trail, 5.4 miles from Crocker Cirque campsite; this trail leads 0.1 mile uphill to Spaulding's 4,010-foot summit, where three short side paths lead to limited views toward Sugarloaf and Abraham.

From the Spaulding Mountain Trail junction, the Appalachian Trail descends 0.8 mile to a side path leading 150 feet to the Spaulding Mountain lean-to, where there is also space for tents. The Appalachian Trail follows moderate terrain south, reaching the Mount Abraham Trail 1.1 miles from the Spaulding lean-to. On this blue-blazed trail, it's 1.7 miles one-way to the 4,043-foot Abraham summit. Although it's relatively flat for the first half mile, after emerging from the woods, the trail climbs over three bumps on a ridge, crossing talus slopes reminiscent of bigger mountains like Washington or Katahdin. But the views from Abraham are among the best in the range. From the Mount Abraham Trail junction, the Appalachian Trail southbound passes a view toward Abraham within 0.2 mile, and then over the wooded top of Lone Mountain in a mile.

Descending, the trail follows and then crosses beautiful Perham Stream (immediately after crossing a logging road), its narrow current choked with moss-covered rocks. The Appalachian Trail crosses a second logging road and, 1.2 miles from Perham Stream, crosses another gem, Sluice Brook, which parallels the trail for 0.7 mile before pouring through a narrow flume. The trail crosses a gravel road and descends very steeply to Orbeton Stream, 5.3 miles from the Spaulding lean-to. I crossed the wide stream on stones in August, but fording it could be difficult in high water. From Orbeton, the Appalachian Trail makes one of its steepest and most arduous ascents in this range, more than two miles to the open ledges of Poplar Ridge, where there are views to the south and east. A half mile beyond the ledges is the Poplar Ridge lean-to (a small brook provides water, but I found it barely trickling in August).

From the shelter, the Appalachian Trail climbs steadily 1.4 miles to the open summit of Saddleback Junior (3,655 feet), with excellent views in all directions. I reached this summit at 7 A.M., early enough to see a cloud tail wave like a flag from the Saddleback summit while fog still sat low in the valleys to the north. Follow white blazes and cairns across the Saddleback Junior top, descend about 500 feet, and then climb steeply 1,000 feet to the open, 4,041-foot summit of the Horn, two miles from Saddleback Junior. Again the views are spectacular, encompassing the Rangeley Lake area and Saddleback Mountain to the west, and extending north to Katahdin and southwest to Washington on a clear day.

Descend south on the Appalachian Trail, crossing mostly open ground with nonstop views, and then ascend Saddleback's ledges to the lower of its two summits. Walk the easy ridge to the true summit, at 4,120 feet, 1.6 miles from the Horn's summit. Continuing south, the Appalachian Trail drops back into the woods a mile below the summit and then crosses a logging road nearly a mile below tree line. The trail crosses a good stream 0.2 mile beyond the logging road and crosses Saddleback Stream 0.6 mile farther. At 3.7 miles from Saddleback's summit, a side path leads a short distance to the Caves, actually passageways through giant boulders that have cleaved from the cliff above over the eons. Just 0.2 mile past the Caves, the trail reaches the Piazza Rock lean-to area, a popular backcountry campsite less than two miles from Route 4. There are tent sites and a large shelter, but this place fills quickly on weekends. A side path off the

Appalachian Trail leads about 200 yards uphill to Piazza Rock, an enormous horizontal slab protruding improbably from the cliff. You can follow the trail up onto the slab with a little scrambling. From the lean-to area, the Appalachian Trail descends south for 1.8 miles to Route 4, this hike's terminus.

User Groups

Hikers only. No wheelchair facilities. Dogs are discouraged along the Appalachian Trail in Maine. This trail should not be attempted in winter except by hikers experienced in mountaineering and prepared for severe winter weather, and is not suitable for skis. Bikes, horses, and hunting are prohibited.

Access and Fees

Parking and access are free. There are three lean-to shelters and one campsite along this section of the Appalachian Trail: the Crocker Cirque campsite, with three tent platforms, lies 0.1 mile down a side path off the Appalachian Trail, 7.3 miles south of Route 27/16; the Spaulding Mountain lean-to is located down a short side path off the Appalachian Trail, 6.2 miles south of the Crocker Cirque campsite; the Poplar Ridge lean-to sits along the Appalachian Trail, eight miles south of the Spaulding Mountain lean-to; and the Piazza Rock lean-to lies on a short side path off the Appalachian Trail, 8.9 miles south of the Poplar Ridge lean-to. For information about a hiker shuttle, free Kennebec River ferry service, and other hiker services along the Appalachian Trail in Maine, contact Steve Longley, P.O. Box 90, Route 201, The Forks, ME 04985, 207/663-4441 or 888/FLOAT-ME (in Maine only), website: www.riversandtrails.com. Stephen Martelli of Stratton also runs a hiker shuttle service to road crossings along the Appalachian Trail between Grafton Notch and Monson; call 207/246-4642.

Maps

For a trail map, refer to map 6 in the *Map and Guide to the Appalachian Trail in Maine,* a set of seven maps and a guidebook for $24.95 from the Maine Appalachian Trail Club or the Appalachian Trail Conference. Also available is the *Rangeley–Stratton/Baxter State Park–Katahdin* map, $7.95 in waterproof Tyvek, which is available in many stores and from the Appalachian Mountain Club, 800/262-4455, website: www.outdoors.org. For topographic area maps, request Sugarloaf Mountain, Black Nubble, Mount Abraham, Redington, and Saddleback Mountain from USGS Map Sales, Federal Center, Box 25286, Denver, CO 80225, 888/ASK-USGS (888/275-8747), website: http://mapping.usgs.gov.

Directions

You need to shuttle two vehicles for this backpacking trip. To do the hike from north to south, as described here, leave one vehicle where the Appalachian Trail crosses Route 4, about 12 miles north of the junction of Routes 4 and 142 in Phillips and 10.1 miles south of the junction of Routes 4 and 16. Then drive to the hike's start, where the Appalachian Trail crosses Route 27/16, 5.3 miles south of where Routes 27 and 16 split in Stratton and 16 miles north of where Routes 27 and 16 split in Kingfield.

Contact

Maine Appalachian Trail Club, P.O. Box 283, Augusta, ME 04332-0283, website: www.matc.org. Appalachian Trail Conference, 799 Washington Street, P.O. Box 807, Harpers Ferry, WV 25425-0807, 304/535-6331, website: www.appalachiantrail.org.

9 SADDLEBACK MOUNTAIN AND THE HORN

southeast of Rangeley

Total distance: 13.4 miles round-trip   **Hiking time:** 8.5 hours

Difficulty: 9   **Rating:** 10

Saddleback Mountain rises to 4,120 feet, offering some of the best views in the state from its summit and the open, three-mile ridge linking it and its neighboring 4,000-footer, The Horn. A round-trip hike on the Appalachian Trail from Route 4 to the true Saddleback summit—the first of its two summits reached from this direction—is a strenuous 10.2-mile day hike. Continuing to The Horn makes the round-trip distance a very challenging 13.4 miles, with a cumulative 3,800 feet of uphill. Although these are among the most sought-after Maine summits, avoid this exposed ridge in inclement weather. Also carry plenty of water, as there is no water source above the outlet to Moose and Deer Pond.

From Route 4, follow the white blazes of the Appalachian Trail northbound. Within 0.1 mile, the trail crosses a bridge over Sandy River and then climbs steadily to the Piazza Rock lean-to and camping area, 1.8 miles from the road (a very popular destination among weekend backpackers). A side path off the Appalachian Trail leads about 200 yards uphill to Piazza Rock, an enormous horizontal slab protruding improbably from the cliff. You can follow the trail up onto the slab with a little scrambling. Following the Appalachian Trail 0.2 mile north of the camping area, pass another side path leading a short distance to the Caves, actually passageways through giant boulders that have cleaved from the cliff above over the eons. Just over a mile beyond the Caves side path, the Appalachian Trail crosses Saddleback Stream, and 0.6 mile farther it crosses the Moose and Deer Pond outlet, the last water source on this hike. At 4.7 miles from Route 4, the trail emerges above tree line on Saddleback and ascends the open ridge another mile to the summit. Views here are spectacular, encompassing the Rangeley Lake area to the west, The Horn to the northeast, and extending north to Katahdin and southwest to Washington on a clear day. The Appalachian Trail continues down into the slight saddle that gives the mountain its name, over Saddleback's second summit, then drops more steeply over ledges for several hundred feet into the col between Saddleback and The Horn. It turns upward again, climbing gently to the 4,041-foot summit of The Horn, 1.6 miles from Saddleback's summit, where again the views are long in every direction. The Appalachian Trail continues north, but this hike returns via the same route you came.

User Groups

Hikers only. No wheelchair facilities. Dogs are discouraged along the Appalachian Trail in Maine. This trail should not be attempted in winter except by hikers experienced in mountaineering and prepared for severe winter weather, and is not suitable for skis. Bikes, horses, and hunting are prohibited.

Access and Fees

Parking and access are free. The Piazza Rock lean-to and camping area is reached via a short side path off the Appalachian Trail, 1.8 miles north of Route 4.

Maps

For a trail map, refer to map 6 in the *Map and Guide to the Appalachian Trail in Maine,* a set of seven maps and a guidebook for $24.95 from the Maine Appalachian Trail Club or the Appalachian Trail Conference. Also available is the *Rangeley–Stratton/Baxter State Park–Katahdin* map, $7.95 in waterproof Tyvek, which is available in many stores and from the Appalachian Mountain Club, 800/262-4455, website: www.outdoors.org. For topographic area maps, request Redington and Saddleback Mountain from USGS Map Sales, Federal Center, Box 25286, Denver, CO 80225, 888/ASK-USGS (888/275-8747), website: http://mapping.usgs.gov.

Directions

Park in the roadside turnout where the Appalachian Trail crosses Route 4, about 12 miles north of the junction of Routes 4 and 142 in Phillips and 10.1 miles south of the junction of Routes 4 and 16 in Rangeley.

Contact

Maine Appalachian Trail Club, P.O. Box 283, Augusta, ME 04332-0283, website: www.matc.org. Appalachian Trail Conference, 799 Washington Street, P.O. Box 807, Harpers Ferry, WV 25425-0807, 304/535-6331, website: www.appalachiantrail.org.

10 PIAZZA ROCK AND THE CAVES
southeast of Rangeley

Total distance: 4 miles round-trip   **Hiking time:** 3 hours

Difficulty: 3   **Rating:** 8

Many Appalachian Trail hikers continue beyond Piazza Rock and the Caves on their way to bag Saddleback Mountain and The Horn. But these two interesting geological formations just a couple miles from the road offer a wonderful destination for a short hike that climbs little more than a few hundred feet—especially suited for children. Piazza Rock is an enormous horizontal slab protruding improbably from the cliff. The Caves are interesting passageways through giant boulders that have cleaved from the cliff above over the eons. The lean-to and camping area nearby provides the option of an overnight trip, though the area is very popular and fills quickly on summer and fall weekends.

From Route 4, follow the white blazes of the Appalachian Trail northbound. Within 0.1 mile, the trail crosses a bridge over Sandy River and then climbs steadily to the Piazza Rock lean-to and camping area, 1.8 miles from the highway. Turn left on a side path that leads about 200 yards uphill to Piazza Rock. You can follow the trail up onto the slab with a little scrambling. Follow the Appalachian Trail 0.2 mile north of the camping area and turn onto another side path leading a short distance to the Caves. Hike back to your vehicle the same way you came.

User Groups

Hikers and snowshoers. No wheelchair facilities. Dogs are discouraged along the Appalachian Trail in Maine. This trail is not suitable for skis. Bikes, horses, and hunting are prohibited.

Access and Fees

Parking and access are free. The Piazza Rock lean-to and camping area is reached via a short side path off the Appalachian Trail, 1.8 miles north of Route 4.

Maps

For a trail map, refer to map 6 in the *Map and Guide to the Appalachian Trail in Maine,* a set of seven maps and a guidebook for $24.95 from the Maine Appalachian Trail Club or the Appalachian Trail Conference. Also available is the *Rangeley-Stratton/Baxter State Park-Katahdin* map, $7.95 in waterproof Tyvek, which is available in many stores and from the Appalachian Mountain Club, 800/262-4455, website: www.outdoors.org. For topographic area maps, request Redington and Saddleback Mountain from USGS Map Sales, Federal Center, Box 25286, Denver, CO 80225, 888/ASK-USGS (888/275-8747), website: http://mapping.usgs.gov.

Directions

Park in the roadside turnout where the Appalachian Trail crosses Route 4, about 12 miles north of the junction of Routes 4 and 142 in Phillips and 10.1 miles south of the junction of Routes 4 and 16 in Rangeley.

Contact

Maine Appalachian Trail Club, P.O. Box 283, Augusta, ME 04332-0283, website: www.matc.org. Appalachian Trail Conference, 799 Washington Street, P.O. Box 807, Harpers Ferry, WV 25425-0807, 304/535-6331, website: www.appalachiantrail.org.

11 OLD BLUE MOUNTAIN
north of Andover

Total distance: 5.6 miles round-trip   **Hiking time:** 4 hours

Difficulty: 8   **Rating:** 9

From the first steps up this remote stretch of the Appalachian Trail to the 3,600-foot summit of Old Blue Mountain, this is a hike without a dull moment. I made this trek on the first weekend of spring—which retains a decidedly wintry feel in the northern mountains—and enjoyed a wilderness experience on a trail that had seen few, if any, hikers all winter. We broke trail through drifted snow deep enough at times to bury the blazes on trees, climbed around and over blown-down trees, and took four hours to hike less than three miles up. For a more moderate yet still fairly remote hiking experience, day hike Old Blue between July and early October—but be prepared for any type of weather. The elevation gain is about 2,200 feet.

The Appalachian Trail leaves South Arm Road (look for a sign a few steps in from the road) and climbs steeply above spectacular Black Brook Notch. Atop the cliffs, watch for an open ledge to the trail's right with an unobstructed view of the notch. The Appalachian Trail then meanders through dense woods, at one point offering a good view toward Old Blue's summit. The summit itself is a broad plateau covered with scrub trees and offering views in all directions. Visible to the south are the Mahoosucs and the slopes of the Sunday River Ski Area; to the northeast are the Saddleback Range and Bigelow Mountain. Descend the same way you came.

User Groups
Hikers and snowshoers. No wheelchair facilities. Dogs are discouraged along the Appalachian Trail in Maine. This trail should not be attempted in winter except by hikers experienced in mountaineering and prepared for severe winter weather, and is not suitable for skis. Bikes, horses, and hunting are prohibited.

Access and Fees
Parking and access are free.

Maps
For a trail map, refer to map 7 in the *Map and Guide to the Appalachian Trail in Maine,* a set of seven maps and a guidebook for $24.95 from the Maine Appalachian Trail Club or the Appalachian Trail Conference. For topographic area maps, request Metallak Mountain and Andover from USGS Map Sales, Federal Center, Box 25286, Denver, CO 80225, 888/ASK-USGS (888/275-8747), website: http://mapping.usgs.gov.

Directions
From the junction of Routes 5 and 120 in Andover, head east on Route 120 for half a mile and then turn left onto South Arm Road. Drive another 7.7 miles into Black Brook Notch to where the Appalachian Trail crosses the road. Park at the roadside.

Contact
Maine Appalachian Trail Club, P.O. Box 283, Augusta, ME 04332-0283, website: www.matc.org. Appalachian Trail Conference, 799 Washington Street, P.O. Box 807, Harpers Ferry, WV 25425-0807, 304/535-6331, website: www.appalachiantrail.org.

12 TUMBLEDOWN MOUNTAIN BROOK TRAIL
northwest of Weld

Total distance: 3.8 miles round-trip   **Hiking time:** 3 hours

Difficulty: 6   **Rating:** 10

Of the two hikes up spectacular Tumbledown Mountain that are described in this guide, this one is significantly easier and more appropriate for children and casual hikers, although it climbs a little more in elevation—about 1,900 feet. (See the following listing for Tumbledown Mountain Loop Trail for another option and more description of Tumbledown.) All trail junctions are marked with signs. The Brook Trail follows an old logging road for its first mile and then climbs more steeply for the next half mile to Tumbledown Pond, a scenic alpine tarn tucked amid Tumbledown's three summits. From the pond, turn left (west) on the Tumbledown Ridge Trail and hike up a moderately steep, open ridge of rock for 0.4 mile to East Peak, where there are sweeping mountain views to the east, south, and west, all the way to Mount Washington in New Hampshire.

This hike ends here and returns the way you came. But to reach West Peak—the true summit at 3,068 feet—follow the Tumbledown Ridge Trail another 0.3 mile west; it drops down into the saddle between the peaks and then climbs the rocky ridge to West Peak (adding 0.6 mile to this hike's distance). See the special note in the Tumbledown Mountain Loop Trail listing for a third possible hike in this area.

a hiker atop Tumbledown Mountain

User Groups

Hikers and dogs. No wheelchair facilities. This trail may be difficult to snowshoe and is not suitable for bikes, horses, or skis. Hunting is allowed in season.

Access and Fees

Parking and access are free.

Maps

For a contour map of trails, obtain the *Camden–Pleasant–Weld/Mahoosuc–Evans map,* $7.95 in waterproof Tyvek, from the Appalachian Mountain Club, 800/262-4455, website: www.outdoors.org. For a topographic area map, request Weld, Madrid, Roxbury, and Jackson Mountain from USGS Map Sales, Federal Center, Box 25286, Denver, CO 80225, 888/ASK-USGS (888/275-8747), website: http://mapping.usgs.gov.

Directions

From the junction of Routes 142 and 156 in Weld, drive 2.4 miles north on Route 142 to Weld Corner. Turn left onto West Side Road at the Mount Blue State Park sign. Continue 0.5 mile and bear right on a dirt road. Drive 2.3 miles on that road, passing the Mountain View Cemetery, and then bear right again on another dirt road, heading toward Byron Notch. From that intersection, it's 1.6 miles to the Brook Trail; park at the roadside.

Contact

There is no contact agency for this hike.

13 TUMBLEDOWN MOUNTAIN LOOP TRAIL

northwest of Weld

Total distance: 4.2 miles round-trip   **Hiking time:** 4 hours

Difficulty: 7   **Rating:** 10

With a 700-foot cliff on its south face, a pristine alpine pond, and more than a half mile of open, rocky ridge, Tumbledown Mountain seems far taller than 3,068 feet. The views from the ridge and the two peaks (East and West) take in a landscape of mountains and lakes offering few, if any, signs of human presence. As a pair of peregrine falcons circled overhead, I stood alone on the West Peak, enjoying a sunny July day and long views of mountains and lakes to the east, south, and west, all the way to Mount Washington and the White Mountains in New Hampshire (the tall ridge looming in the distance to the southwest). Of the two hikes up Tumbledown described in this guide, this 4.2-mile trek is far and away more difficult; some hikers will not feel comfortable climbing up through the wet, fallen boulders near the top of the Loop Trail. (See the previous listing, Tumbledown Mountain Brook Trail, for an easier route up Tumbledown.) All trail junctions are marked with signs. No trail exists to the north peak, which, along with Jackson Mountain, blocks views to the north. The hike climbs about 1,700 feet.

Begin on the Loop Trail, which enters the woods across from the dirt parking lot. The trail soon begins a very steep ascent of 1.3 miles to the Great Ledges, a flat, open shelf below the towering cliff of Tumbledown. The trail trends to the right along the ledges for nearly 0.2 mile and then turns steeply upward again. Just before reaching the saddle between the East and West peaks—1.9 miles from the trailhead—you have to scramble up through a passage between boulders that typically runs with water. In the saddle, turn left (west) on the Tumbledown Ridge Trail for the 0.1-mile, moderate climb to West Peak, the true summit at 3,068 feet. Double back to the saddle, then follow the Tumbledown Ridge Trail 0.2 mile to East Peak. From here, it's nearly a half mile down the Tumbledown Ridge Trail to Tumbledown Pond and the junction with the Brook Trail. Turn right (south) on the Brook Trail, which leads 1.5 miles to the road; it descends steeply at first, but the last mile follows an old logging road.

Special note: Ken Morgan, an avid hiker in Maine, recommends another loop hike up Tumbledown Mountain and Little Jackson Mountain via the Parker's Ridge Trail, Pond Link Trail, and Little Jackson Trail, saying the views from the upper parts of the first and last of those trails are fabulous.

User Groups

Hikers only. No wheelchair facilities. A sign at the Loop Trail's start advises against bringing children or dogs on this trail because of its difficulty. This trail would be very difficult to snowshoe and is not suitable for bikes, dogs, horses, or skis. Hunting is allowed in season.

Access and Fees

Parking and access are free.

Maps

For a contour map of trails, obtain the *Camden-Pleasant-Weld/Mahoosuc-Evans map,* $7.95 in waterproof Tyvek, from the Appalachian Mountain Club, 800/262-4455, website: www.outdoors.org. For topographic area maps, request Weld, Madrid, Roxbury, and Jackson Mountain from USGS Map Sales, Federal Center, Box 25286, Denver, CO 80225, 888/ASK-USGS (888/275-8747), website: http://mapping.usgs.gov.

Directions

From the junction of Routes 142 and 156 in Weld, drive 2.4 miles north on Route 142 to Weld Corner. Turn left onto West Side Road at the Mount Blue State Park sign. Continue 0.5 mile and bear right on a dirt road. Drive 2.3 miles on that road, passing the Mountain View Cemetery, and then bear right again on another dirt road (there's no sign), heading toward Byron Notch. From that intersection, it's 1.6 miles to the Brook Trail (park at the roadside) and three miles to the Loop Trail (park in a dirt lot on the left). For this hike, you need to either leave vehicles at each trailhead, or park at the Loop Trail and walk the 1.4 miles on the dirt road between the two trailheads at the hike's end.

Contact

There is no contact agency for this hike.

14 TABLE ROCK, GRAFTON NOTCH
in Grafton Notch State Park

Total distance: 2.5 miles round-trip   **Hiking time:** 1.5 hours

Difficulty: 4   **Rating:** 9

Flanked to the south by Old Speck Mountain and to the north by Baldpate Mountain, Grafton Notch takes a deep bite out of this western Maine stretch of the Appalachians and marks the northern terminus of the Mahoosuc Range. Perched hundreds of feet up Baldpate Mountain, the broad, flat Table Rock overlooks the notch. Visible from Route 26, it affords commanding views of the notch and Old Speck. This 2.5-mile loop over Table Rock employs the orange-blazed Table Rock Trail, which ascends very steeply and relentlessly for a mile. The difficult section can be avoided by hiking the more moderate Appalachian Trail and the upper part of the Table Rock Trail both ways, instead of just on the descent, as described here. But while it was physically demanding, I enjoyed the steep trail stretch, particularly when it emerged at the slab caves below Table Rock. The vertical ascent is nearly 1,000 feet.

From the parking lot, pick up the white-blazed Appalachian Trail heading north, crossing the highway. After reentering the woods, follow the Appalachian Trail for 0.1 mile and then turn right at the sign for Table Rock. The trail almost immediately grows steep, emerging a mile later at the so-called slab caves, which are actually intriguing cavities amid boulders rather than true caves. The trail turns right and circles around and up onto Table Rock. To descend, walk off the back of Table Rock, following the blue-blazed trail for 0.5 mile to the left until reaching the Appalachian Trail. Turn left (south), and follow the Appalachian Trail nearly a mile back to Route 26. Cross the highway to the parking lot.

User Groups

Hikers only. No wheelchair facilities. Dogs are discouraged along the Appalachian Trail in Maine. This trail would be difficult to snowshoe and is not suitable for skis. Bikes, horses, and hunting are prohibited.

Access and Fees

Grafton Notch State Park is open from May 15 to October 15, though the trails are accessible year-round. Visitors using the parking lot at this trailhead are asked to pay a self-service fee of $1 per adult and 50 cents per child. There is a box beside the parking lot.

Maps

A very basic map of Grafton Notch State Park trails is available from park rangers, who are usually on duty at high-traffic areas such as Screw Auger Falls; it can also be obtained through the park office or the Maine Bureau of Parks and Lands. For a contour map of trails, refer to map 7 in the *Map and Guide to the Appalachian Trail in Maine,* a set of seven maps and a guidebook for $24.95 from the Maine Appalachian Trail Club or the Appalachian Trail Conference. For a topographic area map, request Old Speck Mountain from USGS Map Sales, Federal Center, Box 25286, Denver, CO 80225, 888/ASK-USGS (888/275-8747), website: http://mapping.usgs.gov.

Directions

This hike begins from a large parking lot (marked by a sign reading "Hiking Trail") where the Appalachian Trail crosses Route 26 in Grafton Notch State Park, 6.7 miles north of the sign at the state park's southern entrance and 1.8 miles south of the sign at the state park's northern entrance.

Contact

Grafton Notch State Park, 1941 Bear River Road, Newry, ME 04261, 207/824-2912 or 207/624-6080 off-season. Maine Department of Conservation, Bureau of Parks and Lands, 286 Water Street, Key Bank Plaza, 3rd and 5th floors, Augusta, ME 04333-0022, 207/287-3821, website: www.state.me.us/doc/parks/. Maine Appalachian Trail Club, P.O. Box 283, Augusta, ME 04332-0283, website: www.matc.org. Appalachian Trail Conference, 799 Washington Street, P.O. Box 807, Harpers Ferry, WV 25425-0807, 304/535-6331, website: www.appalachiantrail.org.

15 MOTHER WALKER FALLS
in Grafton Notch State Park

Total distance: 0.2 miles round-trip   **Hiking time:** 0.25 hour

Difficulty: 1   **Rating:** 7

This short walk on an easy, wide path leads to a couple of viewpoints above what is more of a gorge than a falls. From the turnout, walk down the stairs. A gravel path leads both to the right and to the left, and both directions lead a short distance to views into the narrow gorge, in which the stream drops through several short steps for 100 yards or more. To the right, the walkway ends at a fence. If you go left, you have greater liberty to explore the stream and gorge. It can be difficult to get a good view into the gorge because of the forest's density and terrain's rugged nature along the stream.

User Groups
Hikers, snowshoers, and dogs. Dogs must be leashed. No wheelchair facilities. This trail is not suitable for bikes, horses, or skis. Hunting is allowed in season.

Access and Fees
Parking and access are free.

Maps
Although no map is needed for this walk, a very basic map of Grafton Notch State Park trails is available from park rangers, who are usually on duty at Screw Auger Falls; it can also be obtained through the park office or the Maine Bureau of Parks and Lands. For a topographic area map, request Old Speck Mountain from USGS Map Sales, Federal Center, Box 25286, Denver, CO 80225, 888/ASK-USGS (888/275-8747), website: http://mapping.usgs.gov.

Directions
This hike begins from a roadside turnout marked by a sign for Mother Walker Falls, on Route 26 in Grafton Notch State Park, 2.2 miles north of the sign at the state park's southern entrance, and 6.3 miles south of the sign at the state park's northern entrance.

Contact
Grafton Notch State Park, 1941 Bear River Road, Newry, ME 04261, 207/824-2912 or 207/624-6080 off-season. Maine Department of Conserva-

tion, Bureau of Parks and Lands, 286 Water Street, Key Bank Plaza, 3rd and 5th floors, Augusta, ME 04333-0022, 207/287-3821, website: www.state.me.us/doc/parks/.

16 SCREW AUGER FALLS
in Grafton Notch State Park

Total distance: 0.1 miles round-trip   **Hiking time:** 0.25 hour

Difficulty: 1   **Rating:** 9

A popular swimming hole for families and a scenic attraction for tourists, Screw Auger Falls lies just a few minutes' stroll down a flat walkway from the parking lot. The Bear River pours over smooth stone slabs, tumbling through the impressive waterfall and a tight gorge of water-sculpted rock reminiscent of Southwestern slot canyons (albeit on a smaller scale). While today it sits in the heart of 3,192-acre Grafton Notch State Park, the falls once sported a water-powered log saw. Up until the early 20th century, the logging community of Grafton, with a population of more than 100, sprawled up through the notch. Interestingly, the town's children attended school during the summer because the notch road was often impassable in winter.

User Groups
Hikers, dogs, and wheelchair users. Dogs must be leashed. This trail is not suitable for bikes, horses, or skis. Hunting is allowed in season.

Access and Fees
Parking and access are free.

Maps
Although no map is needed for this walk, a very basic map of Grafton Notch State Park trails is available from park rangers, who are usually on duty at Screw Auger Falls; it can also be obtained through the park office or the state Bureau of Parks and Lands. For a topographic area map, request Old Speck Mountain from USGS Map Sales, Federal Center, Box 25286, Denver, CO 80225, 888/ASK-USGS (888/275-8747), website: http://mapping.usgs.gov.

Directions
This hike begins from a large parking lot marked by a sign for Screw Auger Falls, on Route 26 in Grafton Notch State Park, one mile north of

the sign at the state park's southern entrance and 7.5 miles south of the sign at the state park's northern entrance.

Contact
Grafton Notch State Park, 1941 Bear River Road, Newry, ME 04261, 207/824-2912 or 207/624-6080 off-season. Maine Department of Conservation, Bureau of Parks and Lands, 286 Water Street, Key Bank Plaza, 3rd and 5th floors, Augusta, ME 04333-0022, 207/287-3821, website: www.state.me.us/doc/parks/.

17 EYEBROW TRAIL
in Grafton Notch State Park

Total distance: 2.3 miles round-trip   **Hiking time:** 1.5 hours

Difficulty: 4   **Rating:** 9

The Eyebrow Trail is a rugged side loop off the Appalachian Trail that offers a spectacular Grafton Notch view from the crest of Old Speck Mountain's towering cliffs, which are visible from the parking lot. Be forewarned: Parts of the trail are severely eroded and could be unpleasant, especially in wet weather. The elevation gain is about 1,000 feet.

From the parking lot, walk southbound on the white-blazed Appalachian Trail for about 100 yards and then bear right onto the Eyebrow Trail. The trail climbs very steeply over rugged terrain—at one point traversing an exposed slab of rock that could be dangerous when wet or icy. A bit more than a mile from the trailhead, the Eyebrow Trail passes over a series of four ledges. The view of Grafton Notch from the first ledge, a small overlook, is pretty good; the third ledge's view is largely obscured by trees. But from the second and fourth ledges you get an excellent, cliff-top view of Grafton Notch. The summit of Old Speck Mountain (see listing in this chapter) looms high to the right, Table Rock (see listing in this chapter) is distinguishable on the face of Baldpate Mountain directly across the notch, and Sunday River Whitecap rises prominently to the southeast. After enjoying the view, continue along the Eyebrow Trail 0.1 mile to its upper junction with the Appalachian Trail. Turn left and descend the Appalachian Trail for 1.1 miles back to the trailhead.

User Groups
Hikers only. No wheelchair facilities. Dogs are discouraged along the Appalachian Trail in Maine. This trail should not be attempted in winter except by hikers experienced in mountaineering and prepared for severe winter weather, and is not suitable for skis. Bikes, horses, and hunting are prohibited.

Access and Fees

Grafton Notch State Park is open from May 15 to October 15, though the trails are accessible year-round. Visitors using the parking lot at this trailhead are asked to pay a self-service fee of $1 per adult and 50 cents per child. There is a box beside the parking lot. The Old Speck summit and northeast slopes are within Grafton Notch State Park in Maine.

Maps

Map 1 in the *Map and Guide to the Appalachian Trail in New Hampshire and Vermont,* an eight-map set and guidebook available for $18.95 ($12.95 for the maps alone) from the Appalachian Trail Conference, covers the entire Mahoosuc Range. So does the *Camden-Pleasant-Weld/Mahoosuc-Evans map,* $7.95 in waterproof Tyvek, available in many stores and from the Appalachian Mountain Club, 800/262-4455, website: www.outdoors .org. Map 7 in the *Map and Guide to the Appalachian Trail in Maine,* a set of seven maps and a guidebook for $24.95 from the Appalachian Trail Conference, covers just the Appalachian Trail in Maine, including this hike. For a topographic area map, request Old Speck Mountain from USGS Map Sales, Federal Center, Box 25286, Denver, CO 80225, 888/ASK-USGS (888/275-8747), website: http://mapping.usgs.gov.

Directions

Park in the large parking lot located where the white-blazed Appalachian Trail crosses Route 26 (marked by a sign reading "Hiking Trail"), 6.7 miles north of the sign at the state park's southern entrance and 1.8 miles south of the sign at the state park's northern entrance.

Contact

Grafton Notch State Park, 1941 Bear River Road, Newry, ME 04261, 207/824-2912 or 207/624-6080 off-season. Maine Department of Conservation, Bureau of Parks and Lands, 286 Water Street, Key Bank Plaza, 3rd and 5th floors, Augusta, ME 04333-0022, 207/287-3821, website: www .state.me.us/doc/parks/. Appalachian Mountain Club Pinkham Notch Visitor Center, P.O. Box 298, Gorham, NH 03581, 603/466-2721, website: www.outdoors.org. Appalachian Trail Conference, 799 Washington Street, P.O. Box 807, Harpers Ferry, WV 25425-0807, 304/535-6331, website: www.appalachiantrail.org.

18 STEP FALLS

south of Grafton Notch State Park, in Newry

Total distance: 1 mile round-trip   **Hiking time:** 0.5 hour

Difficulty: 1   **Rating:** 9

On a typical, stiflingly hot and humid July day, I walked these cool hemlock woods to the lower part of Step Falls. Seeing it for the first time, I thought, "Nice." Then I rounded a bend in Wight Brook for my first glimpse of the upper falls and thought, "Wow!" I won't try to build up these falls with some verbose description—this is the sort of place you should discover without expectations.

From the parking lot, follow the obvious, white-blazed trail for 0.5 mile to the falls. The trail is an easy, flat walk; take care not to wander off it onto false trails, because such roaming tramples vegetation. Return the same way.

User Groups

Hikers and snowshoers. No wheelchair facilities. This trail is not suitable for bikes, dogs, horses, or skis. Hunting is prohibited.

Access and Fees

Parking and access are free. The preserve is closed from dusk to dawn.

Maps

No map is needed for this easy walk. But for a topographic area map, request Old Speck Mountain from USGS Map Sales, Federal Center, Box 25286, Denver, CO 80225, 888/ASK-USGS (888/275-8747), website: http://mapping.usgs.gov.

Directions

This hike begins from a large dirt parking lot off Route 26, 0.6 mile south of the Grafton Notch State Park southern entrance. Watch for a dirt road, marked by a small sign, on the south side of a small bridge over Wight Brook; it leads 100 feet to the parking area.

Contact

The Nature Conservancy Maine Chapter, Fort Andross, 14 Maine Street, Suite 401, Brunswick, ME 04011, 207/729-5181, email: naturemaine@tnc.org, website: http://nature.org.

19 OLD SPECK MOUNTAIN
in Grafton Notch State Park

Total distance: 7.6 miles round-trip   **Hiking time:** 5 hours

Difficulty: 9   **Rating:** 7

This 7.6-mile round-trip hike brings you to the summit of Maine's fourth-highest peak and one of the state's 14 4,000-footers at 4,180 feet—a summit that lacked views until a fire tower was built there in 1999, replacing an old, unsafe tower. Now you can climb the tower for 360-degree views. Also, an area was cleared at the summit to land a helicopter carrying building supplies for the tower, opening up views north to the Baldpate Range. There are good views of the Mahoosuc Range from about a half mile south of the summit of Old Speck on the Mahoosuc Trail/Appalachian Trail; that distance is not calculated in this hike's total mileage. There are also views along the Old Speck Trail, which coincides with the Appalachian Trail, from the shoulder of Old Speck out over the vast sweep of woodlands to the north. You can also turn onto the upper part of the Eyebrow Trail and hike just 0.1 mile to a ledge with a wonderful view of Grafton Notch. This hike's other attractions are the brook cascades, which the trail parallels lower on the mountain. The hike climbs about 2,700 feet in elevation.

From the parking lot in Grafton Notch, follow the white blazes of the Appalachian Trail/Old Speck Trail southbound. At 3.5 miles, the trail reaches a junction with the Mahoosuc Trail. Turn left for the easy, final 0.3-mile climb to Old Speck's summit. Head back along the same route.

User Groups
Hikers only. No wheelchair facilities. Dogs are discouraged along the Appalachian Trail in Maine. This trail should not be attempted in winter except by hikers experienced in mountaineering and prepared for severe winter weather, and is not suitable for skis. Bikes, horses, and hunting are prohibited.

Access and Fees
Grafton Notch State Park is open from May 15 to October 15, though the trails are accessible year-round. Visitors using the parking lot at this trailhead are asked to pay a self-service fee of $1 per adult and 50 cents per child. There is a box beside the parking lot. The Old Speck summit and northeast slopes are within Grafton Notch State Park in Maine.

Maps
Map 1 in the *Map and Guide to the Appalachian Trail in New Hampshire and Vermont,* an eight-map set and guidebook available for $18.95 ($12.95

for the maps alone) from the Appalachian Trail Conference, covers the entire Mahoosuc Range. So does the *Camden–Pleasant–Weld/Mahoosuc–Evans map*, $7.95 in waterproof Tyvek, available in many stores and from the Appalachian Mountain Club, 800/262-4455, website: www.outdoors .org. Map 7 in the *Map and Guide to the Appalachian Trail in Maine*, a set of seven maps and a guidebook for $24.95 from the Appalachian Trail Conference, covers just the Appalachian Trail in Maine, including this hike. For a topographic area map, request Old Speck Mountain from USGS Map Sales, Federal Center, Box 25286, Denver, CO 80225, 888/ASK-USGS (888/275-8747), website: http://mapping.usgs.gov.

Directions
Park in the large parking lot located where the white-blazed Appalachian Trail crosses Route 26 (marked by a sign reading "Hiking Trail"), 6.7 miles north of the sign at the state park's southern entrance and 1.8 miles south of the sign at the state park's northern entrance.

Contact
Grafton Notch State Park, 1941 Bear River Road, Newry, ME 04261, 207/824-2912 or 207/624-6080 off-season. Maine Department of Conservation, Bureau of Parks and Lands, 286 Water Street, Key Bank Plaza, 3rd and 5th floors, Augusta, ME 04333-0022, 207/287-3821, website: www .state.me.us/doc/parks/. Appalachian Mountain Club Pinkham Notch Visitor Center, P.O. Box 298, Gorham, NH 03581, 603/466-2721, website: www.outdoors.org. Appalachian Trail Conference, 799 Washington Street, P.O. Box 807, Harpers Ferry, WV 25425-0807, 304/535-6331, website: www.appalachiantrail.org.

20 MAHOOSUC NOTCH
south of Grafton Notch State Park

Total distance: 6.5 miles round-trip   **Hiking time:** 6 hours

Difficulty: 8   **Rating:** 10

While backpacking the northern Mahoosuc Range with a friend a few years back, I was descending toward our introduction to Mahoosuc Notch—which bears a reputation as the hardest mile on the Appalachian Trail—when we encountered another backpacker. He had just come through the notch, so we curiously inquired about it. He smiled wickedly and said, "The notch was full of surprises this morning." Indeed. On a 70-degree Indian summer day, we dropped into the notch and immediately the temperature plummeted about 20 degrees. Giant boulders, which over the eons have toppled off the towering cliffs that embrace the notch, lay strewn about its floor, a maze of stone through which we picked our careful way, crawling through cavelike passages, constantly scrambling over and around obstacles.

Mahoosuc Notch can be day hiked via the Notch Trail from Success Pond Road when the road is passable; it's 6.5 miles round-trip, climbs a cumulative 1,300 feet or so, and can easily take several hours. Follow the white blazes of the Appalachian Trail carefully through the notch. From Success Pond Road, the trail ascends gently eastward. At 2.2 miles, it reaches a junction with the Mahoosuc Trail, which coincides with the Appalachian Trail. Continue straight ahead (northbound) on the Appalachian Trail, soon entering the boulder realm of the notch. Upon reaching the opposite end—you will know when you're through it—turn around and return the way you came. For a two- or three-day loop that incorporates the notch and allows you to avoid backtracking, see the following listing for the Mahoosuc Range.

User Groups

Hikers only. No wheelchair facilities. Dogs are discouraged along the Appalachian Trail in Maine. Bikes, horses, and hunting are prohibited.

Access and Fees

Parking and access are free. Success Pond Road, a private logging road that parallels the Mahoosuc Range on its west side, isn't maintained in winter and may not be passable due to mud in spring; it may also be difficult to follow because side roads branch from it.

Maps

For a map of trails, see Map 1 in the *Map and Guide to the Appalachian Trail in New Hampshire and Vermont,* an eight-map set and guidebook available for $18.95 ($12.95 for the maps alone) from the Appalachian Trail Conference, covers the entire Mahoosuc Range. Or the *Camden-Pleasant-Weld/Mahoosuc-Evans map,* $7.95 in waterproof Tyvek, available in many stores and from the Appalachian Mountain Club, 800/262-4455, website: www.outdoors.org. For topographic area maps, request Success Pond and Old Speck Mountain from USGS Map Sales, Federal Center, Box 25286, Denver, CO 80225, 888/ASK-USGS (888/275-8747), website: http://mapping.usgs.gov.

Directions

The Mahoosuc Notch Trail begins on the dirt Success Pond Road, which runs south from Route 26, 2.8 miles north of where the white-blazed

Appalachian Trail crosses the highway in Grafton Notch State Park. To access Success Pond Road from the south, drive north on Route 16 from its southern junction with U.S. 2 in Gorham for about 4.5 miles and turn east on the Cleveland Bridge across the Androscoggin River in Berlin. Bear left onto Unity Street; go through traffic lights 0.7 mile from Route 16, and then continue 0.1 mile and bear right onto Hutchins Street. Drive 0.8 mile farther and turn sharply left, passing the paper company mill yard. Just 0.3 mile farther, turn right onto Success Pond Road. From Hutchins Street, it's about 11 miles to the trailhead parking area on the right at the Notch Trail sign.

Contact

Appalachian Mountain Club Pinkham Notch Visitor Center, P.O. Box 298, Gorham, NH 03581, 603/466-2721, website: www.outdoors.org. Appalachian Trail Conference, 799 Washington Street, P.O. Box 807, Harpers Ferry, WV 25425-0807, 304/535-6331, website: www.appalachiantrail.org.

21 THE MAHOOSUC RANGE

between Shelburne, New Hampshire, and
Grafton Notch State Park

Total distance: 30.6 miles one-way   **Hiking time:** 4–5 days

Difficulty: 9   **Rating:** 10

I've considered the Mahoosucs one of my favorite New England mountain ranges since my first foray into this wild, remote string of rugged hills one March weekend several years ago. A friend and I spent three days here and saw no one else; and the hiker log in our shelter indicated no more than a half-dozen people had visited since November. On an autumn trip here, I enjoyed one of my finest sunrises ever from the open south summit of Fulling Mill Mountain. Among the trek's many highlights are the ridge walk over Goose Eye Mountain, and Mahoosuc Notch, a boulder-strewn cleft in the range, often referred to as the hardest mile on the Appalachian Trail. The Mahoosucs grow much busier from July through October than they are in March, of course, and their popularity has mushroomed in recent years.

Only one peak in the Mahoosucs—Old Speck—rises above 4,000 feet, but there's nary a flat piece of earth through the entire range. Read: Very tough hiking. This trek traverses the Mahoosucs on the Appalachian Trail from U.S. 2 in Shelburne, New Hampshire, to Grafton Notch, Maine, a 30.6-mile outing that can easily take five days. For a shorter trip, consider a two- or three-day hike from Grafton Notch to either the Mahoosuc Notch Trail (see previous listing) or the Carlo Col Trail.

Beginning on an old woods road, the Centennial Trail ascends steadily, and steeply at times, to the Mount Hayes eastern summit at 2.8 miles, which offers good views of the Carter-Moriah Range and the northern Presidentials to the south and southwest. At 3.1 miles, turn right (north) on the Mahoosuc Trail, which coincides with the Appalachian Trail. (Just 0.2 mile to the left is a good view from the Mount Hayes summit.) At 4.9 miles, the Appalachian Trail passes over the open summit of Cascade Mountain, and at 6.1 miles a side path leads 0.2 mile to the Trident Col campsite. It skirts Page Pond at 7.1 miles, and at 7.7 miles a side path leads to views from Wocket Ledge. At 8.8 miles, the trail runs along the north shore of Dream Lake; at the lake's far end, the Peabody Brook Trail diverges right, leading 3.1 miles south to North Road. (The Dryad Falls Trail branches east from the Peabody Brook Trail 0.1 mile from the Appalachian Trail and leads 1.8 miles to the Austin Brook Trail.) At 11 miles, the Appalachian Trail descends to Gentian Pond and a lean-to near its shore.

Continuing northbound, the trail climbs steeply up Mount Success, reaching the summit at 13.8 miles. After the Success Trail diverges left (west) at 14.4 miles (leading 2.4 miles to Success Pond Road), the Appalachian Trail descends steeply and then climbs to the Carlo Col Trail junction at 16.2 miles. (That trail leads 0.2 mile to the Carlo Col shelter and 2.6 miles west to Success Pond Road.) At 16.6 miles it passes over Mount Carlo's open summit, descends, and then climbs—very steeply near the top—to Goose Eye Mountain's high ridge at 18 miles. Walk the open ridge to the left a short distance for the terrific view from the west peak, where the Goose Eye Trail diverges left (west), leading 3.1 miles to Success Pond Road. Then turn north again on the Appalachian Trail, descend, and follow it as it skirts the 3,794-foot east peak, around which the Appalachian Trail was rerouted in the 1990s because of damage by hikers to fragile alpine vegetation on its summit. (The two Wright Trail branches reach the Appalachian Trail immediately south and north of the east peak, both leading east about four miles to the Sunday River Ski Area road in Ketchum.) Descend again, climb over the summit of North Peak at 19.6 miles, and reach the Full Goose shelter at 20.6 miles. The Appalachian Trail climbs steeply north from the shelter to the barren South Peak summit, with views in nearly every direction. It swings left and then descends steeply to the junction with the Mahoosuc Notch Trail at 22.1 miles (the trail leads 2.2 miles west to Success Pond Road).

The next trail mile traverses the floor of Mahoosuc Notch, flanked by tall cliffs that usually leave the notch in cool shadow. Follow the white blazes carefully through the jumbled terrain of boulders, where carrying a backpack can be very difficult. At the notch's far end, at 23.1 miles, the Appalachian Trail swings uphill for the sustained climb of Mahoosuc Arm, passes ledges with good views, and then drops downhill to beautiful Speck Pond—at 3,430 feet one of the highest ponds in Maine. There is a lean-to just above the pond's shore, at 25.7 miles; nearby, the Speck Pond Trail descends west 3.6 miles to Success Pond Road. From the shelter, the Appalachian Trail ascends north up Old Speck Mountain, traversing open ledges with excellent views to the south, then reentering the woods to reach a junction with the Old Speck Trail at 26.8 miles (where the Mahoosuc Trail ends). From that junction, the Old Speck Trail continues straight ahead 0.3 mile over easy ground to the wooded 4,180-foot summit of Old Speck, where an abandoned fire tower stands. The Appalachian Trail coincides with the Old Speck Trail for the circuitous, 3.5-mile descent to Grafton Notch, culminating at the parking lot.

User Groups

Hikers only. No wheelchair facilities. Dogs are discouraged along the Appalachian Trail in Maine. This trail should not be attempted in winter except by hikers experienced in mountaineering and prepared for severe winter weather, and is not suitable for skis. Bikes, horses, and hunting are prohibited.

Access and Fees

Parking and access are free. Camping is permitted only at the five back-country campsites along the Appalachian Trail through the Mahoosuc Range; backpackers must stay in the shelters or use the tent platforms and pay a fee of $8 per person per night. The Old Speck summit and northeast slopes are within Grafton Notch State Park in Maine, but the rest of the Mahoosucs are on private property and not a part of the White Mountain National Forest.

Maps

Map 1 in the *Map and Guide to the Appalachian Trail in New Hampshire and Vermont,* an eight-map set and guidebook available for $18.95 ($12.95 for the maps alone) from the Appalachian Trail Conference, covers the entire Mahoosuc Range. So does the *Camden-Pleasant-Weld/Mahoosuc-Evans map,* $7.95 in waterproof Tyvek, available in many stores and from the Appalachian Mountain Club, 800/262-4455, website: www.outdoors .org. Map 7 in the *Map and Guide to the Appalachian Trail in Maine,* a set of seven maps and a guidebook for $24.95 from the ATC, covers just the Appalachian Trail in Maine (roughly the northern half of the Mahoosuc Range). For topographic area maps, request Berlin, Shelburne, Success

Pond, Gilead, and Old Speck Mountain from USGS Map Sales, Federal Center, Box 25286, Denver, CO 80225, 888/ASK-USGS (888/275-8747), website: http://mapping.usgs.gov.

Directions

You need to shuttle two vehicles for this backpacking trip. To hike the range from south to north, as described here, leave one vehicle in the large parking lot located where the white-blazed Appalachian Trail crosses Route 26 in Grafton Notch State Park (marked by a sign reading "Hiking Trail"), 6.7 miles north of the sign at the state park's southern entrance and 1.8 miles south of the sign at the state park's northern entrance. To reach the start of this hike, turn north off U.S. 2 onto North Road in Shelburne, New Hampshire, about 3.2 miles east of the southern junction of U.S. 2 and Route 16 in Gorham. Cross the Androscoggin River, turn left onto Hogan Road, and continue 0.2 mile to a small parking area for the Centennial Trail.

Contact

Appalachian Mountain Club Pinkham Notch Visitor Center, P.O. Box 298, Gorham, NH 03581, 603/466-2721, website: www.outdoors.org. Appalachian Trail Conference, 799 Washington Street, P.O. Box 807, Harpers Ferry, WV 25425-0807, 304/535-6331, website: www.appalachiantrail.org. Grafton Notch State Park, 1941 Bear River Road, Newry, ME 04261, 207/824-2912 or 207/624-6080 off-season. Maine Department of Conservation, Bureau of Parks and Lands, 286 Water Street, Key Bank Plaza, 3rd and 5th floors, Augusta, ME 04333-0022, 207/287-3821, website: www.state.me.us/doc/parks/.

22 THE ROOST

White Mountain National Forest, south of Gilead

Total distance: 1 mile round-trip   **Hiking time:** 0.75 hour

Difficulty: 2   **Rating:** 8

From the turnout, walk south across the bridge and turn left (east) on the Roost Trail. Cross two small brooks within the first quarter mile and then walk an old woods road. Less than 0.5 mile from the trailhead, turn left (where indicated by an arrow and yellow blazes). Cross a brook and climb steeply uphill for the final 0.2 mile to the rocky knob of a summit, where the views are largely obscured by trees. Follow the view sign and trail downhill for 0.1 mile to open ledges with a good view overlooking the

Wild River Valley. Turn around and return the way you came. The elevation gain is about 500 feet.

User Groups
Hikers, snowshoers, and dogs. No wheelchair facilities. This trail is not suitable for bikes, horses, or skis. Hunting is allowed in season.

Access and Fees
Parking and access are free. Route 113 through Evans Notch is not maintained in winter, and gates are used to close off a 9.1-mile stretch of the highway. But you can drive to parking areas near the gates and ski or snowshoe the road beyond the gates to access this area. The northern gate on Route 113 is 1.6 miles south of the junction of U.S. 2 and Route 133 in Gilead. The southern gate sits on the Maine–New Hampshire line, 0.2 mile south of Brickett Place in North Chatham and immediately north of the White Mountain National Forest Basin Recreation Area entrance. The distance given for this hike is from the trailhead.

Maps
For a contour map of trails, get the *Map of Cold River Valley and Evans Notch* for $6 from Chatham Trails Association President Allen Cressy, P.O. Box 74, Bethel, ME 04217, 207/824-0508; the *Carter Range-Evans Notch/North Country-Mahoosuc* map, $7.95 in waterproof Tyvek, available in many stores and from the Appalachian Mountain Club, 800/262-4455, website: www.outdoors.org; or the *Trail Map and Guide to the White Mountain National Forest* for $4.95 from the DeLorme Publishing Company, 800/642-0970. For a topographic area map, request Speckled Mountain from USGS Map Sales, Federal Center, Box 25286, Denver, CO 80225, 888/ASK-USGS (888/275-8747), website: http://mapping.usgs.gov.

Directions
Drive to a turnout just north of the bridge over Evans Brook on Route 113, 3.7 miles south of the junction of Route 113 and U.S. 2 in Gilead and seven miles north of where Route 113 crosses the Maine–New Hampshire border.

Contact
White Mountain National Forest Supervisor, 719 North Main Street, Laconia, NH 03246, 603/528-8721, TDD for the hearing impaired 603/528-8722, website: www.fs.fed.us/r9/white.

23 MOUNT CARIBOU

White Mountain National Forest, south of Gilead

Total distance: 7.3 miles round-trip　　　　　　**Hiking time:** 4.5 hours

Difficulty: 8　　　　　　　　　　　　　　　　　　　　　　**Rating:** 9

I first attempted this hike on a winter backpacking trip, when a friend and I had to walk the road for three miles to the trailhead but never reached the summit because the trail became difficult to follow under a blanket of snow. Months later, in shorts and a T-shirt, I completed this scenic 7.3-mile loop over Mount Caribou, a hill with unusually excellent summit views for its 2,828-foot elevation. There are also beautiful cascades and falls along the Caribou Trail. Mount Caribou lies within the Caribou–Speckled Mountain Wilderness of the White Mountain National Forest. This loop gains more than 1,800 feet in elevation.

The Caribou Trail–Mud Brook Trail loop begins and ends at the parking area; this 7.3-mile hike follows it clockwise. Yellow blazes mark both trails only sporadically, though the paths are well used and obvious (except when covered with snow). Hike north (left from the parking area) on the Caribou Trail, crossing a wooden footbridge over a brook at 0.3 mile. About a half mile past the footbridge, the trail crosses Morrison Brook and trends in a more easterly direction—making several more stream crossings over the next two miles, some of which could be difficult at high water times. One stretch of about a half mile makes five crossings near several waterfalls and cascades, including 25-foot Kees Falls. Three miles from the trailhead, the Caribou Trail reaches a junction with the Mud Brook Trail, marked by a sign. Turn right (south) on the Mud Brook Trail and follow it 0.5 mile, climbing steadily, to the open ledges of the summit. From various spots on the ledges you enjoy views of western Maine's low mountains and lakes in virtually every direction. Numerous false trails lead through the summit's scrub brush, so take care to follow cairns and faint yellow blazes over the summit, continuing on the Mud Brook Trail. A half mile below the summit, the trail traverses a clifftop with a good view east. From the summit, it's nearly four miles back to the parking area. Along its lower two miles, the trail parallels and twice crosses Mud Brook.

User Groups

Hikers, snowshoers, and dogs. No wheelchair facilities. This trail is not suitable for bikes, horses, or skis. Hunting is allowed in season.

Access and Fees

Parking and access are free. Route 113 through Evans Notch is not maintained in winter, and gates are used to close off a 9.1-mile stretch of the highway. But you can drive to parking areas near the gates and ski or snowshoe the road beyond the gates to access this area. The northern gate on Route 113 is 1.6 miles south of the junction of U.S. 2 and Route 133 in Gilead. The southern gate sits on the Maine–New Hampshire line, 0.2 mile south of Brickett Place in North Chatham and immediately north of the White Mountain National Forest Basin Recreation Area entrance. The distance given for this hike is from the trailhead.

Maps

For a contour map of trails, get the *Map of Cold River Valley and Evans Notch* for $6 from Chatham Trails Association President Allen Cressy, P.O. Box 74, Bethel, ME 04217, 207/824-0508; the *Carter Range-Evans Notch/North Country-Mahoosuc* map, $7.95 in waterproof Tyvek, available in many stores and from the Appalachian Mountain Club, 800/262-4455, website: www.outdoors.org; or the *Trail Map and Guide to the White Mountain National Forest* for $4.95 from the DeLorme Publishing Company, 800/642-0970. For a topographic area map, request Speckled Mountain from USGS Map Sales, Federal Center, Box 25286, Denver, CO 80225, 888/ASK-USGS (888/275-8747), website: http://mapping.usgs.gov.

Directions

The hike begins from a parking lot on Route 113, 4.8 miles south of its junction with U.S. 2 in Gilead and 5.9 miles north of where Route 113 crosses the Maine–New Hampshire border.

Contact

White Mountain National Forest Supervisor, 719 North Main Street, Laconia, NH 03246, 603/528-8721, TDD for the hearing impaired 603/528-8722, website: www.fs.fed.us/r9/white.

24 EAST ROYCE

White Mountain National Forest, south of Gilead

Total distance: 2.8 miles round-trip   **Hiking time:** 2 hours

Difficulty: 7   **Rating:** 9

From the parking lot, the trail immediately crosses a braided stream and begins a steep climb—both portents of what lies ahead on this short but rigorous 2.8-mile hike. The hike up East Royce makes several stream crossings, passing picturesque waterfalls and cascades, and ascends a relentlessly steep mountainside. I hustled up here one morning after a day of heavy downpours and found the streams swelled nearly to bursting. The summit proves worth the effort, with sweeping views that encompass the dramatic cliffs of West Royce, the peaks of South and North Baldface, and the lakes and lower hills of western Maine. The hike ascends about 1,700 feet.

From the parking lot, follow the East Royce Trail a mile to where the Royce Connector Trail enters from the left. Turn right with the East Royce Trail, reaching open ledges that involve somewhat exposed scrambling within 0.25 mile, and the summit just 0.1 mile farther.

Special note: Across Route 113 from the parking area, the Spruce Hill Trail enters the woods beside a series of cascades worth checking out when the water is high.

User Groups

Hikers, snowshoers, and dogs. No wheelchair facilities. This trail is not suitable for bikes, horses, or skis. Hunting is allowed in season.

Access and Fees

Parking and access are free. Route 113 through Evans Notch is not maintained in winter, and gates are used to close off a 9.1-mile stretch of the highway. But you can drive to parking areas near the gates, and ski or snowshoe the road beyond the gates to access this area. The northern gate on Route 113 is 1.6 miles south of the junction of U.S. 2 and Route 133 in Gilead. The southern gate sits on the Maine–New Hampshire line, 0.2 mile south of Brickett Place in North Chatham and immediately north of the White Mountain National Forest Basin Recreation Area entrance. The distance given for this hike is from the trailhead.

Maps

For a contour map of trails, get the *Map of Cold River Valley and Evans Notch* for $6 from Chatham Trails Association President Allen Cressy, P.O. Box 74, Bethel, ME 04217, 207/824-0508; the *Carter Range–Evans Notch/North Country–Mahoosuc* map, $7.95 in waterproof Tyvek, available in many stores and from the Appalachian Mountain Club, 800/262-4455, website: www.outdoors.org; or the *Trail Map and Guide to the White Mountain National Forest* for $4.95 from the DeLorme Publishing Company, 800/642-0970. For a topographic area map, request Speckled Mountain from USGS Map Sales, Federal Center, Box 25286, Denver, CO 80225, 888/ASK-USGS (888/275-8747), website: http://mapping.usgs.gov.

Directions

The East Royce Trail begins at a parking lot on the west side of Route 113,

7.6 miles south of the junction of U.S. 2 and Route 113 in Gilead and 3.1 miles north of where Route 113 crosses the Maine–New Hampshire border.

Contact
White Mountain National Forest Supervisor, 719 North Main Street, Laconia, NH 03246, 603/528-8721, TDD for the hearing impaired 603/528-8722, website: www.fs.fed.us/r9/white.

25 SPECKLED AND BLUEBERRY MOUNTAINS
White Mountain National Forest, south of Gilead

Total distance: 7.9 miles round-trip   **Hiking time:** 5 hours

Difficulty: 8   **Rating:** 9

The views from the barren Speckled Mountain summit are among the best in the area. My wife and I had this summit and the cliffs of Blueberry Mountain to ourselves one summer afternoon when the wind blew hard enough to knock us around. This hike's cumulative elevation gain is about 2,400 feet.

From the parking area, pick up the Bickford Brook Trail. At 0.6 mile, turn right at the sign for the Blueberry Ridge Trail. Immediately the trail makes a stream crossing at a narrow gorge that definitely could be dangerous during high water. (If the stream is impassable or if you would prefer a less strenuous hike to the summit of Speckled Mountain, skip this trail and follow the Bickford Brook Trail all the way to the summit, an 8.6-mile round-trip. That option would be the easier route on snowshoes as well.) Continue up the Blueberry Ridge Trail for 0.7 mile to a junction with the Lookout Loop, a 0.5-mile detour out to the Blueberry Mountain cliffs and a great panoramic view of lakes and hills to the south and east, including Pleasant Mountain (see listing in this chapter). The Lookout Loop rejoins the Blueberry Ridge Trail; follow it to the right. (Hikers seeking a shorter day can turn left and descend the Blueberry Ridge and Bickford Brook Trails, a round-trip of 3.1 miles.) It ascends the two-mile ridge, much of it open, with wide views over your shoulder of the peaks across Evans Notch: East and West Royce, Meader, and North and South Baldface. At the upper junction with the Bickford Brook Trail, turn right (east) for the easy 0.5-mile hike to the Speckled Mountain summit, a bald crown of rock with great views in almost every direction. Descend the same way, except stay on the Bickford Brook Trail all the way (4.3 miles) back to the parking area.

User Groups

Hikers, snowshoers, and dogs. No wheelchair facilities. This trail is not suitable for bikes, horses, or skis. Hunting is allowed in season.

Access and Fees

Parking and access are free. Route 113 through Evans Notch is not maintained in winter, and gates are used to close off a 9.1-mile stretch of the highway. But you can drive to parking areas near the gates, and ski or snowshoe the road beyond the gates to access this area. The northern gate on Route 113 is 1.6 miles south of the junction of U.S. 2 and Route 133 in Gilead. The southern gate sits on the Maine–New Hampshire line, 0.2 mile south of Brickett Place in North Chatham and immediately north of the White Mountain National Forest Basin Recreation Area entrance. The distance given for this hike is from the trailhead.

Maps

For a contour map of trails, get the *Map of Cold River Valley and Evans Notch* for $6 from Chatham Trails Association President Allen Cressy, P.O. Box 74, Bethel, ME 04217, 207/824-0508; the *Carter Range–Evans Notch/North Country–Mahoosuc* map, $7.95 in waterproof Tyvek, available in many stores and from the Appalachian Mountain Club, 800/262-4455, website: www.outdoors.org; or the *Trail Map and Guide to the White Mountain National Forest* for $4.95 from the DeLorme Publishing Company, 800/642-0970. For a topographic area map, request Speckled Mountain from USGS Map Sales, Federal Center, Box 25286, Denver, CO 80225, 888/ASK-USGS (888/275-8747), website: http://mapping.usgs.gov.

Directions

This hike begins at Brickett Place, a parking area beside a brick building on Route 113 in North Chatham, 0.2 mile north of where Route 113 crosses the Maine–New Hampshire border and 10.5 miles south of the junction of Route 113 and U.S. 2 in Gilead.

Contact

White Mountain National Forest Supervisor, 719 North Main Street, Laconia, NH 03246, 603/528-8721, TDD for the hearing impaired 603/528-8722, website: www.fs.fed.us/r9/white.

26 SABATTUS MOUNTAIN
outside Center Lovell

Total distance: 1.5 miles round-trip

Hiking time: 1 hour

Difficulty: 2

Rating: 9

This short but popular local hike leads to the top of a sheer drop of hundreds of feet, providing wide views of nearly unbroken forest and mountains, including Pleasant Mountain (see listing in this chapter) to the south and the White Mountains to the east. This is a great hike for young children and fall foliage lovers. Follow the wide trail, which ascends steadily—and at times steeply—for 0.75 mile to the summit. Walk the clifftop to the right for the best views of the Whites. Return the same way.

User Groups
Hikers, snowshoers, and dogs. No wheelchair facilities. This trail is not suitable for bikes, horses, or skis. Hunting is allowed in season.

Access and Fees
Parking and access are free.

Maps
No map is needed for this hike. The *Camden Pleasant-Weld/Mahoosuc-Evans map* shows the location of Sabattus Mountain, but not its trail; the map costs $7.95 in waterproof Tyvek, from the Appalachian Mountain Club, 800/262-4455, website: www.outdoors.org. For a topographic area map, request Center Lovell from USGS Map Sales, Federal Center, Box 25286, Denver, CO 80225, 888/ASK-USGS (888/275-8747), website: http://mapping.usgs.gov.

Directions
From the Center Lovell Inn on Route 5 in Center Lovell, drive north for 0.2 mile on Route 5 and turn right on Sabattus Road. Continue for 1.5 miles and then bear right on the dirt Sabattus Mountain Road. Park in a small dirt lot or at the roadside 0.3 mile farther. The trail begins across the road from the lot.

Contact
There is no contact agency for this hike.

27 JOCKEY CAP
east of Fryeburg

Total distance: 0.4 miles round-trip   **Hiking time:** 0.5 hour

Difficulty: 2   **Rating:** 7

This short walk in Fryeburg—just down the road from North Conway, New Hampshire—leads to the top of what a sign along the trail describes as "the largest boulder in the United States." While that claim's veracity might be questionable, the hike does nonetheless provide a nice walk to a good view of the surrounding countryside, including Mounts Washington and Chocorua in the White Mountains.

Follow the wide and obvious trail into the woods. As the cliffs on the face of Jockey Cap come into view through the trees, the trail circles to the left around the boulder and emerges from the woods at a spot where you can safely walk up onto the cap. Return the same way.

User Groups
Hikers, snowshoers, and dogs. No wheelchair facilities. This trail is not suitable for bikes, horses, or skis. Hunting is prohibited.

Access and Fees
Parking and access are free. The trail is open to the public year-round.

Maps
No map is needed for this short walk, but for a topographic area map, request Fryeburg from USGS Map Sales, Federal Center, Box 25286, Denver, CO 80225, 888/ASK-USGS (888/275-8747), website: http://mapping.usgs.gov.

Directions
From the junction of U.S. 302, Route 5, and Route 113 in Fryeburg, drive east on U.S. 302 for one mile and park at the Jockey Cap Country Store on the left. The Jockey Cap Trail begins at a gate between the store and the cabins to the right.

Contact
This trail crosses private land owned by the Jockey Cap Motel and Country Store, 207/935-2306, and land owned by the town of Fryeburg and managed by its recreation department, 207/935-3933.

28 PLEASANT MOUNTAIN
between Fryeburg, Denmark, and Bridgeton

Total distance: 5.7 miles round-trip   **Hiking time:** 3.5 hours

Difficulty: 7   **Rating:** 9

Rising barely more than 2,000 feet above sea level, Pleasant Mountain is probably one of the finest low-elevation ridge walks in New England. Walking the ridge brings you alternately through beautiful forest, over open ledges, and to several distinct summit humps with sweeping views. Big Bald Peak may be the nicest stretch of the ridge, though the views from the main summit are excellent also. The cumulative elevation gain is about 1,600 feet.

For a shorter hike, go to either the main summit via the Ledges Trail (3.6 miles, 2.5 hours round-trip) or to Big Bald Peak via the Bald Peak Trail (2.2 miles, 1.5 hours). For the full loop, begin on the Bald Peak Trail, ascending steadily beside a stream; watch for short waterfalls and a miniature flume. You'll pass the Sue's Way Trail and North Ridge Trail entering from the right, but stay left, climbing steeply to Big Bald Peak, then following the Bald Peak Trail southward along the ridge, with excellent views. The Bald Peak Trail eventually joins the wide Fire Warden's Trail. Turn left for the 2,006-foot summit of Pleasant Mountain. Continue over the summit to pick up the Ledges Trail, which descends along open ledges with terrific views to the south. The lower sections of this trail can be muddy and running with water. At the road, if you did not shuttle two vehicles, turn left and walk 1.5 miles to the Bald Peak Trailhead.

User Groups
Hikers, snowshoers, and dogs. No wheelchair facilities. This trail is not suitable for bikes, horses, or skis. Hunting is allowed in season.

Access and Fees
Parking and access are free.

Maps
See the *Camden-Pleasant-Weld/Mahoosuc-Evans map,* $7.95 in waterproof Tyvek, available in many stores and from the Appalachian Mountain Club, 800/262-4455, website: www.outdoors.org. For a topographic area map, request Pleasant Mountain from USGS Map Sales, Federal Center, Box 25286, Denver, CO 80225, 888/ASK-USGS (888/275-8747), website: http://mapping.usgs.gov.

Directions

From the junction of U.S. 302 and Route 93, west of Bridgeton, drive 4.5 miles west on 302 and turn left onto Mountain Road (heading toward the Shawnee Peak Ski Area). Drive another 1.8 miles to a turnout at the Bald Peak Trailhead (marked by a sign on the right). If you have two vehicles, leave one at the Ledges Trailhead (marked by a sign) 1.5 miles farther down the road. Otherwise, you walk that stretch of road to finish this loop.

Contact

There is no contact agency for this hike.

29 BURNT MEADOW MOUNTAIN
outside Brownfield

Total distance: 2.4 miles round-trip

Hiking time: 2 hours

Difficulty: 2

Rating: 7

A nice, short local hike, this hill near Brownfield has an open summit with views in almost every direction, from the White Mountains to the lakes of western Maine. When my wife and I hiked it one July afternoon, we found ripe blueberries to nibble on. This hike gains about 1,200 feet in elevation.

From the parking area, walk uphill to the old T-bar of a former ski area. Turn left and follow the T-bar and a worn footpath uphill. Ignore the sign with an arrow pointing to the right, which you encounter within the first half mile, and continue straight ahead under the T-bar. The trail grows quite steep, with lots of loose stones and dirt. Footing may become very tricky here in spring. Where the T-bar ends in a small clearing, turn left onto a trail marked by blue blazes, which leads at a more moderate angle to the summit. Watch for a good view from ledges on the left before reaching the summit. The broad top of Burnt Meadow Mountain offers views to the west, north, and south; continue over it and you get views to the south and east. Descend the way you came.

User Groups

Hikers, snowshoers, and dogs. No wheelchair facilities. This trail is not suitable for bikes, horses, or skis. Hunting is allowed in season.

Access and Fees

Parking and access are free.

Maps

For a topographic area map, request Brownfield from USGS Map Sales, Federal Center, Box 25286, Denver, CO 80225, 888/ASK-USGS (888/275-8747), website: http://mapping.usgs.gov.

Directions

From the junction of Route 5/113 and Route 160 in East Brownfield, turn west on Route 160 and continue 1.1 miles. Turn left, staying on Route 160, and continue another 0.3 mile. Turn right onto the paved Fire Lane 32. The parking area is 0.2 mile farther. The trailhead isn't marked, but there's an obvious parking area. The trail starts at the parking area's right side.

Contact

There is no contact agency for this hike.

30 MOUNT CUTLER

in Hiram

Total distance: 2.6 miles round-trip   **Hiking time:** 1.5 hours

Difficulty: 2   **Rating:** 8

Mount Cutler rises abruptly from the Saco River valley in Hiram and is really a nice hike up a relatively small hill. Cross the railroad tracks, turn left, and then enter the woods on the right at a wide trail. Soon you branch right onto a red-blazed trail. The blazes appear sporadically at times, and on rocks rather than on trees higher up the mountain, making the trail potentially difficult to follow (particularly in winter). The trail ascends steep ledges overlooking the town of Hiram and grows narrow; care is needed over the ledges. But once you gain the ridge, the walking grows much easier as you pass through forests with a mix of hardwoods and hemlocks, and traverse open areas with sweeping views. The east summit ledges, with views of the Saco Valley, are a good destination for a round-trip hike of about 1.5 miles. Continue on the trail along the ridge and into a saddle, where there's a birch tree grove. A faint footpath leads up the left side of the slope to the main summit, which is wooded. Just beyond it and to the right, however, is an open area with great views toward Pleasant Mountain and the White Mountains.

User Groups

Hikers, snowshoers, and dogs. No wheelchair facilities. This trail is not suitable for bikes, horses, or skis. Hunting is allowed in season.

Access and Fees

Parking and access are free.

Maps

For topographic area maps, request Hiram and Cornish from USGS Map Sales, Federal Center, Box 25286, Denver, CO 80225, 888/ASK-USGS (888/275-8747), website: http://mapping.usgs.gov.

Directions

From the junction of Route 117 and Route 5/113, drive over the concrete bridge; take an immediate left and then a right onto Mountain View Avenue. Drive about 0.1 mile and park at the roadside near the railroad tracks.

Contact

There is no contact agency for this hike.

31 DOUGLAS HILL

south of Sebago

Total distance: 1.2 miles round-trip

Hiking time: 0.5 hour

Difficulty: 2

Rating: 7

This 169-acre preserve formerly owned by The Nature Conservancy is now owned by the town of Sebago. A short walk to the hill's open summit and its stone tower gives you expansive views of Sebago Lake, Pleasant Mountain, and the mountains to the northwest as far as Mount Washington.

From the registration box, walk through the stone pillars, follow the yellow-blazed Woods Trail a short distance, and then bear left onto the Ledges Trail (also blazed yellow). This trail leads over interesting open ledges with good views, though they are slick when wet. At the summit, climb the stone tower's steps; on top is a diagram identifying the distant peaks. A nature trail, blazed orange, makes a 0.75-mile loop off the summit and returns to it. Descend back to the parking lot via the Woods Trail.

User Groups

Hikers only. No wheelchair facilities. This trail is not suitable for bikes or horses and is not open in winter. Dogs are prohibited. Hunting is allowed in season.

Access and Fees

Parking and access are free; just register at the trailhead. The preserve is open only during daylight hours.

Maps

A free guide and map to Douglas Hill may be available at the trailhead registration box. For topographic area maps, request Steep Falls and North Sebago from USGS Map Sales, Federal Center, Box 25286, Denver, CO 80225, 888/ASK-USGS (888/275-8747), website: http://mapping.usgs.gov.

Directions

From the junction of Routes 107 and 114 in East Sebago, drive 0.5 mile north on Route 107 and turn left onto Douglas Mountain Road (which is one mile south of Sebago center). Drive 0.8 mile to a hilltop and take a sharp left. In another half mile, turn left into a small parking area.

Contact

Sebago Town Hall, 207/787-2457.

32 MOUNT AGAMENTICUS

west of Ogunquit

Total distance: 1 mile round-trip   **Hiking time:** 0.75 hour

Difficulty: 2   **Rating:** 7

This one-mile hike up and down tiny Agamenticus is an easy walk to a summit with a fire tower that offers 360-degree views of the Seacoast region and southern Maine and New Hampshire. From the parking area, follow the trail along an old woods road, soon climbing moderately. The trail ascends ledges, crosses the summit road, and emerges after half a mile at the summit. Return the way you came or descend the summit road.

User Groups

Hikers, snowshoers, and dogs. No wheelchair facilities. This trail is not suitable for bikes, horses, or skis. Hunting is allowed in season.

Access and Fees

Parking and access are free.

Maps

No map is needed for this hike. For topographic area maps, request York

Harbor and North Berwick from USGS Map Sales, Federal Center, Box 25286, Denver, CO 80225, 888/ASK-USGS (888/275-8747), website: http://mapping.usgs.gov.

Directions

Take I-95 to Exit 4 in Ogunquit. At the end of the off-ramp, turn left, passing over the highway, and then immediately turn right onto Mountain Road. Follow it for about 2.7 miles to the base of the Agamenticus summit road and a dirt parking area.

Contact

The Nature Conservancy Maine Chapter, Fort Andross, 14 Maine Street, Suite 401, Brunswick, Maine 04011, 207/729-5181, email: naturemaine@tnc.org, website: http://nature.org. The Nature Conservancy Southern Maine field office, 207/646-1788.

Resources

COURTESY OF THE MAINE OFFICE OF TOURISM

Resources

Public Lands Agencies

Acadia National Park
P.O. Box 177
Eagle Lake Rd.
Bar Harbor, ME 04609-0177
207/288-3338, fax 207/288-5507
website: www.nps.gov/acad

Baxter State Park
64 Balsam Dr.
Millinocket, ME 04462-2190
207/723-5140
website: www.baxterstatepark
authority.com

Maine Bureau of Parks and Lands
Department of Conservation
mailing address: 22 State
House Station
Augusta, ME 04333-0022

207/287-2211, fax 207/287-2400
physical address: 286 Water St.
Key Bank Plaza, Augusta, ME
website: www.state.me.us/
doc/parks.htm

**White Mountain National
Forest Supervisor**
719 North Main St.
Laconia, NH 03246
603/528-8721 or
TDD 603/528-8722
website: www.fs.fed.us/r9/white

Map Sources

DeLorme Publishing Company
800/253-5081
website: www.DeLorme.com

Trails Illustrated
800/962-1643
website: http://maps.national
geographic.com/trails

United States Geological Survey
Information Services
Box 25286
Denver, CO 80225
888/ASK-USGS (888/275-8747),
fax 303/202-4693
website: http://mapping.usgs.gov

Trail Clubs and Organizations

Appalachian Mountain Club
5 Joy St.
Boston, MA 02108
617/523-0655
website: www.outdoors.org

Appalachian Mountain Club
  Pinkham Notch Visitor Center
P.O. Box 298
Gorham, NH 03581
603/466-2721
website: www.outdoors.org

Appalachian Trail Conference
799 Washington St.
P.O. Box 807
Harpers Ferry, WV 25425-0807
304/535-6331
website: www.appalachiantrail.org

Maine Appalachian Trail Club
P.O. Box 283
Augusta, ME 04332-0283
website: www.matc.org

Acknowledgments

I want to thank the many people who accompanied me on these trails, in particular my wife and hiking partner, Penny Beach. My parents, Henry and Joanne Lanza, deserve recognition—both for putting up with a son who has shown up at their door a few times since they first got rid of him, and for being good hiking partners. I also want to thank my editors and the rest of the very talented staff at Avalon Travel Publishing.

While I have personally walked every hike described in this book—some of them many times—updating a volume as comprehensive as this one cannot possibly be accomplished without the assistance of many people. To that end, I relied on friends, acquaintances, people active with hiking and conservation groups, and managers of public lands and private reserves to do some on-the-ground "scouting" of trails and send me current reports on the hikes in this book. Much deep appreciation goes out to: Joe Albee, Mike and Rick Baron, Denise Buck, Steve Buck, Ed Hawkins, Joe Kuzneski, Carol Lavoie, Denis Lavoie, Diane Mailloux, Bill Mistretta, Ken Morgan, Brion O'Connor, Ed Poyer, Gerry Prutsman, Keith Ratner, Topher Sharp, and Doug Thompson.

There were also many helpful people at various organizations and public agencies, including: Acadia National Park; Appalachian Mountain Club; Appalachian Trail Conference; Baxter State Park; Bigelow Preserve; Camden Hills State Park; Chatham Trails Association; DeLorme Publishing Company; Friends of Acadia; Maine Appalachian Trail Club; Maine Bureau of Parks and Lands; The Nature Conservancy; Trails Illustrated; White Mountain National Forest.

Index

Notes

Notes

Notes

Notes